THE ESSENTIAL TILLICH

THE ESSENTIAL TILLICH

AN
ANTHOLOGY OF THE WRITINGS OF
PAUL TILLICH

EDITED WITH A PREFACE BY
F. FORRESTER CHURCH

The University of Chicago Press

Published by arrangement with Scribner, an Imprint of Simon & Schuster, Inc.

The University of Chicago Press, Chicago 60637
The University of Chicago Press, Ltd., London
Copyright © 1987 by F. Forrester Church
All rights reserved. Originally published 1987
University of Chicago Press edition 1999
Printed in the United States of America
15 14 13 12 11 10 09 08 07 06   8 7 6 5 4

ISBN-13: 978-0-226-80343-2 (paper)
ISBN-10: 0-226-80343-0 (paper)

Library of Congress Cataloging-in-Publication Data
Tillich, Paul, 1886–1965.
[Selections. 1999]
The essential Tillich : an anthology of the writings of Paul Tillich / edited, with a
preface, by F. Forrester Church.
p.   cm.
Originally published: New York : Macmillan, 1987.
ISBN 0-226-80343-0 (pbk. : alk. paper)
1. Theology, Doctrinal. I. Church, F. Forrester. II. Title.

BT75.2.T482   1999   99-28156
230—dc21   CIP

⊖ The paper used in this publication meets the minimum requirements of the
American National Standard for Information Sciences—Permanence of Paper for
Printed Library Materials. ANSI Z39.48-1992.

For Hannah Tillich

Contents

PART VII
THE FUTURE OF RELIGIONS

PART VIII
LIVING ON THE BOUNDARY

Foreword

I have heard it said that my father's works are difficult to read and hard to understand. It is true. In a few of his works he expresses complex ideas in very complex language—to the distress of many a theology student. But, more often, Tillich makes complex concepts intelligible in language that is remarkable for its clarity and rhythm. Consequently, I am very happy that F. Forrester Church has chosen passages for this book in which Tillich writes about some of his most important concepts in words that are lucid, accessible, and, in the case of the sermons, beautiful.

Around each important concept, Dr. Church has clustered several passages, of varying complexity, from Tillich's books, articles, and sermons which deal, in different ways, with the same idea. In this ingenious format, one passage explicates the other, and a rich, illuminating introduction to Tillich's essential thought becomes available to the student, the church-worker, and any serious reader who has ever asked an existential question.

F. Forrester Church, the editor of this book, is pastor of the Unitarian Church of All Souls in New York City where he preaches compellingly to a congregation that fills the church to overflowing every Sunday. He is sensitive to the anxiety which these disturbing times arouse in us all. He hopes, as I do, that these works by my father, who often gave wise answers to difficult questions, might offer some insight, give some courage, and open up some spiritual avenues as we struggle to come to terms with this deeply troubled world.

MUTIE TILLICH FARRIS

Preface

During his lifetime, Paul Tillich won renown as an apostle to the intellectuals, leaders in government, the arts, and the sciences, who took him seriously because he took them and their skepticism seriously. Since his death, the religious situation has changed dramatically. The church militant, of which Tillich was so chary, with its impatience with tentativeness, openness, and ambiguity, has emerged with power; and the religious academy has followed other academic disciplines into hermetically sealed pockets of specialization. In the latter, Tillich is not forgotten. Dozens of books and articles are published every year that illuminate his contributions to various compartments of theology, philosophy, aesthetics, psychology, and ethics. But Tillich's major contribution, an integrated approach to all of these disciplines from a coherent if nondogmatic point of view, has fallen into the shadows.

I was a senior in high school the year Tillich died. The old voices had failed us, or so we thought. Children of the late '60s, we believed that we were inaugurating a new era. Though I remember those years with more than a little nostalgia, nearly a quarter of a century later, with our collective knowledge and faith continuing to outstrip our collective wisdom, I have come to recognize that, now more than ever, we need a Paul Tillich to guide us through the perils of our age.

The last half of the twentieth century has aptly been described as an age of anxiety, its symbols suggesting estrangement, alienation, and division, both within us and between us. Zealots on the right and left, each with their terrorists for Truth or God, unwittingly contribute to this anxiety, as do Promethean scientists who, by splicing genes and splitting atoms, have begun to unveil the secrets of both creation and armageddon, hitherto the province of God alone. Here on earth God's work has truly become our own, John Kennedy said in his inaugural address. Even to the limited extent that this is so, never before have we been in greater need of theological vision and religious depth. So long as both our faith and our knowledge continue to outstrip our wisdom, Kennedy's vision offers a haunting emblem of our peril, riddled with potentially demonic consequences.

One answer is to retreat from newfound knowledge into the bastions of dogma. Many do. Another is to lapse into the secular idolatries of nationalism, political ideology, personal gratification: The list is endless. Instead, what we need is a theology at once open enough to speak to our situation, humble enough to heal divisions while respecting differences, and powerful enough to liberate us from the tyrannies of our times.

Though he was born one hundred years ago and has been dead for almost a quarter century, Paul Tillich remains the one theologian whose range and method are expansive enough to help us comprehend and confront our predicament. Liberal in the best senses of the word (open, rational, and free), Tillich based the particulars of his faith upon insights from his own tradition and times without denying the validity of experiences profoundly different from his own. In part this is because he lived on the boundary line: between religion and culture; philosophy and theology; America and Europe; the old wisdom and the new knowledge.

He was a true catholic, reverentially attentive to the sacramental nature of creation, but also a true protestant, ever mindful of the corruptions of religion in the name of religion. Ranging freely and with confidence among the disciplines of history, philosophy, political science, psychology, and art, Paul Tillich sought evidence of the eternal in temporal things, seeking through his explorations to project human pictures upon a cosmic screen.

Perceiving sin in brokenness (alienation, estrangement, and

division), he sought evidence of salvation in wholeness (self-acceptance, forgiveness, and reconciliation). Knowing his own weaknesses, which—not unique to him—were many, he enjoined in both his preaching and teaching the injunction of Micah to do justice, love mercy, and walk humbly with our God.

I am a parish minister. During the nine years I have served my congregation, the Unitarian Church of All Souls in Manhattan, I have learned far more about religion than I ever did, either in my Masters or my Ph.D. program, at Harvard. But my first encounter with Paul Tillich was at Harvard, where he taught after leaving Union Theological Seminary and before going to the University of Chicago. By the time I entered Harvard, Tillich had been gone for more than a decade and was dead five years. Though I was assigned several of his books, no member of the faculty and no graduate student identified him- or herself to me as a "Tillichean." There were liberationist theologians of every possible stripe, and neo-Barthians, and Bultmanians, and disciples of Bonhoeffer and Brunner. Many had been influenced by Tillich, but none professed allegiance to "the Tillich school."

That's because there is no Tillich school, and can be none, which, ironically, is precisely why his witness is so needed today. In a time of growing tribalism, Tillich was a religious diplomat at large, respectful of differences, chary of absolutes, devout and yet skeptical, mindful of the limits of all theology, including his own. He had something to say about everything, but never the final word. He spoke to his own situation from his own tradition, recognizing that others, to follow him, would have to do the same. This was not mere relativism. By positing a God beyond "God"—Being itself, the Ground of Being—he acknowledged the limits of human knowledge, while stretching it to the utmost. This combination of true humility and untrammeled openness is a model for any of us—theologian or struggling believer—who seeks both deeper insight into the nature of reality and a form of discourse that remains potentially inclusive in a time of growing polarization.

My own definition of religion is a simple one, simpler than

any with which Tillich would likely have been comfortable. *Religion is our human response to the dual reality of being alive and having to die.* Accordingly, all of us are religious, to one degree or another. We struggle, some of us intensively, some only when the roof falls in, to make whatever sense we can of life and death.

The reason Tillich's writings have such power for me is that nothing human—or divine—is alien to him. Responding in depth to the dual reality of being alive and having to die, he garners meaning wherever meaning is to be found. Avoiding false distinctions between the sacred and the profane, he gathers the pieces together. A piece of art and a piece of scripture; a piece of creation and a piece of destruction; a piece of carefully plotted thought and a piece of mystical inspiration: All make up Paul Tillich's mosaic. Then he invites us to discover our own.

What follows is the essential Tillich in so far as Tillich himself—his approach to theology as much as its specifics—is essential. More than ever before it is essential that we counter our own dogmas with rationality, and our own narrow rationality with journeys into the transrational realm. Tillich reminds us that to build secure bunkers and fly either the banner of empirically demonstrated fact or that of revealed truth, is in each instance to lapse into idolatry, revering the part over the whole, contributing to divisiveness in a divided world.

A word about my approach and my selections. The former is based upon my belief that in an age of specialization the professional theologian has increasingly little to say to people in the pew. Despite my academic training, there are many books of theology, no doubt subtle and brilliant, that I cannot begin to understand. On the other hand, if cut off from the academy, preachers and laypeople often become provincial, their prophecy political more than theological, and their theology unnuanced, defensive, and uncritical, both blindered and blind.

Paul Tillich is perhaps the last major theologian who preached as tellingly as he taught. His language changed as did his images, but not his message. It remained the same, in impact and moment, precisely because he adapted his discourse to his audience. He says at one point that the best of his theology is in his preaching. Surely the heart of his theology is there. Until theologians can liberate themselves from the private and privileged discourse of the academy, the impact of their ideas, however enlightened or well-intentioned, will be limited. By speaking as eloquently from the pulpit as he did from the lectern, Tillich proved that despite having gone abroad, he could bring his faith home.

Accordingly, in each chapter I have included at least one of Tillich's sermons or addresses delivered to a nonacademic audience. These are chosen both on their own merits and also to illumine the selections with which they are juxtaposed: at least one brief definitional piece (often from Tillich's three-volume *Systematic Theology*); and one or more expository pieces (often a key chapter from one of his major books).

My selections are dictated by three criteria. First, to cover the major areas of Tillich's thought and teaching. Second, to connect the parts, within and between each section, in such a way that they would compose a coherent whole. And third, to ensure that the selections speak as directly to our present situation as they did to his own.

I have chosen eight areas for my focus: Ultimate Concern; Symbols of Faith; The Protestant Principle; Addressing the Situation; Love, Power, and Justice; The Courage to Be; The Future of Religions; and, Living on the Boundary. Two dimensions of Tillich's thought are not fully represented but only hinted at here. The first is his important and illuminating interpretive criticism of the arts, especially the visual arts. The second is his groundbreaking work, more than a dozen essays, in psychiatry and religion. In addition, Tillich's early socialist writings are not proportionately represented. None of these, including the selection that is included, fully translates to the situation today.

A word of appreciation to Michelle Rapkin and Charles Scribner III at Macmillan for the confidence they expressed by inviting me to edit this volume, and to Charles and Steven Wilburn for their loving oversight of the entire project. Terrence J. Mulry of

Harvard Divinity School assisted in my research and helped me with my selections. Donald Brenneis of Pitzer College also aided in my research and my thanks to Carolyn Kleinmann who read the galleys. I am especially indebted to the Tillich family for their encouragement and support.

My final hope is that some of you who read this selection of Paul Tillich's writings will be inspired to share some of the pleasure that I have had by turning to the works themselves. In their entirety, one encounters a man of rare genius and perspicuity, a modern man whose heart was in Jerusalem, whose spirit was with the ancient Greeks, and whose soul was committed to a better future, one he would not share, but nonetheless strove mightily to bring about.

F. FORRESTER CHURCH
Unitarian Church of All Souls
New York City
December 1, 1986

THE
ESSENTIAL
TILLICH

Invocation:
The Lost Dimension
in Religion

Being religious means asking passionately the question of the meaning of our existence and being willing to receive answers, even if the answers hurt. Such an idea of religion makes religion universally human, but it certainly differs from what is usually called religion. It does not describe religion as the belief in the existence of gods or one God, and as a set of activities and institutions for the sake of relating oneself to these beings in thought, devotion and obedience. No one can deny that the religions which have appeared in history are religions in this sense. Nevertheless, religion in its innermost nature is more than religion in this narrower sense. It is the state of being concerned about one's own being and being universally.

There are many people who are ultimately concerned in this way who feel far removed, however, from religion in the narrower sense, and therefore from every historical religion. It often happens that such people take the question of the meaning of their life infinitely seriously and reject any historical religion just for this reason. They feel that the concrete religions fail to express their profound concern adequately. They are religious while rejecting the religions. It is this experience which forces us to

From Paul Tillich, "The Lost Dimension in Religion," *The Saturday Evening Post* 230, no. 50 (June 14, 1958): p. 29, 76, 78–79. Reprinted by permission of *The Saturday Evening Post*. Copyright © 1958 by The Curtis Publishing Co.

distinguish the meaning of religion as living in the dimension of depth from particular expressions of one's ultimate concern in the symbols and institutions of a concrete religion. If we now turn to the concrete analysis of the religious situation of our time, it is obvious that our key must be the basic meaning of religion and not any particular religion, not even Christianity. What does this key disclose about the predicament of man in our period?

If we define religion as the state of being grasped by an infinite concern we must say: Man in our time has lost such infinite concern. And the resurgence of religion is nothing but a desperate and mostly futile attempt to regain what has been lost.

How did the dimension of depth become lost? Like any important event, it has many causes, but certainly not the one which one hears often mentioned from ministers' pulpits and evangelists' platforms, namely that a widespread impiety of modern man is responsible. Modern man is neither more pious nor more impious than man in any other period. The loss of the dimension of depth is caused by the relation of man to his world and to himself in our period, the period in which nature is being subjected scientifically and technically to the control of man. In this period, life in the dimension of depth is replaced by life in the horizontal dimension. The driving forces of the industrial society of which we are a part go ahead horizontally and not vertically. In popular terms this is expressed in phrases like "better and better," "bigger and bigger," "more and more." One should not disparage the feeling which lies behind such speech. Man is right in feeling that he is able to know and transform the world he encounters without a foreseeable limit. He can go ahead in all directions without a definite boundary.

A most expressive symbol of this attitude of going ahead in the horizontal dimension is the breaking through of the space which is controlled by the gravitational power of the earth into the world-space. It is interesting that one calls this world-space simply "space" and speaks, for instance, of space travel, as if every trip were not travel into space. Perhaps one feels that the true nature of space has been discovered only through our entering into indefinite world-space. In any case, the predominance of the horizontal dimension over the dimension of depth has been immensely increased by the opening of the space beyond the space of earth.

If we now ask what does man do and seek if he goes ahead in the horizontal dimension, the answer is difficult. Sometimes one is inclined to say that the mere movement ahead without an end, the intoxication with speeding forward without limits, is what satisfies him. But this answer is by no means sufficient. For on his way into space and time man changes the world he encounters. And the changes made by him change himself. He transforms everything he encounters into a tool; and in doing so he himself becomes a tool. But if he asks, a tool for what, there is no answer.

One does not need to look far beyond everyone's daily experience in order to find examples to describe this predicament. Indeed our daily life in office and home, in cars and airplanes, at parties and conferences, while reading magazines and watching television, while looking at advertisements and hearing radio, are in themselves continuous examples of a life which has lost the dimension of depth. It runs ahead, every moment is filled with something which must be done or seen or said or planned. But no one can experience depth without stopping and becoming aware of himself. Only if he has moments in which he does not care about what comes next can he experience the meaning of this moment here and now and ask himself about the meaning of his life. As long as the preliminary, transitory concerns are not silenced, no matter how interesting and valuable and important they may be, the voice of the ultimate concern cannot be heard. This is the deepest root of the loss of the dimension of depth in our period—the loss of religion in its basic and universal meaning.

If the dimension of depth is lost, the symbols in which life in this dimension has expressed itself must also disappear. I am speaking of the great symbols of the historical religions in our Western world, of Judaism and Christianity. The reason that the religious symbols became lost is not primarily scientific criticism, but it is a complete misunderstanding of their meaning; and only because of this misunderstanding was scientific critique able, and even justified, in attacking them. The first step toward the nonreligion of the Western world was made by religion itself. When it defended its great symbols, not as symbols, but as literal stories, it had already lost the battle. In doing so the theologians (and today many religious laymen) helped to transfer the powerful expressions of the dimension of depth into objects or happenings on the horizontal plane. There the symbols lose their power and meaning and become an easy prey to physical, biological and historical attack.

If the symbol of creation which points to the divine ground of everything is transferred to the horizontal plane, it becomes a story of events in a removed past for which there is no evidence, but which contradicts every piece of scientific evidence. If the symbol of the Fall of Man, which points to the tragic estrangement of man and his world from their true being, is transferred to the horizontal plane, it becomes a story of a human couple a few thousand years ago in what is now present-day Iraq. One of the most profound psychological descriptions of the general human predicament becomes an absurdity on the horizontal plane. If the symbols of the Saviour and the salvation through Him which point to the healing power in history and personal life are transferred to the horizontal plane, they become stories of a half-divine being coming from a heavenly place and returning to it. Obviously, in this form, they have no meaning whatsoever for people whose view of the universe is determined by scientific astronomy.

If the idea of God (and the symbols applied to Him) which expresses man's ultimate concern is transferred to the horizontal plane, God becomes a being among others whose existence or nonexistence is a matter of inquiry. Nothing, perhaps, is more symptomatic of the loss of the dimension of depth than the permanent discussion about the existence or nonexistence of God

—a discussion in which both sides are equally wrong, because the discussion itself is wrong and possible only after the loss of the dimension of depth.

When in this way man has deprived himself of the dimension of depth and the symbols expressing it, he then becomes a part of the horizontal plane. He loses his self and becomes a thing among things. He becomes an element in the process of manipulated production and manipulated consumption. This is now a matter of public knowledge. We have become aware of the degree to which everyone in our social structure is managed, even if one knows it and even if one belongs himself to the managing group. The influence of the gang mentality on adolescents, of the corporation's demands on the executives, of the conditioning of everyone by public communication, by propaganda and advertising under the guidance of motivation research, et cetera, have all been described in many books and articles.

Under these pressures, man can hardly escape the fate of becoming a thing among the things he produces, a bundle of conditioned reflexes without a free, deciding and responsible self. The immense mechanism, set up by man to produce objects for his use, transforms man himself into an object used by the same mechanism of production and consumption.

But man has not ceased to be man. He resists this fate anxiously, desperately, courageously. He asks the question, for what? And he realizes that there is no answer. He becomes aware of the emptiness which is covered by the continuous movement ahead and the production of means for ends which become means again without an ultimate end. Without knowing what has happened to him, he feels that he has lost the meaning of life, the dimension of depth.

Out of this awareness the religious question arises and religious answers are received or rejected. Therefore, in order to describe the contemporary attitude toward religion, we must first point to the places where the awareness of the predicament of Western man in our period is most sharply expressed. These places are the great art, literature and, partly at least, the philosophy of our time. It is both the subject matter and the style of these creations which show the passionate and often tragic struggle about the meaning of life in a period in which man has lost the dimension of depth. This art, literature, philosophy is not religious in the narrower sense of the word; but it asks the religious question more radically and more profoundly than most directly religious expressions of our time.

It is the religious question which is asked when the novelist describes a man who tries in vain to reach the only place which could solve the problem of his life, or a man who disintegrates under the memory of a guilt which persecutes him, or a man who never had a real self and is pushed by his fate without resistance to death, or a man who experiences a profound disgust of everything he encounters.

It is the religious question which is asked when the poet opens up the horror and the fascination of the demonic regions of his soul, or if he leads us into the deserts and empty places of our being, or if he shows the physical and moral mud under the surface of life, or if he sings the song of transitoriness, giving words to the ever-present anxiety of our hearts.

It is the religious question which is asked when the playwright shows the illusion of a life in a ridiculous symbol, or if he lets the emptiness of a life's work end in self-destruction, or if he confronts us with the inescapable bondage to mutual hate and guilt, or if he leads us into the dark cellar of lost hopes and slow disintegration.

It is the religious question which is asked when the painter breaks the visible surface into pieces, then reunites them into a great picture which has little similarity with the world at which we normally look, but which expresses our anxiety and our courage to face reality.

It is the religious question which is asked when the architect, in creating office buildings or churches, removes the trimmings taken over from past styles because they cannot be considered an honest expression of our own period. He prefers the seeming poverty of a purpose-determined style to the deceptive richness of imitated styles of the past. He knows that he gives no final answer, but he does give an honest answer. . . .

Is there an answer? There is always an answer, but the answer may not be available to us. We may be too deeply steeped in the predicament out of which the question arises to be able to answer it. To acknowledge this is certainly a better way toward a real answer than to bar the way to it by deceptive answers. And it may be that in this attitude the real answer (within available limits) is given. The real answer to the question of how to regain the dimension of depth is not given by increased church membership or church attendance, nor by conversion or healing experiences. But it is given by the awareness that we have lost the decisive dimension of life, the dimension of depth, and that there is no easy way of getting it back. Such awareness is in itself a state of being grasped by that which is symbolized in the term, dimension of depth. He who realizes that he is separated from the ultimate source of meaning shows by this realization that he is not only separated but also reunited. And this is just our situation. What we need above all—and partly have—is the radical realization of our predicament, without trying to cover it up by secular or religious ideologies. The revival of religious interest would be a creative power in our culture if it would develop into a movement of search for the lost dimension of depth.

This does not mean that the traditional religious symbols should be dismissed. They certainly have lost their meaning in the literalistic form into which they have been distorted, thus producing the critical reaction against them. But they have not lost their genuine meaning, namely, of answering the question which is implied in man's very existence in powerful, revealing and saving symbols. If the resurgence of religion would produce a new understanding of the symbols of the past and their relevance for our situation, instead of premature and deceptive answers, it would become a creative factor in our culture and a saving factor for many who live in estrangement, anxiety and despair. The religious answer has always the character of "in spite of." In spite of the loss of dimension of depth, its power is present, and most present in those who are aware of the loss and are striving to regain it with ultimate seriousness.

PART I
ULTIMATE
CONCERN

I
God

GOD is the answer to the question implied in man's finitude; he is the name for that which concerns man ultimately. This does not mean that first there is a being called God and then the demand that man should be ultimately concerned about him. It means that whatever concerns a man ultimately becomes god for him, and, conversely, it means that a man can be concerned ultimately only about that which is god for him. The phrase "being ultimately concerned" points to a tension in human experience. On the one hand, it is impossible to be concerned about something which cannot be encountered concretely, be it in the realm of reality or in the realm of imagination. Universals can become matters of ultimate concern only through their power of representing concrete experiences. The more concrete a thing is, the more the possible concern about it. The completely concrete being, the individual person, is the object of the most radical concern—the concern of love. On the other hand, ultimate concern must transcend every preliminary finite and concrete concern. It must transcend the whole realm of finitude in order to be the answer to the question implied in finitude. But in transcending the finite the religious concern loses the concreteness of a being-to-being relationship. It tends to become not only absolute but also abstract, provoking reactions from the concrete element. This is the inescapable inner tension in the idea of God. The conflict between the

From Paul Tillich, *Systematic Theology, Vol. 1* (Chicago: University of Chicago Press), 211. Reprinted by permission of University of Chicago Press. Copyright © 1973 by Paul Tillich.

concreteness and the ultimacy of the religious concern is actual wherever God is experienced and this experience is expressed, from primitive prayer to the most elaborate theological system. It is the key to understanding the dynamics of the history of religion.

2
What Faith
Is

I. FAITH AS ULTIMATE CONCERN

Faith is the state of being ultimately concerned: the dynamics of faith are the dynamics of man's ultimate concern. Man, like every living being, is concerned about many things, above all about those which condition his very existence, such as food and shelter. But man, in contrast to other living beings, has spiritual concerns—cognitive, aesthetic, social, political. Some of them are urgent, often extremely urgent, and each of them as well as the vital concerns can claim ultimacy for a human life or the life of a social group. If it claims ultimacy it demands the total surrender of him who accepts this claim, and it promises total fulfillment even if all other claims have to be subjected to it or rejected in its name. If a national group makes the life and growth of the nation its ultimate concern, it demands that all other concerns, economic well-being, health and life, family, aesthetic and cognitive truth, justice and humanity, be sacrificed. The extreme nationalisms of our century are laboratories for the study of what ultimate concern means in all aspects of human existence, including the smallest concern of one's daily life. Everything is centered in the only god, the nation—a god who certainly proves

From Paul Tillich, *Dynamics of Faith* (New York: Harper & Row), 1–29. Reprinted by permission of Harper & Row Publishers, Inc. Copyright © 1957 by Paul Tillich.

to be a demon, but who shows clearly the unconditional character of an ultimate concern.

But it is not only the unconditional demand made by that which is one's ultimate concern, it is also the promise of ultimate fulfillment which is accepted in the act of faith. The content of this promise is not necessarily defined. It can be expressed in indefinite symbols or in concrete symbols which cannot be taken literally, like the "greatness" of one's nation in which one participates even if one has died for it, or the conquest of mankind by the "saving race," etc. In each of these cases it is "ultimate fulfillment" that is promised, and it is exclusion from such fulfillment which is threatened if the unconditional demand is not obeyed.

An example—and more than an example—is the faith manifest in the religion of the Old Testament. It also has the character of ultimate concern in demand, threat and promise. The content of this concern is not the nation—although Jewish nationalism has sometimes tried to distort it into that—but the content is the God of justice, who, because he represents justice for everybody and every nation, is called the universal God, the God of the universe. He is the ultimate concern of every pious Jew, and therefore in his name the great commandment is given: "You shall love the Lord your God with all your heart, and with all your soul, and with all your might" (Deut. 6:5). This is what ultimate concern means and from these words the term "ultimate concern" is derived. They state unambiguously the character of genuine faith, the demand of total surrender to the subject of ultimate concern. The Old Testament is full of commands which make the nature of this surrender concrete, and it is full of promises and threats in relation to it. Here also are the promises of symbolic indefiniteness, although they center around fulfillment of the national and individual life, and the threat is the exclusion from such fulfillment through national extinction and individual catastrophe. Faith, for the men of the Old Testament, is the state of being ultimately and unconditionally concerned about Jahweh and about what he represents in demand, threat and promise.

Another example—almost a counter-example, yet nevertheless equally revealing—is the ultimate concern with "success" and with social standing and economic power. It is the god of many people in the highly competitive Western culture and it does what every ultimate concern must do: it demands unconditional surrender to its laws even if the price is the sacrifice of genuine human relations, personal conviction and creative *eros*. Its threat is social and economic defeat, and its promise—indefinite as all such promises—the fulfillment of one's being. It is the breakdown of this kind of faith which characterizes and makes religiously important most contemporary literature. Not false calculations but a misplaced faith is revealed in novels like *Point of No Return*. When fulfilled, the promise of this faith proves to be empty.

Faith is the state of being ultimately concerned. The content matters infinitely for the life of the believer, but it does not matter for the formal definition of faith. And this is the first step we have to make in order to understand the dynamics of faith.

2. FAITH AS A CENTERED ACT

Faith as ultimate concern is an act of the total personality. It happens in the center of the personal life and includes all its elements. Faith is the most centered act of the human mind. It is not a movement of a special section or a special function of man's total being. They all are united in the act of faith. But faith is not the sum total of their impacts. It transcends every special impact as well as the totality of them and it has itself a decisive impact on each of them.

Since faith is an act of the personality as a whole, it participates in the dynamics of personal life. These dynamics have been described in many ways, especially in the recent developments of analytic psychology. Thinking in polarities, their tensions and their possible conflicts, is a common characteristic of most of them. This makes the psychology of personality highly dynamic and requires a dynamic theory of faith as the most personal of all personal acts. The first and decisive polarity in analytic psychology is that between the so-called unconscious and the conscious. Faith as an act of the total personality is not imaginable without the participation of the unconscious elements in the personality structure. They are always present and decide largely about the content of faith. But, on the other hand, faith is a conscious act and the unconscious elements participate in the creation of faith only if they are taken into the personal center which transcends each of them. If this does not happen, if unconscious forces determine the mental status without a centered act, faith does not occur, and compulsions take its place. For faith is a matter of freedom. Freedom is nothing more than the possibility of centered personal acts. The frequent discussion in which faith and freedom are contrasted could be helped by the insight that faith is a free, namely, centered act of the personality. In this respect freedom and faith are identical. . . .

3. THE SOURCE OF FAITH

Faith is a total and centered act of the personal self, the act of unconditional, infinite and ultimate concern. The question now arises: what is the source of this all-embracing and all transcending concern? The word "concern" points to two sides of a relationship, the relation between the one who is concerned and his concern. In both respects we have to imagine man's situation in itself and in his world. The reality of man's ultimate concern reveals something about his being, namely, that he is able to transcend the flux of relative and transitory experiences of his ordinary life. Man's experiences, feelings, thoughts are conditioned and finite. They not only come and go, but their content is of finite and conditional concern—unless they are elevated to unconditional validity. But this presupposes the general possibility of doing so; it presupposes the element of infinity in man. Man is able to understand in an immediate personal and central act the meaning of the ultimate, the unconditional, the absolute, the infinite. This alone makes faith a human potentiality.

Human potentialities are powers that drive toward actualization. Man is driven toward faith by his awareness of the infinite to which he belongs, but which he does not own like a possession. This is in abstract terms what concretely appears as the "restlessness of the heart" within the flux of life.

The unconditional concern which is faith is the concern about the unconditional. The infinite passion, as faith has been described, is the passion for the infinite. Or, to use our first term, the ultimate concern is concern about what is experienced as ultimate. In this way we have turned from the subjective meaning of faith as a centered act of the personality to its objective meaning, to what is meant in the act of faith. It would not help at this point of our analysis to call that which is meant in the act of faith "God" or "a god." For at this step we ask: what in the idea of God constitutes divinity? The answer is: it is the element of the unconditional and of ultimacy. This carries the quality of divinity. If this is seen, one can understand why almost every thing "in heaven and on earth" has received ultimacy in the history of human religion. But we also can understand that a critical principle was and is at work in man's religious consciousness, namely, that which is really ultimate over against what claims to be ultimate but is only preliminary, transitory, finite.

The term "ultimate concern" unites the subjective and the objective side of the act of faith—the *fides qua creditur* (the faith through which one believes) and the *fides quae creditur* (the faith which is believed). The first is the classical term for the centered act of the personality, the ultimate concern. The second is the classical term for that toward which this act is directed, the ultimate itself, expressed in symbols of the divine. This distinction is very important, but not ultimately so, for the one side cannot be without the other. There is no faith without a content toward which it is directed. There is always something meant in the act of faith. And there is no way of having the content of faith except in the act of faith. All speaking about divine matters which is not done in the state of ultimate concern is meaningless. Because that which is meant in the act of faith cannot be approached in any other way than through an act of faith.

In terms like ultimate, unconditional, infinite, absolute, the difference between subjectivity and objectivity is overcome. The ultimate of the act of faith and the ultimate that is meant in the act of faith are one and the same. This is symbolically expressed by the mystics when they say that their knowledge of God is the knowledge God has of himself; and it is expressed by Paul when he says (I Cor. 13) that he will know as he is known, namely, by God. God never can be object without being at the same time subject. Even a successful prayer is, according to Paul (Rom. 8), not possible without God as Spirit praying within us. The same experience expressed in abstract language is the disappearance of the ordinary subject-object scheme in the experience of the ultimate, the unconditional. In the act of faith that which is the source of this act is present beyond the cleavage of subject and object. It is present as both and beyond both.

This character of faith gives an additional criterion for distinguishing true and false ultimacy. The finite which claims infinity without having it (as, e.g., a nation or success) is not able to transcend the subject-object scheme. It remains an object which the believer looks at as a subject. He can approach it with ordinary knowledge and subject it to ordinary handling. There are, of course, many degrees in the endless realm of false ultimacies. The nation is nearer to true ultimacy than is success. Nationalistic ecstasy can produce a state in which the subject is almost swallowed by the object. But after a period the subject emerges again, disappointed radically and totally, and by looking at the nation in a skeptical and calculating way does injustice even to its justified claims. The more idolatrous a faith the less it is able to overcome the cleavage between subject and object. For that is the difference between true and idolatrous faith. In true faith the ultimate concern is a concern about the truly ultimate; while in idolatrous faith preliminary, finite realities are elevated to the rank of ultimacy. The inescapable consequence of idolatrous faith is "existential disappointment," a disappointment which penetrates into the very existence of man! This is the dynamics of idolatrous faith: that it is faith, and as such, the centered act of a personality; that the centering point is something which is more or less on the periphery; and that, therefore, the act of faith leads to a loss of the center and to a disruption of the personality. The ecstatic character of even an idolatrous faith can hide this consequence only for a certain time. But finally it breaks into the open.

4. FAITH AND THE DYNAMICS OF THE HOLY

He who enters the sphere of faith enters the sanctuary of life. Where there is faith there is an awareness of holiness. This seems to contradict what has just been said about idolatrous faith. But it does not contradict our analysis of idolatry. It only contradicts the popular way in which the word "holy" is used. What concerns one ultimately becomes holy. The awareness of the holy is awareness of the presence of the divine, namely of the content of our ultimate concern. This awareness is expressed in a grand way in the Old Testament from the visions of the patriarchs and Moses to the shaking experiences of the great prophets and psalmists. It is a presence which remains mysterious in spite of its appearance, and it exercises both an attractive and a repulsive function on those who encounter it. In his classical book, *The Idea of the Holy*, Rudolph Otto has described these two functions as the fascinating and the shaking character of the holy. (In Otto's terminology: *mysterium fascinans et tremendum.*) They can be found in all religions because they are the way in which man always encounters the representations of his ultimate concern. The reason for these two effects of the holy is obvious if we see the relation of the experience of the holy to the experience of ultimate concern. The human heart seeks the infinite because that is where the finite wants to rest. In the infinite it sees its own fulfillment. This is the reason for the ecstatic attraction and fascination of everything in which ultimacy is manifest. On the other hand, if ultimacy is manifest and exercises its fascinating attraction, one realizes at the same time the infinite distance of the finite from the infinite and, consequently, the negative judgment over any finite attempts to reach the infinite. The feeling of being consumed in the presence of the divine is a profound expression of man's relation to the holy. It is implied in every genuine act of faith, in every state of ultimate concern.

This original and only justified meaning of holiness must replace the currently distorted use of the word. "Holy" has become identified with moral perfection, especially in some Protestant groups. The historical causes of this distortion give a new insight into the nature of holiness and of faith. Originally, the holy has meant what is apart from the ordinary realm of things and experiences. It is separated from the world of finite relations. This is the reason why all religious cults have separated holy places and activities from all other places and activities. Entering the sanctuary means encountering the holy. Here the infinitely removed makes itself near and present, without losing its remoteness. For this reason, the holy has been called the "entirely other," namely, other than the ordinary course of things or—to refer to a former statement—other than the world which is determined by the cleavage of subject and object. The holy transcends this realm; this is its mystery and its unapproachable character. There is no conditional way of reaching the unconditional; there is no finite way of reaching the infinite.

The mysterious character of the holy produces an ambiguity in man's ways of experiencing it. The holy can appear as creative and as destructive. Its fascinating element can be both creative and destructive (referring again to the fascinating character of the nationalistic idolatry), and the terrifying and consuming element can be destructive and creative (as in the double function of Siva or Kali in Indian thought). This ambiguity, of which we still find traces in the Old Testament, is reflected in the ritual or quasi-ritual activities of religions and quasi religions (sacrifices of others or one's bodily or mental self) which are strongly ambiguous. One can call this ambiguity divine-demonic, whereby the divine is characterized by the victory of the creative over the destructive possibility of the holy, and the demonic is character-ized by the victory of the destructive over the creative possibility of the holy. In this situation, which is most profoundly understood in the prophetic religion of the Old Testament, a fight has been waged against the demonic-destructive element in the holy. And this fight was so successful that the concept of the holy was changed. Holiness becomes justice and truth. It is creative and not destructive. The true sacrifice is obedience to the law. This is the line of thought which finally led to the identification of holiness with moral perfection. But when this point is reached, holiness loses its meaning as the "separated," the "transcending," the "fascinating and terrifying," the "entirely other." All this is gone, and the holy has become the morally good and the logically true. It has ceased to be the holy in the genuine sense of the word. Summing up this development, one could say that the holy originally lies below the alternative of the good and the evil; that it is both divine and demonic; that with the reduction of the demonic possibility the holy itself becomes transformed in its meaning; that it becomes rational and identical with the true and the good; and that its genuine meaning must be rediscovered.

These dynamics of the holy confirm what was said about the dynamics of faith. We have distinguished between true and idolatrous faith. The holy which is demonic, or ultimately de-structive, is identical with the content of idolatrous faith. Idola-trous faith is still faith. The holy which is demonic is still holy. This is the point where the ambiguous character of religion is most visible and the dangers of faith are most obvious: the danger of faith is idolatry and the ambiguity of the holy is its demonic possibility. Our ultimate concern can destroy us as it can heal us. But we never can be without it.

5. FAITH AND DOUBT

We now return to a fuller description of faith as an act of the human personality, as its centered and total act. An act of faith is an act of a finite being who is grasped by and turned to the infinite. It is a finite act with all the limitations of a finite act, and it is an act in which the infinite participates beyond the limitations of a finite act. Faith is certain in so far as it is an experience of the holy. But faith is uncertain in so far as the infinite to which it is related is received by a finite being. This element of uncertainty in faith cannot be removed, it must be accepted. And the element in faith which accepts this is courage. Faith includes an element of immediate awareness which gives certainty and an element of uncertainty. To accept this is courage. In the courageous standing of uncertainty, faith shows most visibly its dynamic character.

If we try to describe the relation of faith and courage, we must use a larger concept of courage than that which is ordinarily used. Courage as an element of faith is the daring self-affirmation of one's own being in spite of the powers of "nonbeing" which are the heritage of everything finite. Where there is daring and courage there is the possibility of failure. And in every act of faith this possibility is present. The risk must be taken. Whoever makes his nation his ultimate concern needs courage in order to maintain this concern. Only certain is the ultimacy as ultimacy, the infinite passion as infinite passion. This is a reality given to the self with his own nature. It is as immediate and as much beyond doubt as the self is to the self. It *is* the self in its self-transcending quality. But there is not certainty of this kind about the content of our ultimate concern, be it nation, success, a god, or the God of the Bible: they all are contents without immediate awareness. Their acceptance as matters of ultimate concern is a risk and therefore an act of courage. There is a risk if what was considered as a matter of ultimate concern proves to be a matter of preliminary and transitory concern—as, for example, the nation. The risk to faith in one's ultimate concern is indeed the greatest risk man can run. For if it proves to be a failure, the meaning of one's life breaks down; one surrenders oneself, including truth and justice, to something which is not worth it. One has given away one's personal center without having a chance to regain it. The

reaction of despair in people who have experienced the breakdown of their national claims is an irrefutable proof of the idolatrous character of their national concern. In the long run this
is the inescapable result of an ultimate concern, the subject matter of which is not ultimate. And this is the risk faith must take;
this is the risk which is unavoidable if a finite being affirms itself.
Ultimate concern is ultimate risk and ultimate courage. It is not
risk and needs no courage with respect to ultimacy itself. But it
is risk and demands courage if it affirms a concrete concern. And
every faith has a concrete element in itself. It is concerned about
something or somebody. But this something or this somebody
may prove to be not ultimate at all. Then faith is a failure in its
concrete expression, although it is not a failure in the experience
of the unconditional itself. A god disappears; divinity remains.
Faith risks the vanishing of the concrete god in whom it believes.
It may well be that with the vanishing of the god the believer
breaks down without being able to reestablish his centered self
by a new content of his ultimate concern. This risk cannot be
taken away from any act of faith. There is only one point which
is a matter not of risk but of immediate certainty and herein lies
the greatness and the pain of being human; namely, one's standing between one's finitude and one's potential infinity.

All this is sharply expressed in the relation of faith and doubt.
If faith is understood as belief that something is true, doubt is
incompatible with the act of faith. If faith is understood as being
ultimately concerned, doubt is a necessary element in it. It is a
consequence of the risk of faith.

The doubt which is implicit in faith is not a doubt about facts
or conclusions. It is not the same doubt which is the lifeblood of
scientific research. Even the most orthodox theologian does not
deny the right of methodological doubt in matters of empirical
inquiry or logical deduction. A scientist who would say that a
scientific theory is beyond doubt would at that moment cease to
be scientific. He may believe that the theory can be trusted for
all practical purposes. Without such belief no technical application of a theory would be possible. One could attribute to this

kind of belief pragmatic certainty sufficient for action. Doubt in this case points to the preliminary character of the underlying theory.

There is another kind of doubt, which we could call skeptical in contrast to the scientific doubt which we could call methodological. The skeptical doubt is an attitude toward all the beliefs of man, from sense experiences to religious creeds. It is more an attitude than an assertion. For as an assertion it would conflict with itself. Even the assertion that there is no possible truth for man would be judged by the skeptical principle and could not stand as an assertion. Genuine skeptical doubt does not use the form of an assertion. It is an attitude of actually rejecting any certainty. Therefore, it can not be refuted logically. It does not transform its attitude into a proposition. Such an attitude necessarily leads either to despair or cynicism, or to both alternately. And often, if this alternative becomes intolerable, it leads to indifference and the attempt to develop an attitude of complete unconcern. But since man is that being who is essentially concerned about his being, such an escape finally breaks down. This is the dynamics of skeptical doubt. It has an awakening and liberating function, but it also can prevent the development of a centered personality. For personality is not possible without faith. The despair about truth by the skeptic shows that truth is still his infinite passion. The cynical superiority over every concrete truth shows that truth is still taken seriously and that the impact of the question of an ultimate concern is strongly felt. The skeptic, so long as he is a serious skeptic, is not without faith, even though it has no concrete content.

The doubt which is implicit in every act of faith is neither the methodological nor the skeptical doubt. It is the doubt which accompanies every risk. It is not the permanent doubt of the scientist, and it is not the transitory doubt of the skeptic, but it is the doubt of him who is ultimately concerned about a concrete content. One could call it the existential doubt, in contrast to the methodological and the skeptical doubt. It does not question whether a special proposition is true or false. It does not reject every concrete truth, but it is aware of the element of insecurity in every existential truth. At the same time, the doubt which is implied in faith accepts this insecurity and takes it into itself in an act of courage. Faith includes courage. Therefore, it can include the doubt about itself. Certainly faith and courage are not identical. Faith has other elements besides courage and courage has other functions beyond affirming faith. Nevertheless, an act in which courage accepts risks belongs to the dynamics of faith.

This dynamic concept of faith seems to give no place to that restful affirmative confidence which we find in the documents of all great religions, including Christianity. But this is not the case. The dynamic concept of faith is the result of a conceptual analysis, both of the subjective and of the objective side of faith. It is by no means the description of an always actualized state of the mind. An analysis of structure is not the description of a state of things. The confusion of these two is a source of many misunderstandings and errors in all realms of life. An example, taken from the current discussion of anxiety, is typical of this confusion. The description of anxiety as the awareness of one's finitude is sometimes criticized as untrue from the point of view of the ordinary state of the mind. Anxiety, one says, appears under special conditions but is not an ever present implication of man's finitude. Certainly anxiety as an acute experience appears under definite conditions. But the underlying structure of finite life is the universal condition which makes the appearance of anxiety under special conditions possible. In the same way doubt is not a permanent experience within the act of faith. But it is always present as an element in the structure of faith. This is the difference between faith and immediate evidence either of perceptual or of logical character. There is no faith without an intrinsic "in spite of" and the courageous affirmation of oneself in the state of ultimate concern. This intrinsic element of doubt breaks into the open under special individual and social conditions. If doubt appears, it should not be considered as the negation of faith, but as an element which was always and will always be present in the act of faith. Existential doubt and faith are poles of the same reality, the state of ultimate concern.

The insight into this structure of faith and doubt is of tremendous practical importance. Many Christians, as well as members of other religious groups, feel anxiety, guilt and despair about what they call "loss of faith." But serious doubt is confirmation of faith. It indicates the seriousness of the concern, its unconditional character. This also refers to those who as future or present ministers of a church experience not only scientific doubt about doctrinal statements—this is as necessary and perpetual as theology is a perpetual need—but also existential doubt about the message of their church, e.g., that Jesus can be called the Christ. The criterion according to which they should judge themselves is the seriousness and ultimacy of their concern about the content of both their faith and their doubt.

6. FAITH AND COMMUNITY

The last remarks about faith and doubt in relation to religious creeds have led us to those problems which are ordinarily dominant in the popular mind in the discussion of faith. Faith is seen in its doctrinal formulations or in its legally dogmatic expressions. It is seen in its sociological setting more than in its character as a personal act. The historical causes of this attitude are obvious. The periods of suppression of the autonomous mind, culturally and religiously, in the name of the doctrinal formulations of a special faith, are remembered by the following generations. The life-and-death struggle of rebellious autonomy with the powers of religious suppression has left a deep scar in the "collective unconscious." This is true even in the present period, when the kind of suppression that existed at the end of the Middle Ages and in the period of the religious wars is a thing of the past. Therefore, it is not futile to defend the dynamic concept of faith against the accusation that it would lead back to new forms of orthodoxy and religious suppression. Certainly, if doubt is considered an intrinsic element of faith, the autonomous creativity of the human mind is in no way restricted. But, one will ask, is not this concept of faith incompatible with the "community of faith" which is a decisive reality in all religions? Is not the dynamic idea of faith an expression of Protestant individualism and humanistic autonomy? Can a community of faith—e.g., a church—accept a faith which includes doubt as an intrinsic element and calls the seriousness of doubt an expression of faith? And even if it could allow such an attitude in its ordinary members, how could it permit the same in its leaders?

The answers to these often rather passionately asked questions are many-sided and involved. At the present point the obvious and yet significant assertion must be made that the act of faith, like every act in man's spiritual life, is dependent on language and therefore on community. For only in the community of spiritual beings is language alive. Without language there is no act of faith, no religious experience! This refers to language generally and to the special language in every function of man's spiritual life. The religious language, the language of symbol and myth, is created in the community of believers and cannot be fully understood outside this community. But within it, the religious language enables the act of faith to have a concrete content. Faith needs its language, as does every act of the personality; without language it would be blind, not directed toward a content, not conscious of itself. This is the reason for the predominant significance of the community of faith. Only as a member of such a community (even if in isolation or expulsion) can man have a content for his ultimate concern. Only in a community of language can man actualize his faith.

But now one will repeat the question and ask: if there is no faith without community of faith, is it not necessary that the community formulate the content of its faith in a definite way as a creedal statement and demand that every member of the community accept it? Certainly this is the way in which the creeds came into existence. This is the reason for their dogmatic and legal fixation! But this does not explain the tremendous power of these expressions of the communal faith over groups and individuals from generation to generation. Nor does it explain the fanaticism with which doubts and deviations were suppressed, not only by external power, but even more by the mechanisms of inner suppression. These mechanisms had been planted into the individual mind and were most effective even without pressure from outside. In order to understand these facts we must remember that faith as the state of ultimate concern includes total surrender to the content of this concern in a centered act of the personality. This means that the existence of the personality in the ultimate sense is at stake. Idolatrous concern and devotion may destroy the center of the personality. If, as in the Christian Church, in centuries of strife the content of the communal faith has been defended against idolatrous intrusions and has been formulated as a defense against such intrusions, it is understandable that every deviation from these formulations is considered destructive for the "soul" of the Christian. He is thought to have fallen under demonic influences. Ecclesiastical punishments are attempts to save him from demonic self-destruction. In these measures the concern which is the content of faith is taken absolutely seriously. It is a matter of eternal life and death.

But it is not only the individual for whom subjection to the established creed is of decisive importance. It is also the community of faith as such which must be protected against the distorting influences of individuals. The Church excludes from its community those who are thought to have denied the foundations of the Church. This is the meaning of the concept of "heresy." The heretic is not one who has erroneous beliefs (this is a possible implication of heresy, but not its essence), but the heretic is one who has turned away from the true to a false, idolatrous concern. Therefore, he may influence others in the same direction, destroy them, and undermine the community. If the civil authorities consider the Church as the basis of the conformity and cultural substance without which a society cannot live, they persecute the heretic as a civil criminal and use means of indoctrination and external pressure by which they try to keep the unity of the religio-political realm. However, if this point is reached, the re-action of man's spiritual autonomy begins to work and, if victo-rious, removes not only the political enforcement of a creedal system but the creedal system itself—and, beyond this, often faith itself. But this proves to be impossible. It can be and has always been done only through the power of another ultimate concern. Faith stands against faith in the world historical struggles be-tween the Church and its liberal critics. Even the faith of the liberal needs expression and some communal formulation, and it needs to be defended against authoritarian attacks. Even more: the ultimate concern of the liberal needs concrete contents, as does every ultimate concern. He also lives in institutions of a definite historical character. He, too, has a special language and uses special symbols. His faith is not the abstract affirmation of freedom, but is the faith in freedom as an element in the con-creteness of a total situation. If he undercuts this concreteness in the name of freedom, he produces a vacuum into which an-tiliberal forces easily enter. Only creative faith can resist the onslaught of destructive faith. Only the concern with what is truly ultimate can stand against idolatrous concerns.

All this drives to the question: how is a community of faith possible without suppression of the autonomy of man's spiritual life? The first answer is based on the relation of the civil au-thorities to the community of faith. Even if a society is practically identical with a community of faith and the actual life of the group is determined by the spiritual substance of a church, the civil authorities should as such remain neutral and risk the rise of dissident forms of faith. If they try to enforce spiritual con-formity, and are successful, they have removed the risk and cour-age which belong to the act of faith. They have transformed faith into a behavior pattern which does not admit alternatives, and which loses its character of ultimacy even if the fulfillment of the religious duties is done with ultimate concern. However, such a situation has become rare in our period. In most societies the civil authorities have to deal with different communities of faith, unable to enforce the one or the other in all members of the society. In this case the spiritual substance of the social group is determined by the common denominator of the different groups and their common tradition. This denominator may be more secular or more religious. In any case it is an outgrowth of faith, and its expression—as in the American Constitution—is affirmed in an attitude which sometimes has the unconditional character of an ultimate concern, but more often the conditional character of a preliminary concern of highest degree. Just for this reason the civil authorities should not try to prohibit the expression of doubt about such a basic law, although they must enforce the legal consequences of it.

The second step in the solution of the problem deals with faith and doubt within the community of faith itself. The question is whether the dynamic concept of faith is incompatible with a community which needs creedal expressions of the concrete elements in its ultimate concern. The answer which follows from the preceding analyses is that no answer is possible if the character of the creed excludes the presence of doubt. The concept of the "infallibility" of a decision by a council or a bishop or a book excludes doubt as an element of faith in those who subject themselves to these authorities. They may have to struggle within themselves about their subjection; but after they have made the decision, no doubt can be admitted by them about the infallible statements of the authorities. This faith has become static, a nonquestioning surrender not only to the ultimate, which is affirmed in the act of faith, but also to its concrete elements as formulated by the religious authorities. In this way something preliminary and conditional—the human interpretation of the content of faith from the Biblical writers to the present—receives ultimacy and is elevated above the risk of doubt. The fight against the idolatrous implication of this kind of static faith was waged first by Protestantism and then, when Protestantism itself became static, by Enlightenment. This protest, however insufficient its expression, aimed originally at a dynamic faith and not at the negation of faith, not even at the negation of creedal formulations.

So we stand again before the question: how can a faith which has doubt as an element within itself be united with creedal statements of the community of faith? The answer can only be that creedal expressions of the ultimate concern of the community must include their own criticism. It must become obvious in all of them—be they liturgical, doctrinal or ethical expressions of the faith of the community—that they are not ultimate. Rather, their function is to point to the ultimate which is beyond all of them. This is what I call the "Protestant principle," the critical element in the expression of the community of faith and consequently the element of doubt in the act of faith. Neither the doubt nor the critical element is always actual, but both must always be possible within the circle of faith. From the Christian point of view, one would say that the Church with all its doctrines and institutions and authorities stands under the prophetic judgment and not above it. Criticism and doubt show that the community of faith stands "under the Cross," if the Cross is understood as the divine judgment over man's religious life, and even over Christianity, though it has accepted the sign of the Cross. In this way the dynamic faith which we first have described in personal terms is applied to the community of faith. Certainly, the life of a community of faith is a continuous risk, if faith itself is understood as a risk. But this is the character of dynamic faith, and the consequence of the Protestant principle.

3
Our Ultimate Concern

Now as they went on their way, he entered a village; and a woman named Martha received him into her house. And she had a sister called Mary, who sat at the Lord's feet and listened to his teaching. But Martha was distracted with much serving; and she went to him and said, "Lord, do you not care that my sister has left me to serve alone? Tell her then to help me." But the Lord answered, "Martha, Martha, you are anxious and troubled about many things; one thing is needful. Mary has chosen the good portion, which shall not be taken away from her."

—LUKE 10:38–42

THE WORDS Jesus speaks to Martha belong to the most famous of all the words in the Bible. Martha and Mary have become symbols for two possible attitudes towards life, for two forces in man and in mankind as a whole, for two kinds of concern. Martha is concerned about many things,

From Paul Tillich, *The New Being* (New York: Charles Scribner's Sons), 152–60. Reprinted by permission of Charles Scribner's Sons. Copyright © 1955 by Paul Tillich.

but all of them are finite, preliminary, transitory. Mary is concerned about one thing, which is infinite, ultimate, lasting.

Martha's way is not contemptible. On the contrary, it is the way which keeps the world running. It is the driving force which preserves and enriches life and culture. Without it Jesus could not have talked to Mary and Mary could not have listened to Jesus. Once I heard a sermon dedicated to the justification and glorification of Martha. This can be done. There are innumerable concerns in our lives and in human life generally which demand attention, devotion, passion. But they do not demand *infinite* attention, *unconditional* devotion, *ultimate* passion. They are important, often very important for you and for me and for the whole of mankind. But they are not *ultimately* important. And therefore Jesus praises not Martha, but Mary. She has chosen the right thing, the one thing man needs, the only thing of ultimate concern for every man.

The hour of a church service and every hour of meditative reading is dedicated to listening in the way Mary listened. Something is being said to us, to the speaker as well as to the listeners, something about which we may become infinitely concerned. This is the meaning of every sermon. It shall awaken infinite concern.

What does it mean to be concerned about something? It means that we are involved in it, that a part of ourselves is in it, that we participate with our hearts. And it means even more than that. It points to the way in which we are involved, namely, *anxiously*. The wisdom of our language often identifies concern with anxiety. Wherever we are involved we feel anxiety. There are many things which interest us, which provoke our compassion or horror. But they are not our real concern; they do not produce this driving, torturing anxiety which is present when we are genuinely and seriously concerned. In our story, Martha was seriously concerned. Let us try to remember what gives us concern in the course of an average day, from the moment of awakening to the last moment before falling asleep, and even beyond that, when our anxieties appear in our dreams.

We are concerned about our work; it is the basis of our existence. We may love it or hate it; we may fulfill it as a duty or as a hard necessity. But anxiety grasps us whenever we feel the limits of our strength, our lack of efficiency, the struggle with our laziness, the danger of failure. We are concerned about our relationships to others. We cannot imagine living without their benevolence, their friendship, their love, their communion in body and soul. But we are worried and often in utter despair when we think about the indifference, the outbursts of anger and jealousy, the hidden and often poisonous hostility we experience in ourselves as well as in those we love. The anxiety about losing them, about having hurt them, about not being worthy of them, creeps into our hearts and makes our love restless. We are concerned about ourselves. We feel responsible for our development towards maturity, toward strength in life, wisdom in mind, and perfection in spirit. At the same time, we are striving for happiness, we are concerned about our pleasures and about "having a good time," a concern which ranks very high with us. But our anxiety strikes us when we look at ourselves in the mirror of self-scrutiny or of the judgments of others. We feel that we have made the wrong decision, that we have started on the wrong road, that we are failing before men and before ourselves. We compare ourselves with others and feel inferior to them, and we are depressed and frustrated. We believe that we have wasted our happiness either by pursuing it too eagerly and confusing happiness with pleasure or by not being courageous enough to grasp the right moment for a decision which might have brought us happiness.

We cannot forget the most natural and most universal concern of everything that lives, the concern for the preservation of life —for our daily bread. There was a time in recent history in which large groups in the Western world had almost forgotten this concern. Today, the simple concern for food and clothing and shelter is so overwhelming in the greater part of mankind that it has almost suppressed most of the other human concerns, and it has absorbed the minds of all classes of people.

But, someone may ask, do we not have higher concerns than those of our daily life? And does not Jesus Himself witness to them? When He is moved by the misery of the masses does He not consecrate the social concern which has grasped many people in our time, liberating them from many worries of their daily lives? When Jesus is moved by pity for the sick and heals them, does He not thereby consecrate the concern shared by medical and spiritual healers? When He gathers around Him a small group in order to establish community within it, does He not thereby consecrate the concern about all communal life? When He says that He has come to bear witness to the truth, does He not consecrate the concern for truth, and the passion for knowledge which is such a driving force in our time? When He is teaching the masses and His disciples, does He not consecrate the concern for learning and education? And when He tells the parables, and when He pictures the beauty of nature and creates sentences of classic perfection, does He not consecrate the concern for beauty, and the elevation of mind it gives, and the peace after the restlessness of our daily concerns?

But are these noble concerns the "one thing" that is needed and the right thing that Mary has chosen? Or are they perhaps the highest forms of what Martha represents? Are we still, like Martha, concerned about many things even when we are concerned about great and noble things?

Are we really beyond anxiety when we are socially concerned and when the mass of misery and social injustice, contrasted with our own favored position, falls upon our conscience and prevents us from breathing freely and happily while we are forced to heave the sighs of hundreds of people all over the world? And do you know the agony of those who want to heal but know it is too late; of those who want to educate and meet with stupidity, wickedness and hatred; of those who are obliged to lead and are worn out by the people's ignorance, by the ambitions of their opponents, by bad institutions and bad luck? These anxieties are greater than those about our daily life. And do you know what tremendous anxiety is connected with every honest inquiry, the anxiety about falling into error, especially when one takes new and untrod paths of thought? Have you ever experienced the almost intolerable feeling of emptiness when you turned from a great work of art to the demands, ugliness and worries of your daily life? Even this is not the "one thing" we need as Jesus indicated when He spoke of the beauties of the Temple being doomed to destruction. Modern Europe has learned that the millennia of human creativity of which it boasted were not that "one thing needful," for the monuments of these millennia now lie in ruins.

Why are the many things about which we are concerned connected with worry and anxiety? We give them our devotion, our strength, our passion and we must do so; otherwise we would not achieve anything. Why, then, do they make us restless in the deepest ground of our hearts, and why does Jesus dismiss them as not ultimately needed?

As Jesus indicates in His words about Mary, it is because they can be taken from us. They all come to an end; all our concerns are finite. In the short span of our lives many of them have already disappeared and new ones have emerged which also will disappear. Many great concerns of the past have vanished and more will come to an end, sooner or later. The melancholy law of transitoriness governs even our most passionate concerns. The anxiety of the end dwells in the happiness they give. Both the things about which we are concerned and we ourselves come to an end. There will be a moment—and perhaps it is not far away—when we shall no longer be concerned about any of these concerns, when their finitude will be revealed in the experience of our own finitude—of our own end.

But we maintain our preliminary concerns as if they were ultimate. And they keep us in their grasp if we try to free ourselves from them. Every concern is tyrannical and wants our whole heart and our whole mind and our whole strength. Every concern tries to become our ultimate concern, our god. The concern about our work often succeeds in becoming our god, as does the concern about another human being, or about pleasure. The concern about science has succeeded in becoming the god of a whole era in history, the concern about money has become an even more important god, and the concern about the nation the most important god of all. But these concerns are finite, they conflict with each other, they burden our consciences because we cannot do justice to all of them.

We may try to dismiss all concerns and to maintain a cynical unconcern. We determine that nothing shall concern us any more, except perhaps casually, but certainly not seriously. We try to be unconcerned about ourselves and others, about our work and our pleasures, about necessities and luxuries, about social and political matters, about knowledge and beauty. We may even feel that this unconcern has something heroic about it. And one thing is true: It is the only alternative to having an ultimate concern. Unconcern or ultimate concern—those are the only alternatives. The cynic is concerned, passionately concerned, about one thing, namely, his unconcern. This is the inner contradiction of all unconcern. Therefore, there is only one alternative, which is ultimate concern.

What, then, is the one thing that we need? What is the right thing that Mary has chosen? Like our story, I hesitate to answer, for almost any answer will be misunderstood. If the answer is "religion," this will be misunderstood as meaning a set of beliefs and activities. But, as other New Testament stories show, Martha was at least as religious as Mary. Religion can be a human concern on the same level as the others, creating the same anxiety as the others. Every page of the history and psychology of religion demonstrates this. There are even special people who are supposed to cultivate this particular human concern. They are called by a highly blasphemous name: religionists—a word that reveals more about the decay of religion in our time than does anything else. If religion is the special concern of special people and not the ultimate concern of everybody, it is nonsense or blasphemy. So we ask again, what is the one thing we need? And again it is difficult to answer. If we answer "God," this will also be misunderstood. Even God can be made a finite concern, an object among other objects; in whose existence some people believe and some do not. Such a God, of course, cannot be our ultimate concern. Or we make Him a person like other persons with whom it is useful to have a relationship. Such a person may support our finite concerns, but He certainly cannot be our ultimate concern.

The one thing needed—this is the first and in some sense the last answer I can give—is to be concerned ultimately, unconditionally, infinitely. This is what Mary was. It is this that Martha felt and what made her angry, and it is what Jesus praises in Mary. Beyond this, not much has been said or could be said about Mary, and it is less than what has been said about Martha. *But Mary was infinitely concerned.* This is the one thing needed.

If, in the power and passion of such an ultimate concern, we look at our finite concerns, at the Martha sphere of life, everything seems the same and yet everything is changed. We are still concerned about all these things but differently—the anxiety is gone! It still exists and tries to return. But its power is broken; it cannot destroy us any more. He who is grasped by the one thing that is needed has the many things under his feet. They concern him but not ultimately, and when he loses them he does not lose the one thing he needs and that cannot be taken from him.

PART II

SYMBOLS OF FAITH

4
The Meaning of Symbol

M AN'S ULTIMATE CONCERN must be expressed symbolically, because symbolic language alone is able to express the ultimate. This statement demands explanation in several respects. In spite of the manifold research about the meaning and function of symbols which is going on in contemporary philosophy, every writer who uses the term "symbol" must explain his understanding of it.

Symbols have one characteristic in common with signs; they point beyond themselves to something else. The red sign at the street corner points to the order to stop the movements of cars at certain intervals. A red light and the stopping of cars have essentially no relation to each other, but conventionally they are united as long as the convention lasts. The same is true of letters and numbers and partly even words. They point beyond themselves to sounds and meanings. They are given this special function by convention within a nation or by international conventions, as the mathematical signs. Sometimes such signs are called symbols; but this is unfortunate because it makes the distinction between signs and symbols more difficult. Decisive is the fact that signs do not participate in the reality of that to which they point, while symbols do. Therefore, signs can be replaced for reasons of expediency or convention, while symbols cannot.

From Paul Tillich, *Dynamics of Faith* (New York: Harper & Row), 41–43. Reprinted by permission of Harper & Row Publishers, Inc. Copyright © 1957 by Paul Tillich.

This leads to the second characteristic of the symbol: It participates in that to which it points: the flag participates in the power and dignity of the nation for which it stands. Therefore, it cannot be replaced except after an historic catastrophe that changes the reality of the nation which it symbolizes. An attack on the flag is felt as an attack on the majesty of the group in which it is acknowledged. Such an attack is considered blasphemy.

The third characteristic of a symbol is that it opens up levels of reality which otherwise are closed for us. All arts create symbols for a level of reality which cannot be reached in any other way. A picture and a poem reveal elements of reality which cannot be approached scientifically. In the creative work of art we encounter reality in a dimension which is closed for us without such works. The symbol's fourth characteristic not only opens up dimensions and elements of reality which otherwise would remain unapproachable but also unlocks dimensions and elements of our soul which correspond to the dimensions and elements of reality. A great play gives us not only a new vision of the human scene, but it opens up hidden depths of our own being. Thus we are able to receive what the play reveals to us in reality. There are within us dimensions of which we cannot become aware except through symbols, as melodies and rhythms in music.

Symbols cannot be produced intentionally—this is the fifth characteristic. They grow out of the individual or collective unconscious and cannot function without being accepted by the unconscious dimension of our being. Symbols which have an especially social function, as political and religious symbols, are created or at least accepted by the collective unconscious of the group in which they appear.

The sixth and last characteristic of the symbol is a consequence of the fact that symbols cannot be invented. Like living beings, they grow and die. They grow when the situation is ripe for them, and they die when the situation changes. The symbol of the "king" grew in a special period of history, and it died in most parts of the world in our period. Symbols do not grow because people are longing for them, and they do not die because of scientific or practical criticism. They die because they can no longer produce response in the group where they originally found expression.

These are the main characteristics of every symbol. Genuine symbols are created in several spheres of man's cultural creativity. We have mentioned already the political and the artistic realm. We could add history and, above all, religion, whose symbols will be our particular concern.

5

The Nature of Religious Language

HE FACT that there is so much discussion about the meaning of symbols going on in this country as well as in Europe is a symptom of something deeper, something both negative and positive in its import. It is a symptom of the fact that we are in a confusion of language in theology and philosophy and related subjects which has hardly been surpassed at any time in history. Words do not communicate to us any more what they originally did and what they were invented to communicate. This has something to do with the fact that our present culture has no clearing house such as medieval scholasticism was, Protestant scholasticism in the seventeenth century at least tried to be, and philosophers like Kant tried to renew. We have no such clearing house, and this is the one point at which we might be in sympathy with the present day so-called logical positivists or symbolic logicians or logicians generally. They at least try to produce a clearing house. The only criticism is that this clearing house is a very small room, perhaps only a corner of a house, and not a real house. It excludes most of life. But it could become useful if it increased in reach and acceptance of realities beyond the mere logical calculus.

The positive point is that we are in a process in which a very important thing is being rediscovered: namely, that there are

From Paul Tillich, "Religious Symbols and Our Knowledge of God," *Christian Scholar* (September 1955), 189–197. Reprinted by permission of *Soundings* magazine. Copyright © 1955 by *Soundings* magazine.

levels of reality of great difference, and that these different levels demand different approaches and different languages; not everything in reality can be grasped by the language which is most adequate for mathematical sciences. The insight into this situation is the most positive side of the fact that the problem of symbols is again taken seriously.

I

Let us proceed with the intention of clearing concepts as much as we are able, and let us take five steps, the first of which is the discussion of "symbols and signs." Symbols are similar to signs in one decisive respect: both symbols and signs point beyond themselves to something else. The typical sign, for instance the red light at the corner of the street, does not point to itself but it points to the necessity of cars stopping. And every symbol points beyond itself to a reality for which it stands. In this, symbols and signs have an essential identity—they point beyond themselves. And this is the reason that the confusion of language mentioned above has also conquered the discussion about symbols for centuries and has produced confusion between signs and symbols. The first step in any clearing up of the meaning of symbols is to distinguish it from the meaning of signs.

The difference, which is a fundamental difference between them, is that signs do not participate in any way in the reality and power of that to which they point. Symbols, although they are not the same as that which they symbolize, participate in its meaning and power. The difference between symbol and sign is the participation in the symbolized reality which characterizes the symbols, and the nonparticipation in the "pointed-to" reality which characterizes a sign. For example, letters of the alphabet as they are written, an "A" or an "R" do not participate in the sound to which they point; on the other hand, the flag participates in the power of the king or the nation for which it stands and which it symbolizes. There has, therefore, been a fight since the days of William Tell as to how to behave in the presence of the flag. This would be meaningless if the flag did not participate as a symbol in the power of that which it symbolizes. The whole monarchic idea is itself entirely incomprehensible, if you do not understand that the king always is both: on the one hand, a symbol of the power of the group of which he is the king and on the other hand, he who exercises partly (never fully, of course) this power.

But something happened which is very dangerous for all our attempts to find a clearing house for the concepts of symbols and signs. The mathematician has usurped the term "symbol" for mathematical "sign," and this makes a disentanglement of the confusion almost impossible. The only thing we can do is to distinguish different groups, signs which are called symbols, and genuine symbols. The mathematical signs are signs which are wrongly called symbols.

Language is a very good example of the difference between signs and symbols. Words in a language are signs for a meaning which they express. The word "desk" is a sign which points to something quite different—namely, the thing on which a paper is lying and at which we might be looking. This has nothing to do with the word "desk," with these four letters. But there are words in every language which are more than this, and in the moment in which they get connotations which go beyond something to which they point as signs, then they can become symbols; and this is a very important distinction for any speaker. He can speak almost completely in signs, reducing the meaning of his words almost to mathematical signs, and this is the absolute ideal of the logical positivist. The other pole of this is liturgical or poetic language where words have a power through centuries, or more than centuries. They have connotations in situations in which they appear so that they cannot be replaced. They have become not only signs pointing to a meaning which is defined, but also symbols standing for a reality in the power of which they participate.

I I

Now we come to a second consideration dealing with the functions of symbols. The first function is implied in what has already been said—namely, the representative function. The symbol represents something which is not itself, for which it stands and in the power and meaning of which it participates. This is a basic function of every symbol, and therefore, if that word had not been used in so many other ways, one could perhaps even translate "symbolic" as "representative," but for some reason that is not possible. If the symbols stand for something which they are not, then the question is, "Why do we not have that for which they stand directly? Why do we need symbols at all?" And now we come to something which is perhaps the main function of the symbol—namely, the opening up of levels of reality which otherwise are hidden and cannot be grasped in any other way.

Every symbol opens up a level of reality for which nonsymbolic speaking is inadequate. Let us interpret this, or explain this, in terms of artistic symbols. The more we try to enter into the meaning of symbols, the more we become aware that it is a function of art to open up levels of reality; in poetry, in visual art, and in music, levels of reality are opened up which can be opened up in no other way. Now if this is the function of art, then certainly artistic creations have symbolic character. You can take that which a landscape of Rubens, for instance, mediates to you. You cannot have this experience in any other way than through this painting made by Rubens. This landscape has some heroic character; it has character of balance, of colors, of weights, of values, and so on. All this is very external. What this mediates to you cannot be expressed in any other way than through the painting itself. The same is true also in the relationship of poetry and philosophy. The temptation may often be to confuse the issue by bringing too many philosophical concepts into a poem. Now this is really the problem; one cannot do this. If one uses philosophical language or scientific language, it does not mediate the same thing which is mediated in the use of really poetic language without a mixture of any other language.

This example may show what is meant by the phrase "opening up of levels of reality." But in order to do this, something else must be opened up—namely, levels of the soul, levels of our interior reality. And they must correspond to the levels in exterior reality which are opened up by a symbol. So every symbol is two edged. It opens up reality and it opens up the soul. There are, of course, people who are not opened up by music or who are not opened up by poetry, or more of them (especially in Protestant America) who are not opened up at all by visual arts. The "opening up" is a two-sided function—namely, reality in deeper levels and the human soul in special levels.

If this is the function of symbols then it is obvious that symbols cannot be replaced by other symbols. Every symbol has a special function which is just *it* and cannot be replaced by more or less adequate symbols. This is different from signs, for signs can always be replaced. If one finds that a green light is not so expedient as perhaps a blue light (this is not true, but could be true), then we simply put on a blue light, and nothing is changed. But a symbolic word (such as the word "God") cannot be replaced. No symbol can be replaced when used in its special function. So one asks rightly, "How do symbols arise, and how do they come to an end?" As different from signs, symbols are born and die. Signs are consciously invented and removed. This is a fundamental difference.

"Out of what womb are symbols born?" Out of the womb which is usually called today the "group unconscious" or "collective unconscious," or whatever you want to call it—out of a group which acknowledges, in this thing, this word, this flag, or whatever it may be, its own being. It is not invented intentionally; and even if somebody would try to invent a symbol, as sometimes happens, then it becomes a symbol only if the unconscious of a group says "yes" to it. It means that something is opened up by it in the sense which I have just described. Now this implies further that in the moment in which this inner situation of the human group to a symbol has ceased to exist, then the symbol dies. The symbol does not "say" anything any more. In this way, all of the polytheistic gods have died; the situation in which they were born has changed or does not exist any more, and so the symbols died. But these are events which cannot be described in terms of intention and invention.

III

Now we come to a third consideration—namely, the nature of religious symbols. Religious symbols do exactly the same thing as all symbols do—namely, they open up a level of reality, which otherwise is not opened at all, which is hidden. We can call this the depth dimension of reality itself, the dimension of reality which is the ground of every other dimension and every other depth, and which therefore, is not one level beside the others but is the fundamental level, the level below all other levels, the level of being itself, or the ultimate power of being. Religious symbols open up the experience of the dimension of this depth in the human soul. If a religious symbol has ceased to have this function, then it dies. And if new symbols are born, they are born out of a changed relationship to the ultimate ground of being, i.e., to the Holy.

The dimension of ultimate reality is the dimension of the Holy. And so we can also say, religious symbols are symbols of the Holy. As such they participate in the holiness of the Holy according to our basic definition of a symbol. But participation is not identity; they are not themselves *the* Holy. The wholly transcendent transcends every symbol of the Holy. Religious symbols are taken from the infinity of material which the experienced reality gives us. Everything in time and space has become at some time in the history of religion a symbol for the Holy. And this is naturally so, because everything that is in the world we encounter rests on the ultimate ground of being. This is the key to the otherwise extremely confusing history of religion. Those of you who have looked into this seeming chaos of the history of religion in all periods of history from the earliest primitives to the latest developments, will be extremely confused about the chaotic character of this development. The key which makes order out of this chaos is comparatively simple. It is that everything in reality can impress itself as a symbol for a special relationship of the human mind to its own ultimate ground and meaning. So in order to open up the seemingly closed door to this chaos of religious symbols, one simply has to ask, "What is the relationship to the ultimate which is symbolized in these symbols?" And then they cease to be meaningless; and they become, on the contrary, the most revealing creations of the human mind, the most genuine ones, the most powerful ones, those who control the human consciousness, and perhaps even more the unconsciousness, and have therefore this tremendous tenacity which is characteristic of all religious symbols in the history of religion.

Religion, as everything in life, stands under the law of ambiguity, "ambiguity" meaning that it is creative and destructive at the same time. Religion has its holiness and its unholiness, and the reason for this is obvious from what has been said about religious symbolism. Religious symbols point symbolically to that which transcends all of them. But since, as symbols, they participate in that to which they point, they always have the tendency (in the human mind, of course) to replace that to which they are supposed to point, and to become ultimate in themselves. And in the moment in which they do this, they become idols. All idolatry is nothing else than the absolutizing of symbols of the Holy, and making them identical with the Holy itself. In this way, for instance, holy persons can become a god. Ritual acts can take on unconditional validity, although they are only expressions of a special situation. In all sacramental activities of religion, in all holy objects, holy books, holy doctrines, holy rites, you find this danger which we will call "demonization." They become demonic at the moment in which they become elevated to the unconditional and ultimate character of the Holy itself.

IV

Now we turn to a fourth consideration—namely, the levels of religious symbols. There are two fundamental levels in all religious symbols: the transcendent level, the level which goes *beyond* the empirical reality we encounter, and the immanent level, the level which we find *within* the encounter with reality. Let us look at the first level, the transcendent level. The basic symbol on the transcendent level would be God himself. But we cannot simply say that God is a symbol. We must always say two things about him: we must say that there is a nonsymbolic element in our image of God—namely, that he is ultimate reality, being itself, ground of being, power of being; and the other, that he is the highest being in which everything that we have does exist in the most perfect way. If we say this we have in our mind the image of a highest being, a being with the characteristics of highest perfection. That means we have a symbol for that which is not symbolic in the idea of God—namely, "Being Itself."

It is important to distinguish these two elements in the idea of God. Thus all of these discussions going on about God being a person or not a person, God being similar to other beings or not similar, these discussions which have a great impact on the destruction of the religious experience through false interpretations of it, could be overcome if we would say, "Certainly the awareness of something unconditional is in itself what it is, is not symbolic." We can call it *"Being Itself," esse qua esse, esse ipsum*, as the scholastics did. But in our relationship to this ultimate we symbolize and must symbolize. We could not be in communication with God if he were only "ultimate being." But in our relationship to him we encounter him with the highest of what we ourselves are, *person*. And so in the symbolic form of speaking about him, we have both that which transcends infinitely our experience of ourselves as persons, and that which is so adequate to our being persons that we can say, "Thou" to God, and can pray to him. And these two elements must be preserved. If we preserve only the element of the unconditional, then no relationship to God is possible. If we preserve only the element of the ego-thou relationship, as it is called today, we lose the element of the divine—namely, the unconditional which transcends subject and object and all other polarities. This is the first point on the transcendent level.

The second is the qualities, the attributes of God, whatever you say about him: that he is love, that he is mercy, that he is power, that he is omniscient, that he is omnipresent, that he is almighty. These attributes of God are taken from experienced qualities we have ourselves. They cannot be applied to God in the literal sense. If this is done, it leads to an infinite amount of absurdities. This again is one of the reasons for the destruction of religion through wrong communicative interpretation of it. And again the symbolic character of these qualities must be maintained consistently. Otherwise, every speaking about the divine becomes absurd.

A third element on the transcendent level is the acts of God, for example, when we say, "He has created the world," "He has sent his son," "He will fulfill the world." In all these temporal, causal, and other expressions we speak symbolically of God. As an example, look at the one small sentence: *"God has sent his son."* Here we have in the word "has" temporality. But God is beyond *our* temporality, though not beyond every temporality. Here is space; "sending somebody" means moving him from one place to another place. This certainly is speaking symbolically, although spatiality is in God as an element in his creative ground. We say that he "has sent"—that means that he has caused something. In this way God is subject to the category of causality. And when we speak of him and his Son, we have two different substances and apply the category of substance to him. Now all this, if taken literally, is absurd. If it is taken symbolically, it is a profound expression, the ultimate Christian expression, of the relationship between God and man in the Christian experience. But to distinguish these two kinds of speech, the nonsymbolic and the symbolic, in such a point is so important that if we are not able to make understandable to our contemporaries that we speak symbolically when we use such language, they will rightly turn away from us, as from people who still live in absurdities and superstitions.

Now consider the immanent level, the level of the appearances of the divine in time and space. Here we have first of all the incarnations of the divine, different beings in time and space, divine beings transmuted into animals or men or any kinds of other beings as they appear in time and space. This is often forgotten by those within Christianity who like to use in every second theological proposition the word "incarnation." They forget that this is not an especially Christian characteristic, because incarnation is something which happens in paganism all the time. The divine beings always incarnate in different forms. That is very easy in paganism. This is not the real distinction between Christianity and other religions.

Here we must say something about the relationships of the transcendent to the immanent level just in connection with the incarnation idea. Historically, one must say that preceding both of them was the situation in which the transcendent and immanent were not distinguished. In the Indonesian doctrine of "Mana," that divine mystical power which permeates all reality, we have some divine presence which is both immanent in everything as a hidden power, and at the same time transcendent, something which can be grasped only through very difficult ritual activities known to the priest.

Out of this identity of the immanent and the transcendent, the gods of the great mythologies have developed in Greece and in the Semitic nations and in India. There we find incarnations as the immanent element of the divine. The more transcendent the gods become, the more incarnations of personal or sacramental character are needed in order to overcome the remoteness of the divine which develops with the strengthening of the transcendent element.

And from this follows the second element in the immanent religious symbolism, namely, the sacramental. The sacramental is nothing else than some reality becoming the bearer of the Holy in a special way and under special circumstances. In this sense, the Lord's Supper, or better the materials in the Lord's Supper, are symbolic. Now you will ask perhaps, "only symbolic?" That sounds as if there were something more than symbolic, namely, "literal." But the literal is not more but less than symbolic. If we speak of those dimensions of reality which we cannot approach in any other way than by symbols, then symbols are not used in terms of "only" but in terms of that which is necessary, of that which we *must* apply. Sometimes, because of nothing more than the confusion of signs with symbols, the phrase "only a symbol" means "only a sign." And then the question is justified. "Only a sign?" "No." The sacrament is not only a sign. In the famous discussion between Luther and Zwingli, in Marburg in 1529, it was just this point on which the discussion was held. Luther wanted to maintain the genuinely symbolic character of the elements, but Zwingli said that the sacramental materials, bread and wine, are "only symbolic." Thus Zwingli meant that they are only signs pointing to a story of the past. Even in that period there was semantic confusion. And let us not be misled by this. In the real sense of symbol, the sacramental materials are symbols. But if the symbol is used as *only* symbol (i.e., only signs), then of course the sacramental materials are more than this.

Then there is the third element on the immanent level. Many things—like special parts of the church building, like the candles, like the water at the entrance of the Roman Church, like the cross in all churches, especially Protestant churches—were originally only signs, but in use became symbols; call them sign-symbols, signs which have become symbols.

V

And now a last consideration—namely, the truth of religious symbols. Here we must distinguish a negative, a positive, and an absolute statement. First the negative statement. Symbols are independent of any empirical criticism. You cannot kill a symbol by criticism in terms of natural sciences or in terms of historical research. As was said, symbols can only die if the situation in which they have been created has passed. They are not on a level on which empirical criticism can dismiss them. Here are two examples, both connected with Mary, the mother of Jesus, as Holy Virgin. First of all you have here a symbol which has died in Protestantism by the changed situation of the relation to God. The special, direct, immediate relationship to God makes any mediating power impossible. Another reason which has made this symbol disappear is the negation of the ascetic element which is implied in the glorification of virginity. And as long as the Protestant religious situation lasts it cannot be reestablished. It has not died because Protestant scholars have said, "Now there is no empirical reason for saying all this about the Holy Virgin." There certainly is not, but this the Roman Church also knows. But the Roman Church sticks to it on the basis of its tremendous symbolic power which step by step brings her nearer to Trinity itself, especially in the development of the last decade. If this should ever be completed as is now discussed in groups of the Roman Church, Mary would become co-Saviour with Jesus. Then, whether this is admitted or not, she is actually taken into the divinity itself.

Another example is the story of the virginal birth of Jesus. This is from the point of view of historical research a most obviously legendary story, unknown to Paul and to John. It is a late creation, trying to make understandable the full possession of the divine spirit of Jesus of Nazareth. But again its legendary character is not the reason why this symbol will die or has died in many groups of people, in even quite conservative groups within the Protestant churches. The reason is different. The reason is that it is theologically quasi-heretical. It takes away one of the fundamental doctrines of Chalcedon, viz., the classical Christian doctrine that the full humanity of Jesus must be maintained beside his whole divinity. A human being who has no human father has no full humanity. This story then has to be criticized on inner-symbolic grounds, but not on historical grounds. This is the negative statement about the truth of religious symbols. Their truth is their adequacy to the religious situation in which they are created, and their inadequacy to another situation is their untruth. In the last sentence both the positive and the negative statement about symbols are contained.

Religion is ambiguous and every religious symbol may become idolatrous, may be demonized, may elevate itself to ultimate validity although nothing is ultimate but the ultimate itself; no religious doctrine and no religious ritual may be. If Christianity claims to have a truth superior to any other truth in its symbolism, then it is the symbol of the cross in which this is expressed, the cross of the Christ. He who himself embodies the fullness of the divine's presence sacrifices himself in order not to become an idol, another god beside God, a god into whom the disciples wanted to make him. And therefore the decisive story is the story in which he accepts the title "Christ" when Peter offers it to him. He accepts it under the one condition that he has to go to Jerusalem to suffer and to die, which means to deny the idolatrous tendency even with respect to himself. This is at the same time the criterion of all other symbols, and it is the criterion to which every Christian church should subject itself.

6
The Divine Name

*You shall not take the name of the Lord
your God in vain; for the Lord will not
hold him guiltless who takes his name in
vain.*

—EXODUS 20:7

THERE MUST BE something extraordinary about the name if the second commandment tries to protect it as the other commandments try to protect life, honor, property. Of course, God need not protect Himself, but He does protect His name, and so seriously that He adds to this single commandment a special threat. This is done because, within the name, that which bears the name is present. In ancient times, one believed that one held in one's power the being whose hidden name one knew. One believed that the savior-god conquered the demons by discovering the mystery of the power embodied in their names, just as we today try to find out the hidden names

From Paul Tillich *The Eternal Now* (New York: Charles Scribner's Sons), 92–100. Reprinted by permission of Charles Scribner's Sons. Copyright © 1963 by Paul Tillich.

of the powers that disrupt our unconscious depths and drive us
to mental disturbances. If we gain insight into their hidden striving, we break their power. Men have always tried to use the
divine name in the same way, not in order to break its power,
but to harness its power for their own uses. Calling on the name
of God in prayer, for instance, can mean attempting to make God
a tool for our purposes. A name is never an empty sound; it is a
bearer of power; it gives Spiritual Presence to the unseen. This
is the reason the divine name can be taken in vain, and why one
may destroy oneself by taking it in vain. For the invocation of
the holy does not leave us unaffected. If it does not heal us, it
may disintegrate us. This is the seriousness of the use of the
divine name. This is the danger of religion, and even of anti-
religion. For in both the name of God is used as well as misused.

Let us now consider the danger of the use of the word God,
when it is both denied and affirmed, and of the sublime embarrassment of tact, the embarrassment of doubt, and the embarrassment of awe.

I

Not long ago, an intellectual leader was reported as saying, "I
hope for the day when everyone can speak again of God without
embarrassment." These words, seriously meant, deserve thought-
ful consideration, especially in view of the fact that the last fifteen
years have brought to this country an immense increase in the
willingness to use the name of God—an unquestionable and astonishing revival, if not of religion, certainly of religious awareness. Do we hope that this will lead us to a state in which the
name of God will be used without sublime embarrassment, without the restrictions imposed by the fact that in the divine name
there is more present than the name? Is an unembarrassed use
of the divine name desirable? Is unembarrassed religion desir-

able? Certainly not! For the Presence of the divine in the name demands a shy and trembling heart.

Everyone at one time or another finds himself in a situation where he must decide whether he shall use or avoid the name of God, whether he shall talk with personal involvement about religious matters, either for or against them. Making such a decision is often difficult. We feel that we should remain silent in certain groups of people because it might be tactless to introduce the name of God, or even to talk about religion. But our attitude is not unambiguous. We believe we are being tactful, when actually we may be cowardly. And then sometimes we accuse ourselves of cowardice, although it is really tact that prevents us from speaking out. This happens not only to those who would speak out *for* God, but also to those who would speak out *against* God. Whether for or against Him, His name is on our lips and we are embarrassed because we feel that more is at stake than social tact. So we keep silent, uncertain as to whether we are right or wrong. The situation itself is uncertain.

Perhaps we might isolate ourselves or seem ridiculous by even mentioning the divine name, affirming or denying it. But there might also be another present for whom the mention of the divine name would produce a first experience of the Spiritual Presence and a decisive moment in his life. And again, perhaps there may be someone for whom a tactless allusion to God would evoke a definite sense of repulsion against religion. He may now think that religion *as such* is an abuse of the name of God. No one can look into the hearts of others, even if he converses with them intimately. We must risk *now* to talk courageously and *now* to keep silent tactfully. But in no case should we be pushed into a direct affirmation or denial of God which lacks the tact that is born of awe. The sublime embarrassment about His real Presence in and through His name should never leave us.

Many persons have felt the pain of this embarrassment when they have had to teach their children the divine name, and others have felt it perhaps when they tried to protect their children against a divine name that they considered an expression of dangerous superstition. It seems natural to teach children about most objects in nature and history without embarrassment, and there are parents who think it is equally natural to teach them divine things. But I believe that many of us as parents in this situation feel a sublime embarrassment. We know as Jesus knew that children are more open to the divine Presence than adults. It may well be, however, that if we use the divine name easily, we may close this openness and leave our children insensitive to the depth and the mystery of what is present in the divine name. But if we try to withhold it from them, whether because we affirm or because we deny it, emptiness may take hold of their hearts, and they may accuse us later of having cut them off from the most important thing in life. A Spirit-inspired tact is necessary in order to find the right way between these dangers. No technical skill or psychological knowledge can replace the sublimely embarrassed mind of parents or teachers, and especially of teachers of religion.

There is a form of misuse of the name of God that offends those who hear it with a sensitive ear, just because it did not worry those who misused it without sensitivity. I speak now of a public use of the name of God which has little to do with God, but much to do with human purpose—good or bad. Those of us who are grasped by the mystery present in the name of God are often stung when this name is used in governmental and political speeches, in opening prayers for conferences and dinners, in secular and religious advertisements, and in international war propaganda. Often the frequent use of the name of God is praised, as this is an indication that we are a religious nation. And one boasts of this, comparing one's nation with others. Should this be condemned? It is hard *not* to do so, but neither is it easy. If the divine name is used publicly with full conviction, and therefore with embarrassment and Spiritual tact, it may be used without offense, although this is hardly ever so. It is usually taken in vain when used for purposes that are not to the glory of His name.

II

There is another more basic cause for sublime embarrassment about using the divine name—the doubt about God Himself. Such doubt is universally human, and God would not be God if we could possess Him like any object of our familiar world, and verify His reality like any other reality under inquiry. Unless doubt is conquered, there is no faith. Faith must overcome something; it must leap over the ordinary processes that provide evidence, because its object lies above the whole realm where scientific verification is possible. Faith is the courage that conquers doubt, not by removing it, but by taking it as an element into itself. I am convinced that the element of doubt, conquered in faith, is never completely lacking in any serious affirmation of God. It is not always on the surface; but it always gnaws at the depth of our being. We may know people intimately who have a seemingly primitive unshaken faith, but it is not difficult to discover the underswell of doubt that in critical moments surges up to the surface. Religious leaders tell us both directly and indirectly of the struggle in their minds between faith and unfaith. From fanatics of faith we hear beneath their unquestioning affirmations of God the shrill sound of their repressed doubt. It is repressed, but not annihilated.

On the other hand, listening to the cynical denials of God that are an expression of the flight from a meaning of life, we hear the voice of a carefully covered despair, a despair that demonstrates not assurance but doubt about their negation. And in our encounter with those who assume scientific reasons to deny God, we find that they are certain of their denial only so long as they battle—and rightly so—against superstitious ideas of God. When, however, they ask the question of God Who is really God—namely, the question of the meaning of life as a whole and their own life, including their scientific work, their self-assurance tumbles, for neither he who affirms nor he who denies God can be ultimately certain about his affirmation or his denial.

Doubt, and not certitude, is our human situation, whether we affirm or deny God. And perhaps the difference between them is not so great as one usually thinks. They are probably very similar in their mixture of faith and doubt. Therefore, the denial of God, if serious, should not shake us. What should trouble everyone who takes life seriously is the existence of indifference. For he who is indifferent, when hearing the name of God, and feels, at the same time, that the meaning of his life is being questioned, denies his true humanity.

It is doubt in the depth of faith that often produces sublime embarrassment. Such embarrassment can be an expression of conscious or unconscious honesty. Have we not felt how something in us sometimes makes us stop, perhaps only for a moment, when we want to say "God"? This moment of hesitation may express a deep feeling for God. It says something about the power of the divine name, and it says something about him who hesitates to use it. Sometimes we hesitate to use the word "God" even without words, when we are alone; we may hesitate to speak to God even privately and voicelessly, as in prayer. It may be that doubt prevents us from praying. And beyond this we may feel that the abyss between God and us makes the use of His name impossible for us; we do not dare to speak to Him, because we feel Him standing on the other side of the abyss from us. This can be a profound affirmation of Him. The silent embarrassment of using the divine name can protect us against violating the divine mystery.

III

We have considered the silence of tact and the silence of honesty concerning the divine name. But behind them both lies something more fundamental, the silence of awe, that seems to prohibit the speaking of God altogether. But is this the last word demanded by the divine mystery? Must we spread silence around what concerns us more than anything else—the meaning of our existence? The answer is—no! For God Himself has given mankind names for Himself in those moments when He has broken into our finitude and made Himself manifest. We can, and must use these names. For silence has power only if it is the other side of speaking, and in this way becomes itself a kind of speaking. This necessity is both our justification and our being judged, when we gather together in the name of God. We are an assembly where we speak about God. We are a church. The church is the place where the mystery of the holy should be experienced with awe and sacred embarrassment. But is this our experience? Are our prayers, communal or personal, a use or a misuse of the divine name? Do we feel the sublime embarrassment that so many people outside the churches feel? Are we gripped by awe when, as ministers, we point to the Divine Presence in the sacraments? Or, as theological interpreters of the holy, are we too sure that we can really explain Him to others? Is there enough sacred embarrassment in us when fluent Biblical quotations or quick, mechanized words of prayer pour from our mouths? Do we preserve the respectful distance from the Holy-Itself, when we claim to have the truth about Him, or to be at the place of His Presence or to be the administrators of His Power—the proprietors of the Christ? How much embarrassment, how much awe is alive in Sunday devotional services all over the world?

And now let me ask the church and all its members, including you and myself, a bold question. Could it be that, in order to judge the misuse of His name within the church, God reveals Himself from time to time by creating silence about Himself? Could it be that sometimes He prevents the use of His name in order to protect His name, that He withholds from a generation what was natural to previous generations—the use of the word God? Could it be that godlessness is not caused only by human resistance, but also by God's paradoxical action—using men and the forces by which they are driven to judge the assemblies that gather in

His name and take His name in vain? Is the secular silence about God that we experience everywhere today perhaps God's way of forcing His church back to a sacred embarrassment when speaking of Him? It may be bold to ask such questions. Certainly there can be no answer, because we do not know the character of the divine providence. But even without an answer, the question itself should warn all those inside the church to whom the use of His name comes too easily.

Let me close with a few words that are both personal and more than personal. While thinking about this sermon I tried to make it not only one about the divine name, but also about God Himself. Such an attempt stands under the judgment of the very commandment I tried to interpret, for it was a refined way of taking the name of God in vain. We can speak only of the names through which He has made Himself known to us. For He Himself "lives in unapproachable light, whom no man has ever seen nor can see."

7

The Truth of a Religious Symbol

HE TRUTH of a religious symbol has nothing to do with the truth of the empirical assertions involved in it, be they physical, psychological, or historical. A religious symbol possesses some truth if it adequately expresses the correlation of revelation in which some person stands. A religious symbol *is* true if it adequately expresses the correlation of some person with final revelation. A religious symbol can die only if the correlation of which it is an adequate expression dies. This occurs whenever the revelatory situation changes and former symbols becomes obsolete. The history of religion, right up to our own time, is full of dead symbols which have been killed not by a scientific criticism of assumed superstitions but by a religious criticism of religion. The judgment that a religious symbol *is* true is identical with the judgment that the revelation of which it is the adequate expression is true. This double meaning of the truth of a symbol must be kept in mind. A symbol *has* truth: it is adequate to the revelation it expresses. A symbol *is* true: it is the expression of a true revelation.

Theology as such has neither the duty nor the power to confirm or to negate religious symbols. Its task is to interpret them according to theological principles and methods. In the process of interpretation, however, two things may happen: theology may

From Paul Tillich *Systematic Theology, Vol. 1* (Chicago: University of Chicago Press), 240. Reprinted by permission of University of Chicago Press. Copyright © 1973 by Paul Tillich.

discover contradictions between symbols within the theological circle and theology may speak not only as theology but also as religion. In the first case, theology can point out the religious dangers and the theological errors which follow from the use of certain symbols; in the second case, theology can become prophecy, and in this role it may contribute to a change in the revelatory situation.

Religious symbols are double-edged. They are directed toward the infinite which they symbolize *and* toward the finite through which they symbolize it. They force the infinite down to finitude and the finite up to infinity. They open the divine for the human and the human for the divine.

PART III
THE PROTESTANT PRINCIPLE

8
Protestantism

I

Protestantism is understood as a special historical embodiment of a universally significant principle. This principle, in which one side of the divine-human relationship is expressed, is effective in all periods of history; it is indicated in the great religions of mankind; it has been powerfully pronounced by the Jewish prophets; it is manifest in the picture of Jesus as the Christ; it has been rediscovered time and again in the life of the church and was established as the sole foundation of the churches of the Reformation; and it will challenge these churches whenever they leave their foundation.

There is no question here as to whether we are now approaching the end of the Protestant principle. This principle is not a special religious or cultural idea; it is not subject to the changes of history; it is not dependent on the increase or decrease of religious experience or spiritual power. It is the ultimate criterion of all religious and all spiritual experiences; it lies at their base, whether they are aware of it or not. The way in which this principle is realized and expressed and applied and connected with other sides of the divine-human relationship is different in different times and places, groups, and individuals. Protestantism as a principle is eternal and a permanent criterion of everything temporal. Protestantism as the characteristic of a historical period is temporal and subjected to the eternal Protestant principle. It is judged by its own principle, and this judgment might be a negative one. The Protestant era might come to an end. But *if* it came to an end, the Protestant principle would not be refuted. On the contrary, the end of the Protestant era would be another manifestation of the truth and power of the Protestant principle. Will the Protestant era come to an end? Is *that* the judgment of the Protestant principle, as it was the judgment of the prophets that the nation of the prophets would be destroyed? This is a question which, of course, is not to be answered by historical predictions but by an interpretation of Protestantism, its dangers and its promises, its failures and its creative possibilities. . . .

I I

The power of the Protestant principle first became apparent to me in the classes of my theological teacher, Martin Kaehler, a man who in his personality and theology combined traditions of Renaissance humanism and German classicism with a profound understanding of the Reformation and with strong elements of the religious awakening of the middle of the nineteenth century. The historians of theology count him among the "theologians of mediation"—often in a depreciating sense. But *the task of theology is mediation,* mediation between the eternal criterion of truth as it is manifest in the picture of Jesus as the Christ and the changing experiences of individuals and groups, their varying questions and their categories of perceiving reality. If the mediating task of theology is rejected, theology itself is rejected; for the term *theo-logy* implies, as such, a mediation, namely, between the mystery, which is *theos*, and the understanding, which is *logos*. If some biblicists, pietists, evangelicals, and lay Christians are opposed to the mediating function of theology, they deceive themselves, since, in reality, they live by the crumbs falling from the table of the theological tradition which has been created by great mediators. One of the methods of mediation in theology is called "dialectical." Dialectics is the way of seeking for truth by talking with others from different points of view, through "Yes" and "No," until a "Yes" has been reached which is hardened in the fire of many "No's" and which unites the elements of truth promoted in the discussion. It is most unfortunate that in recent years the name "dialectical theology" has been applied to a theology that is strongly opposed to any kind of dialectics and mediation and that constantly repeats the "Yes" to its own and the "No" to any other position. This has made it difficult to use the term "dialectical" to denote theological movements of a really dialectical, that is a mediating, character; and it has resulted in the cheap and clumsy way of dividing all theologians into naturalists and supernaturalists, or into liberals and orthodox. As a theologian who sometimes has been dealt with in this easy way of shelving somebody (for instance, by being called a "neo-supernaturalist") I want to state unambiguously my conviction that these divisions are completely obsolete in the actual work which is done today by every theologian who takes the mediating or dialectical task of theology seriously. Therefore, I would not be ashamed to be called a "theologian of mediation," which, for me, would simply mean: a "theo-logian." There is, of course, danger in all mediation performed by the church, not only in its theological function but also in all its practical functions. The church is often unaware of this danger and falls into a self-surrendering adaptation to its environment. In such situations a prophetic challenge like that given by the "neo-Reformation" theology (as it should be called instead of "dialectical theology") is urgently needed. But, in spite of such a danger, the church as a living reality must permanently mediate its eternal foundation with the demands of the historical situation. The church is by its very nature dialectical and must venture again and again a "theo-logy" of mediation. . . .

The principle of justification through faith refers not only to the religious-ethical but also to the religious-intellectual life. Not only he who is in sin but also he who is in doubt is justified through faith. The situation of doubt, even of doubt about God, need not separate us from God. There is faith in every serious doubt, namely, the faith in the truth as such, even if the only truth we can express is our lack of truth. But if this is experienced in its depth and as an ultimate concern, the divine is present; and he who doubts in such an attitude is "justified" in his thinking. So the paradox got hold of me that he who seriously denies God, affirms him. Without it I could not have remained a theologian. There is, I soon realized, no place *beside* the divine, there is no possible atheism, there is no wall between the religious and the nonreligious. The holy embraces both itself and the secular. Being religious is being unconditionally concerned, whether this concern expresses itself in secular or (in the narrower sense) religious forms. The personal and theological consequences of these ideas for me were immense. Personally, they gave me at the time of their discovery, and always since then, a strong feeling of relief. You cannot reach God by the work of right thinking or by a sacrifice of the intellect or by a submission to strange authorities, such as the doctrines of the church and the Bible. You cannot, and you are not even asked to try it. Neither works of piety nor works of morality nor works of the intellect establish unity with God. They follow from this unity, but they do not make it. They even prevent it if you try to reach it through them. But just as you are justified as a *sinner* (though unjust, you are just), so in the status of *doubt* you are in the status of truth. And if all this comes together and you are desperate about the meaning of life, the seriousness of your despair is the expression of the meaning in which you still are living. This unconditional seriousness is the expression of the presence of the divine in the experience of utter separation from it. It is this radical and universal interpretation of the doctrine of justification through faith which has made me a conscious Protestant. . . .

The radical and universal interpretation of the idea of justification through faith had important theological consequences beyond the personal. If it is valid, no realm of life can exist without relation to something unconditional, to an ultimate concern. Religion, like God, is omnipresent; its presence, like that of God, can be forgotten, neglected, denied. But it is always effective, giving inexhaustible depth to life and inexhaustible meaning to every cultural creation. . . .

It was natural that on the basis of these presuppositions the history of religion and of Christianity required a new interpretation. The early and high Middle Ages received a valuation that they never had received in classical Protestantism. I called them "theonomous" periods, in contrast to the heteronomy of the later Middle Ages and the self-complacent autonomy of modern humanism. "Theonomy" has been defined as a culture in which the ultimate meaning of existence shines through all finite forms of thought and action; the culture is transparent, and its creations are vessels of a spiritual content. "Heteronomy" (with which theonomy is often confused) is, in contrast to it, the attempt of a religion to dominate autonomous cultural creativity from the outside, while self-complacent autonomy cuts the ties of a civilization with its ultimate ground and aim, whereby, in the measure in which it succeeds, a civilization becomes exhausted and spiritually empty. The Protestant principle as derived from the doctrine of justification through faith rejects heteronomy (represented by the doctrine of papal infallibility) as well as a self-complacent autonomy (represented by secular humanism). It demands a self-transcending autonomy, or theonomy. . . .

I I I

Most important for my thought and life was the application of these ideas to the interpretation of history. History became the central problem of my theology and philosophy because of the historical reality as I found it when I returned from the first World War: a chaotic Germany and Europe; the end of the period of the victorious *bourgeoisie* and of the nineteenth-century way of life; the split between the Lutheran churches and the proletariat;

the gap between the transcendent message of traditional Christianity and the immanent hopes of the revolutionary movements. The situation demanded interpretation as well as action. Both were attempted by the German religious-socialist movement, which was founded immediately after the war by a group of people, including myself. The first task we faced was an analysis of the world situation on the basis of contemporary events, viewed in the light of the great criticism of bourgeois culture during the nineteenth and early twentieth centuries, and with the help of the categories derived from the Protestant principle in its application to religion and culture. In this analysis the central proposition of my philosophy of religion proved its significance: Religion is the substance of culture, culture is the expression of religion. . . . An analysis of our situation could not have been attempted by me without my participation in the religious-socialist movement. In speaking about it, I first want to remove some misunderstandings concerning its nature and purpose. This is especially necessary in a country like the United States, where everything critical of nineteenth-century capitalism is denounced as "red" and, consciously or through ignorance, confused with communism of the Soviet type. The most unfortunate consequence of this attitude is the barrier that it erects against any real understanding of what is going on in our world, especially in Europe and Asia, and of the transformations that are taking place in all realms of life, in religion as well as in economy, in science as well as in the arts, in ethics as well as in education, in the whole of human existence. Religious socialism was always interested in human life as a whole and never in its economic basis exclusively. In this it was sharply distinguished from economic materialism, as well as from all forms of "economism." It did not consider the economic factor as an independent one on which all social reality is dependent. It recognized the dependence of economy itself on all other social, intellectual, and spiritual factors, and it created a picture of the total, interdependent structure of our present existence. We understood socialism as a problem not of wages but of a new theonomy in which the question of wages, of social security, is treated in unity with the question of truth, of spiritual security. On the other hand, we realized more than most Christian theologians ever did that there are social structures that unavoidably frustrate any spiritual appeal to the people subjected to them. My entrance into the religious-socialist movement meant for me the definitive break with philosophical idealism and theological transcendentalism. It opened my eyes to the religious significance of political Calvinism and social sectarianism, over against the predominantly sacramental character of my own Lutheran tradition. Religious socialism is not a political party but a spiritual power trying to be effective in as many parties as possible. It had and has sympathizers and foes on the Left as well as on the Right. Yet it stands unambiguously against every form of reaction, whether it be a semifeudal reaction as in Germany; a bourgeois status quo policy as in this country; or the clerical reaction that threatens to develop in large sections of postwar Europe. Religious socialism is not "Marxism," neither political Marxism in the sense of communism nor "scientific" Marxism in the sense of economic doctrines. We have, however, learned more from Marx's dialectical analysis of bourgeois society than from any other analysis of our period. We have found in it an understanding of human nature and history which is much nearer to the classical Christian doctrine of man with its empirical pessimism and its eschatological hope than is the picture of man in idealistic theology.

The most important theoretical work done by religious socialism was the creation of a religious interpretation of history, the first one, so far as I can see, of an especially Protestant character. There were Christian interpretations of history in the early and medieval church, an ecclesiastical or conservative type represented by Augustine and a sectarian or revolutionary type represented by Joachim of Floris. There were and are secular interpretations of history, conservative-pessimistic ones or evolutionary-optimistic ones or revolutionary-utopian ones. . . .

Lutheranism had some affinity to the first type, Calvinism to the second, and sectarianism to the third. But a genuine Protestant interpretation of history was missing. It was the historical situation itself, the gap between conservative Lutheranism and socialist utopianism in Germany, which forced upon us the question of a Protestant interpretation of history. The answer given so far centers around three main concepts: "theonomy," "kairos," and the "demonic." . . . There remains the task of showing the relation of the concepts of "kairos" and of the "demonic" to the Protestant principle.

"Kairos," the "fullness of time," according to the New Testament use of the word, describes the moment in which the eternal breaks into the temporal, and the temporal is prepared to receive it. What happened in the one unique kairos, the appearance of Jesus as the Christ, i.e., as the center of history, may happen in a derived form again and again in the process of time, creating centers of lesser importance on which the periodization of history is dependent. The presence of such a dependent kairos was felt by many people after the first World War. It gave us the impulse to start the religious-socialist movement, the impetus of which was strong enough to survive its destruction in Germany and to spread through many countries, as the work and the decisions of the Oxford conference surprisingly proved. It is the basic trend of the European masses today, as all keen observers agree. "Kairos" is a biblical concept which could not be used by Catholicism because of the latter's conservative hierarchical interpretation of history; and it has not been used by the sects because of their striving toward the final end. The Protestant principle demands a method of interpreting history in which the critical transcendence of the divine over against conservatism and utopianism is strongly expressed and in which, at the same time, the creative omnipresence of the divine in the course of history is concretely indicated. In both respects the concept of "kairos" is most adequate. It continues the Protestant criticism of Catholic historical absolutism; it prevents the acceptance of any kind of utopian belief, progressivistic or revolutionary, in a perfect future; it overcomes Lutheran individualistic transcendentalism; it gives a dynamic historical consciousness in the line of early Christianity and the early Reformation; it provides a theonomous foundation for the creation of the new in history. The idea of "the kairos" unites criticism and creation. And just this is the problem of Protestantism. . . .

The third concept decisive for my interpretation of history is that of "the demonic." It is one of the forgotten concepts of the New Testament, which, in spite of its tremendous importance for Jesus and the apostles, has become obsolete in modern theology. The thing responsible for this neglect was the reaction of the philosophers of the Enlightenment against the superstitious, abominable use of the demonic in the Middle Ages and in orthodox Protestantism. But abuse should not forbid right use. The idea of the demonic is the mythical expression of a reality that was in the center of Luther's experience as it was in Paul's, namely, the structural, and therefore inescapable, power of evil. The Enlightenment, foreshadowed by Erasmus' fight with Luther and by theological humanism, saw only the individual acts of evil, dependent on the free decisions of the conscious personality. It believed in the possibility of inducing the great majority of individuals to follow the demands of an integrated personal and social life by education, persuasion, and adequate institutions. But this belief was broken down not only by the "Storms of Our Times" but also by the new recognition of the destructive mechanisms determining the unconscious trends of individuals and groups. Theologians could reinterpret the badly named but profoundly true doctrine of "original sin" in the light of recent scientific discoveries. The powerful symbol of the demonic was everywhere accepted in the sense in which we had used it, namely, as a "structure of evil" beyond the moral power of good will, producing social and individual tragedy precisely through the inseparable mixture of good and evil in every human act. None of the concepts used by our interpretation of history has found as much response in religious and secular literature as has the concept of the demonic. This response may be interpreted as a symptom of the general feeling for the structural character of evil in our period. If evil has demonic or structural character limiting individual freedom, its conquest can come only by the opposite, the divine structure, that is, by what we have called a structure or "Gestalt" of grace. Luther's fight with Erasmus is typical for the Protestant interpretation of grace. We are justified by grace *alone,* because in our relation to God we are dependent on God, on God alone, and in no way on ourselves; we are grasped by grace, and this is only another way of saying that we have faith. Grace creates the faith through which it is received. Man does not create faith by will or intellect or emotional self-surrender. Grace comes to him; it is "objective," and he may be enabled to receive it, or he may not. The interest of early Protestantism was, however, so much centered around individual justification that the idea of a "Gestalt of grace" in our historical existence could not develop. This development was also prevented by the fact that the Catholic church considered itself as the body of objective grace, thus discrediting the idea of a "Gestalt of grace" for Protestant consciousness. It is obvious that the Protestant principle cannot admit any identification of grace with a visible reality, not even with the church on its visible side. But the negation of a visible "Gestalt of grace" does not imply the negation of the concept as such. The church in its spiritual quality, as an object of faith, is a "Gestalt of grace." . . . And the church as "Gestalt of grace" is older and larger than the Christian churches. Without preparation in all history, without what I later have called the "church in its latency" (abbreviated to the "latent church"), the "manifest" church never could have appeared at a special time. Therefore, grace is in all history, and a continuous fight is going on between divine and demonic structures. The feeling of living in the center of such a fight was the basic impulse of religious socialism, expressing itself in a religious and, I think, essentially Protestant interpretation of history.

IV

In all these ideas—theonomy, the kairos, the demonic, the Gestalt of grace, and the latent church—the Protestant principle appears in its revealing and critical power. But the Protestant principle is not the Protestant reality; and the question had to be asked as to how they are related to one another, how the life of the Protestant churches is possible under the criterion of the Protestant principle, and how a culture can be influenced and transformed by Protestantism. . . . It is not impossible that at some future time people will call the sum total of these transformations the end of the Protestant era. But the end of the Protestant era is, according to the basic distinction between the Protestant principle and Protestant reality, not the end of Protestantism. On the contrary, it may be the way in which the Protestant principle must affirm itself in the present situation. The end of the Protestant era is not the return to the Catholic era and not even, although much more so, the return to early Christianity; nor is it the step to a new form of secularism. It is something beyond all these forms, a new form of Christianity, to be expected and prepared for, but not yet to be named. Elements of it can be described but not the new structure that must and will grow; for Christianity is final only in so far as it has the power of criticizing and transforming each of its historical manifestations; and just this power is the Protestant principle. If the problem is raised of Protestantism as protest and as creation, a large group of questions immediately appear, all of them insufficiently answered in historical Protestantism and all of them driving toward radical transformations. . . . A short account of these problems may show their character and their importance. The sharp distinction between the principle and the actuality of Protestantism leads to the following question: By the power of what reality does the Protestant principle exercise its criticism? There must be such a reality, since the Protestant principle is not mere negation. But if such a reality does exist, how can it escape the Protestant protest? In other words: How can a spiritual Gestalt live if its principle is the protest against itself? How can critical and formative power be united in the reality of Protestantism? The answer is: In the power of the New Being that is manifest in Jesus as the Christ. Here the Protestant protest comes to an end. Here is the bedrock on which it stands and which is not subjected to its criticism. Here is the sacramental foundation of Protestantism, of the Protestant principle, and of the Protestant reality. . . .

The decrease in sacramental thinking and feeling in the churches of the Reformation and in the American denominations is appalling. Nature has lost its religious meaning and is excluded from participation in the power of salvation; the sacraments have lost their spiritual power and are vanishing in the consciousness of most Protestants; the Christ is interpreted as a religious personality and not as the basic sacramental reality, the "New Being." The Protestant protest has rightly destroyed the magical elements in Catholic sacramentalism but has wrongly brought to the verge of disappearance the sacramental foundation of Christianity and with it the religious foundation of the protest itself. It should be a permanent task of Christian theology, of preaching, and of church leadership to draw the line between the spiritual and the magical use of the sacramental element, for this element is the one essential element of every religion, namely, the presence of the divine before our acting and striving, in a "structure of grace" and in the symbols expressing it. C. G. Jung has called the history of Protestantism a history of continuous "iconoclasm" ("the destruction of pictures," that is, of religious symbols) and, consequently, the separation of our consciousness from the universally human "archetypes" that are present in the subconscious of everybody. He is right. Protestants often confuse essential symbols with accidental signs. They often are unaware of the numinous power inherent in genuine symbols, words, acts, persons, things. They have replaced the great wealth of symbols appearing in the Christian tradition by rational concepts, moral laws, and subjective emotions. This also was a consequence of the Protestant protest against the superstitious use of the traditional symbols in Roman Catholicism and in all paganism. But here also the protest has endangered its own basis.

One of the earliest experiences I had with Protestant preaching was its moralistic character or, more exactly, its tendency to overburden the personal center and to make the relation to God dependent on continuous, conscious decisions and experiences. The rediscovery of the unconscious in medical psychology and the insight into the unconscious drives of the mass psyche gave me the key to this basic problem of the Protestant cultus. The loss of sacraments and symbols corresponds to the exclusive emphasis on the center of personality in Protestantism; and both these facts correspond to the rise of the bourgeois ideal of personality, for which the Reformation and the Renaissance are equally responsible. At the same time, personal experience, the intimate observation of many individuals, the knowledge provided by psychotherapy, the trend of the younger generation in Europe toward the vital and prerational side of the individual and social life, the urgent desire for more community and authority and for powerful and dominating symbols—all these seemed to prove that the Protestant-humanist ideal of personality has been undermined and that the Protestant cultus and its personal and social ethics have to undergo a far-reaching transformation. This impression was and is supported by the general development of Western civilization toward more collectivistic forms of political and economic life. The demand for a basic security in social, as well as in spiritual, respects has superseded (though not removed) the liberal demand for liberty. And this demand can no longer be suppressed, for it is rooted in the deepest levels of the men of today, of personalities and groups. Reactionary measures may delay the development, but they cannot stop it. Organization of security (against the devastation coming from the atomic bomb or from permanent unemployment) is impossible without collectivistic measures. The question of whether Protestantism as a determining historical factor will survive is, above all, the question of whether it will be able to adapt itself to the new situation; it is the question of whether Protestantism, in the power of its principle, will be able to dissolve its amalgamation with bourgeois ideology and reality and create a synthesis, in criticism and acceptance, with the new forces that have arisen in the present stage of a revolutionary transformation of man and his world.

This is a challenge for both the individual and the social ethics of Protestantism. . . . Protestantism has not developed a social ethics of its own as Roman Catholicism has done (and codified) in terms of Thomism. The Protestant principle cannot admit an absolute form of social ethics. But, on the other hand, it need not surrender its development to the state, as it did on Lutheran soil, or to society, as it did on Calvinistic soil. Protestantism can and must have social ethics determined by the experience of the kairos in the light of the Protestant principle. . . . Ethics out of the kairos is ethics of love, for love unites the ultimate criterion with the adaptation to the concrete situation.

It is a shortcoming of Protestantism that it never has sufficiently described the place of love in the whole of Christianity. This is due to the genesis and history of Protestantism. The Reformation had to fight against the partly magical, partly moralistic, partly relativistic distortion of the idea of love in later Catholicism. But this fight was only a consequence of Luther's fight against the Catholic doctrine of faith. And so faith and not love occupied the center of Protestant thought. While Zwingli and Calvin, by their humanistic-biblicistic stress on the function of the law, were prevented from developing a doctrine of love, Luther's doctrine of love and wrath (of God and the government) prevented him from connecting love with law and justice. The result was puritanism without love in the Calvinistic countries and romanticism without justice in the Lutheran countries. A fresh interpretation of love is needed in all sections of Protestantism, an interpretation that shows that love is basically not an emotional but an ontological power, that it is the essence of life itself, namely, the dynamic reunion of that which is separated. If love is understood in this way, it is the principle on which all Protestant social ethics is based, uniting an eternal and a dynamic element, uniting power with justice and creativity with form. . . .

Theology is defined as "theonomous metaphysics," a definition that was a first and rather insufficient step toward what I now call the "method of correlation." This method tries to overcome the conflict between the naturalistic and supernaturalistic methods which imperils not only any real progress in the work of systematic theology but also any possible effect of theology on the secular world. The method of correlation shows, at every point of Christian thought, the interdependence between the ultimate questions to which philosophy (as well as pre-philosophical thinking) is driven and the answers given in the Christian message. Philosophy cannot answer ultimate or existential questions *qua* philosophy. If the philosopher tries to answer them (and all creative philosophers have tried to do so), he becomes a theologian. And, conversely, theology cannot answer those questions without accepting their presuppositions and implications. Question and answer determine each other; if they are separated, the traditional answers become unintelligible, and the actual questions remain unanswered. The method of correlation aims to overcome this situation. . . .

Such a method is truly dialectical and therefore opposed to the supernaturalism of later Barthianism as well as to any other type of orthodoxy and fundamentalism. Philosophy and theology are not separated, and they are not identical, but they are correlated, and their correlation is the methodological problem of a Protestant theology.

In this connection I want to say a few words about my relationship to the two main trends in present-day theology, the one called "dialectical" in Europe, "neo-orthodox" in America, the other called "liberal" in Europe (and America) and sometimes "humanist" in America. My theology can be understood as an attempt to overcome the conflict between these two types of theology. It intends to show that the alternative expressed in those names is not valid; that most of the contrasting statements are expressions of an obsolete stage of theological thought; and that, besides many other developments in life and the interpretation of life, the Protestant principle itself prohibits old and new orthodoxy, old and new liberalism. . . .

It was the Protestant principle that gave liberal theology the right and the good conscience to approach the Holy Scripture with the critical methods of historical research and with a complete scientific honesty in showing the mythical and legendary elements in both Testaments. This event, which has no parallel in other religions, is an impressive and glorious vindication of the truth of the Protestant principle. In this respect Protestant theology must always be liberal theology.

It was the Protestant principle that enabled liberal theology to realize that Christianity cannot be considered in isolation from the general religous and cultural, psychologial and sociological, development of humanity; that Christianity, as well as every Christian, is involved in the universal structures and changes of human life; and that, on the other hand, there are anticipations of Christianity in all history. This insight, which is deadly for ecclesiastical and theological arrogance, is strengthening for Christianity in the light of the Protestant principle. In this respect also Protestant theology must be liberal theology.

It was the Protestant principle that destroyed the supra-naturalism of the Roman Catholic system, the dualism between nature and grace, which is ultimately rooted in a metaphysical devaluation of the natural as such. And it was the Protestant principle that showed liberal theology a way of uniting the anti-dualistic emphasis of the Reformation with the ontological universalism and humanism of the Renaissance, thus destroying holy superstitions, sacramental magic, and sacred heteronomy. In this respect above all, Protestant theology must be liberal theology and must remain so even if challenged and suppressed by a period which will prefer security to truth.

But it is also the Protestant principle that has induced orthodox theologians (both old and new) to look at Scripture as Holy Scripture, namely, as the original document of the event which is called "Jesus the Christ" and which is the criterion of all Scripture and the manifestation of the Protestant principle. In this respect Protestant theology must be "ortho-dox" and must always maintain the ground in which the critical power of the Protestant principle is rooted.

It was the Protestant principle that showed orthodox theologians (both old and new) that the history of religion and culture is a history of permanent demonic distortions of revelation and idolatrous confusions of God and man. Therefore, they emphasized and reemphasized the First Commandment, the infinite distance between God and man, and the judgment of the Cross over and against all human possibilities. In this respect also, Protestant theology must be always orthodox, fighting against conscious and unconscious idolatries and ideologies.

Again, it was the Protestant principle that forced the orthodox theologians (both old and new) to acknowledge that man in his very existence is estranged from God, that a distorted humanity is our heritage, and that no human endeavor and no law of progress can conquer this situation but only the paradoxical and reconciling act of the divine self-giving. In this respect above all, Protestant theology must be orthodox at all times.

Is the acceptance of these propositions liberal, is it orthodox theology? I think it is neither the one nor the other. I think it is Protestant and Christian, and, if a technical term is wanted, it is "neodialectical." . . .

What are the chances of historical Protestantism in this period? What are its possible contributions to this period? Will the new era be in any imaginable sense a Protestant era, as the era between the Reformation and the first World War certainly was? A few things are obvious. The wars and the revolutions that mark the first half of the twentieth century are symptoms of the disintegration of life and thought of the liberal *bourgeoisie* and of a radical transformation of Western civilization. In so far as Protestantism is an element in the changing structure of the Western world—and nothing beyond it—it takes part in the process of disintegration and transformation. It is not untouched by the trend toward a more collectivistic order of life, socially as well as spiritually. It is threatened by the dangers of this trend, and it may share in its promises. We are not yet able to have a picture of this coming era and of the situation of Christianity and Protestantism within it. We see elements of the picture which certainly will appear in it, but we do not see the whole. We do not know the destiny and character of Protestantism in this period. We do not know whether it will even desire or deserve the name "Protestantism." All this is unknown. But we know three things: We know the Protestant principle, its eternal significance, and its lasting power in all periods of history. We know, though only fragmentarily, the next steps that Protestantism must take in the light of its principle and in view of the present situation of itself and of the world. And we know that it will take these steps unwillingly, with many discords, relapses, and frustrations, but forced by a power that is not its own.

May I conclude with a personal remark? It was the "ecstatic" experience of the belief in a kairos which, after the first World War, created, or at least initiated, most of the ideas presented in this book. There is no such ecstatic experience after the second World War, but a general feeling that more darkness than light is lying ahead of us. An element of cynical realism is prevailing today, as an element of utopian hope was prevailing at that earlier time. The Protestant principle judges both of them. It justifies the hope, though destroying its utopian form; it justifies the realism, though destroying its cynical form. In the spirit of such a realism of hope, Protestantism must enter the new era, whether this era will be described by later historians as a post-Protestant or as a Protestant era; for, not the Protestant era, but the Protestant principle is everlasting.

9
The Spiritual Presence

I N SO FAR as religion is conquered by the Spiritual Presence, profanization and demonization are conquered. The inner-religious profanization of religion, its transformation into a sacred mechanism of hierarchical structure, doctrine, and ritual, is resisted by the participation of church members in the Spiritual Community, which is the dynamic essence of the churches and of which the churches are both the existential representation and the existential distortion. The freedom of the Spirit breaks through mechanizing profanization—as it did in the creative moments of the Reformation. In doing so it also resists the secular form of profanization, for the secular as secular lives from the protest against the profanization of religion within itself. If this protest becomes meaningless, the functions of morality and culture are opened again for the ultimate, the aim of the self-transcendence of life.

Demonization is also conquered in so far as religion is conquered by the Spiritual Presence. We have distinguished between the demonic that is hidden—the affirmation of a greatness which leads to the tragic conflict with the "great itself"—and the openly demonic—the affirmation of a finite as infinite in the name of the holy. Both the tragic and the demonic are conquered in principle by the Spiritual Presence. Christianity has always claimed

From Paul Tillich, *Systematic Theology, Vol. 3* (Chicago: University of Chicago Press), 244–45. Reprinted by permission of University of Chicago Press. Copyright © 1976 by Paul Tillich.

that neither the death of the Christ nor the suffering of Christians is tragic, because neither is rooted in the affirmation of its greatness but in the participation in the predicament of estranged man to which each belongs and does not belong. If Christianity teaches that the Christ and the martyrs suffered "innocently," this means that their suffering is not based on the tragic guilt of self-affirmed greatness but on their willingness to participate in the tragic consequences of human estrangement.

Self-affirmed greatness in the realm of the holy is demonic. This is true of the claim of a church to represent in its structure the Spiritual Community unambiguously. The consequent will to unlimited power over all things holy and secular is in itself the judgment against a church which makes this claim. The same is true of individuals who, as adherents of a group making such a claim, become self-assured, fanatical, and destructive of life in others and the meaning of life within themselves. But in so far as the divine Spirit conquers religion, it prevents the claim by both the churches and their members. Where the divine Spirit is effective, the claim of a church to represent God to the exclusion of all other churches is rejected. The freedom of the Spirit resists it. And when the divine Spirit is effective, a church member's claim to an exclusive possession of the truth is undercut by the witness of the divine Spirit to his fragmentary as well as ambiguous participation in the truth. The Spiritual Presence excludes fanaticism, because in the presence of God no man can boast about his grasp of God. No one can grasp that by which he is grasped—the Spiritual Presence.

In other connections. I have called this truth the "Protestant principle." It is here that the Protestant principle has its place in the theological system. The Protestant principle is an expression of the conquest of religion by the Spiritual Presence and consequently an expression of the victory over the ambiguities of religion, its profanization, and its demonization. It is Protestant, because it protests against the tragic-demonic self-elevation of religion and liberates religion from itself for the other functions of the human spirit, at the same time liberating these functions from their self-seclusion against the manifestation of the ultimate. The Protestant principle (which is a manifestation of the prophetic Spirit) is not restricted to the churches of the Reformation or to any other church; it transcends every particular church, being an expression of the Spiritual Community. It has been betrayed by every church, including the churches of the Reformation, but it is also effective in every church as the power which prevents profanization and demonization from destroying the Christian churches completely. It alone is not enough; it needs the "Catholic substance," the concrete embodiment of the Spiritual Presence; but it is the criterion of the demonization (and profanization) of such embodiment. It is the expression of the victory of the Spirit over religion.

10
The New Being

> *For neither circumcision counts for anything nor uncircumcision, but a new creation.*
>
> —GALATIANS 6:15

I F I WERE ASKED to sum up the Christian message for our time in two words, I would say with Paul: It is the message of a "New Creation." We have read something of the New Creation in Paul's second letter to the Corinthians. Let me repeat one of his sentences in the words of an exact translation: "If anyone is in union with Christ he is a new being; the old state of things has passed away; there is a new state of things." Christianity is the message of the New Creation, the New Being, the New Reality which has appeared with the appearance of Jesus who for this reason, and just for this reason, is called the Christ. For the Christ, the Messiah, the selected and anointed one is He who brings the new state of things.

From Paul Tillich *The New Being* (New York: Charles Scribner's Sons), 15–24. Reprinted by permission of Charles Scribner's Sons. Copyright © 1955 by Paul Tillich.

We all live in the old state of things, and the question asked of us by our text is whether we *also* participate in the new state of things. We belong to the Old Creation, and the demand made upon us by Christianity is that we *also* participate in the New Creation. We have known ourselves in our old being, and we shall ask ourselves in this hour whether we also have experienced something of a New Being in ourselves.

What is this New Being? Paul answers first by saying what it is *not*. It is neither circumcision, nor uncircumcision, he says. For Paul and for the readers of his letter this meant something very definite. It meant that neither to be a Jew nor to be a pagan is ultimately important; that only one thing counts, namely, the union with Him in whom the New Reality is present. Circumcision or uncircumcision—what does that mean for *us*? It can also mean something very definite, but at the same time something very universal. It means that no religion as such produces the New Being. Circumcision is a religious rite, observed by the Jews; sacrifices are religious rites, observed by the pagans; baptism is a religious rite, observed by the Christians. All these rites do not matter—only a New Creation. And since these rites stand, in the words of Paul, for the whole religion to which they belong, we can say: No religion matters—only a new state of things. Let us think about this striking assertion of Paul. What it says first is that Christianity is more than a religion; it is the message of a New Creation. Christianity as a religion is not important—it is like circumcision or like uncircumcision: no more, no less! Are we able even to imagine the consequences of the apostolic pronouncement for our situation? Christianity in the present world encounters several forms of circumcision and uncircumcision. Circumcision can stand today for everything called religion, uncircumcision for everything called secular, but making half-religious claims. There are the great religions beside Christianity, Hinduism, Buddhism, Islam and the remnants of classical Judaism; they have their myths and their rites—so to speak their "circumcision"—which gives each of them their distinction. There are the secular movements: Fascism and Communism, Secular

Humanism, and Ethical Idealism. They try to avoid myths and rites; they represent, so to speak, uncircumcision. Nevertheless, they also claim ultimate truth and demand complete devotion. How shall Christianity face them? Shall Christianity tell them: Come to us, we are a better religion, our kind of circumcision or uncircumcision is higher than yours? Shall we praise Christianity, our way of life, the religious as well as the secular? Shall we make of the Christian message a success story, and tell them, like advertisers: try it with us, and you will see how important Christianity is for everybody? Some missionaries and some ministers and some Christian laymen use these methods. They show a total misunderstanding of Christianity. The apostle who was a missionary and a minister and a layman all at once says something different. He says: No particular religion matters, neither ours nor yours. But I want to tell you that something has happened that matters, something that judges you and me, your religion and my religion. A New Creation has occurred, a New Being has appeared; and we are all asked to participate in it. And so we should say to the pagans and Jews wherever we meet them: Don't compare your religion and our religion, your rites and our rites, your prophets and our prophets, your priests and our priests, the pious amongst you, and the pious amongst us. All of this is of no avail! And above all don't think that we want to convert you to English or American Christianity, to the religion of the Western World. We do not want to convert you to us, not even to the best of us. This would be of no avail. We want only to show you something we have seen and to tell you something we have heard: That in the midst of the old creation there is a New Creation, and that this New Creation is manifest in Jesus who is called the Christ.

And when we meet Fascists and Communists, Scientific Humanists and Ethical Idealists, we should say to them: Don't boast too much that you have no rites and myths, that you are free from superstitions, that you are perfectly reasonable, uncircumcised in every sense. In the first place, you also have your rites and myths, your bit of circumcision; they are even very important to you. But if you were completely free from them you would have no reason to point to your *un*circumcision. It is of no avail. Don't think that we want to convert you away from your secular state to a religious state, that we want to make you religious and members of a very high religion, the Christian, and of a very great denomination within it, namely, our own. This would be of no avail. We want only to communicate to you an experience we have had that here and there in the world and now and then in ourselves is a New Creation, usually hidden, but sometimes manifest, and certainly manifest in Jesus who is called the Christ.

This is the way we should speak to all those outside the Christian realm, whether they are religious or secular. And we should not be too worried about the Christian religion, about the state of the Churches, about membership and doctrines, about institutions and ministers, about sermons and sacraments. This is circumcision; and the lack of it, the secularization which today is spreading all over the world is uncircumcision. Both are nothing, of no importance, if the ultimate question is asked, the question of a New Reality. *This* question, however, is of infinite importance. We should worry more about it than about anything else between heaven and earth. The New Creation—this is our ultimate concern; this should be our infinite passion—the infinite passion of every human being. This matters; this alone matters ultimately. In comparison with it everything else, even religion or nonreligion, even Christianity or non-Christianity, matters very little—and ultimately nothing.

And now let me boast for a moment about the fact that we are Christians and let us become fools by boasting, as Paul called himself when he started boasting. It is the greatness of Christianity that it can see how small it is. The importance of being a Christian is that we can stand the insight that it is of no importance. It is the spiritual power of religion that he who is religious can fearlessly look at the vanity of religion. It is the maturest fruit of Christian understanding to understand that Christianity, as such, is of no avail. This is boasting, not personal boasting, but boasting about Christianity. As boasting it is foolishness. But as boasting about the fact that there is nothing to boast about, it is wisdom and maturity. Having as having not—this is the right attitude toward everything great and wonderful in life, even religion and Christianity. But it is not the right attitude toward the New Creation. Toward it the right attitude is passionate and infinite longing.

And now we ask again: What is this New Being? The New Being is not something that simply takes the place of the Old Being. But it is a renewal of the Old which has been corrupted, distorted, split and almost destroyed. But not wholly destroyed. Salvation does not destroy creation; but it transforms the Old Creation into a New one. Therefore we can speak of the New in terms of a *re*-newal: The threefold *"re,"* namely, *re*-conciliation, *re*-union, *re*-surrection.

In his letter, Paul combines New Creation with reconciliation. The message of reconciliation is: *Be* reconciled to God. Cease to be hostile to Him, for He is never hostile to you. The message of reconciliation is not that God needs to be reconciled. How could He be? Since He is the source and power of reconciliation, who could reconcile Him? Pagans and Jews and Christians—all of us have tried and are trying to reconcile Him by rites and sacraments, by prayers and services, by moral behavior and works of charity. But if we try this, if we try to give something to Him, to show good deeds which may appease Him, we fail. It is never enough; we never can satisfy Him because there is an infinite demand upon us. And since we cannot appease Him, we grow hostile toward Him. Have you ever noticed how much hostility against God dwells in the depths of the good and honest people, in those who excel in works of charity, in piety and religious zeal? This cannot be otherwise; for one is hostile, consciously or unconsciously, toward those by whom one feels rejected. Everybody is in this predicament, whether he calls that which rejects him "God," or "nature," or "destiny," or "social conditions." Everybody carries a hostility toward the existence into which he has been thrown, toward the hidden powers which determine his life and that of the universe, toward that which makes him guilty and that threatens him with destruction because he has become guilty. We all feel rejected and hostile toward what has rejected us. We all try to appease it and in failing, we become more hostile. This happens often unnoticed by ourselves. But there are two symptoms which we hardly can avoid noticing: The hostility against ourselves and the hostility against others. One speaks so often of pride and arrogance and self-certainty and complacency in people. But this is, in most cases, the superficial level of their being. Below this, in a deeper level, there is self-rejection, disgust, and even hatred of one's self. Be reconciled to God; that means at the same time, be reconciled to ourselves. But we are not; we try to appease ourselves. We try to make ourselves more acceptable to our own judgment and, when we fail, we grow more hostile toward ourselves. And he who feels rejected by God and who rejects himself feels also rejected by the others. As he grows hostile toward destiny and hostile toward himself, he also grows hostile toward other men. If we are often horrified by the unconscious or conscious hostility people betray toward us or about our own hostility toward people whom we believe we love, let us not forget: They feel rejected by us; we feel rejected by them. They tried hard to make themselves acceptable to us, and they failed. We tried hard to make ourselves acceptable to them, and we failed. And their and our hostility grew. Be reconciled with God—that means, at the same time, be reconciled with the others! But it does *not* mean try to reconcile the others, as it does not mean try to reconcile yourselves. Try to reconcile God. You will fail. This is the message: A new reality has appeared in which you *are* reconciled. To enter the New Being we do not need to show anything. We must only be open to be grasped by it, although we have nothing to show.

Being reconciled—that is the first mark of the New Reality. And being reunited is its second mark. Reconciliation makes reunion possible. The New Creation is the reality in which the separated is reunited. The New Being is manifest in the Christ because in Him the separation never overcame the unity between Him and God, between Him and mankind, between Him and

Himself. This gives His picture in the Gospels its overwhelming and inexhaustible power. In Him we look at a human life that maintained the union in spite of everything that drove Him into separation. He represents and mediates the power of the New Being because He represents and mediates the power of an undisrupted union. Where the New Reality appears, one feels united with God, the ground and meaning of one's existence. One has what has been called the love of one's destiny, and what, today, we might call the courage to take upon ourselves our own anxiety. Then one has the astonishing experience of feeling reunited with one's self, not in pride and false self-satisfaction, but in a deep self-acceptance. One accepts one's self as something which is eternally important, eternally loved, eternally accepted. The disgust at one's self, the hatred of one's self has disappeared. There is a center, a direction, a meaning for life. All healing—bodily and mental—creates this reunion of one's self with one's self. Where there is real healing, *there* is the New Being, the New Creation. But real healing is not where only a part of body or mind is reunited with the whole, but where the whole itself, our whole being, our whole personality is united with itself. The New Creation is healing creation because it creates reunion with oneself. And it creates reunion with the others. Nothing is more distinctive of the Old Being than the separation of man from man. Nothing is more passionately demanded than social healing, than the New Being within history and human relationships. Religion and Christianity are under strong accusation that they have not brought reunion into human history. Who could deny the truth of this challenge. Nevertheless, mankind still lives; and it could not live any more if the power of separation had not been permanently conquered by the power of reunion, of healing, of the New Creation. Where one is grasped by a human face as human, although one has to overcome personal distaste, or racial strangeness, or national conflicts, or the differences of sex, of age, of beauty, of strength, of knowledge, and all the other innumerable causes of separation—*there* New Creation happens! Mankind lives because this happens again and again. And if the Church which is the assembly of God has an ultimate significance, this is its significance: That here the reunion of man to man is pronounced and confessed and realized, even if in fragments and weaknesses and distortions. The Church is the place where the reunion of man with man is an actual event, though the Church of God is permanently betrayed by the Christian churches. But, although betrayed and expelled, the New Creation saves and preserves that by which it is betrayed and expelled: churches, mankind and history.

The Church, like all its members, relapses from the New into the Old Being. Therefore, the third mark of the New Creation is re-surrection. The word "resurrection" has for many people the connotation of dead bodies leaving their graves or other fanciful images. But resurrection means the victory of the New state of things, the New Being born out of the death of the Old. Resurrection is not an event that might happen in some remote future, but it is the power of the New Being to create life out of death, here and now, today and tomorrow. Where there is a New Being, *there* is resurrection, namely, the creation into eternity out of every moment of time. The Old Being has the mark of disintegration and death. The New Being puts a new mark over the old one. Out of disintegration and death something is born of eternal significance. That which is immersed in dissolution emerges in a New Creation. Resurrection happens *now*, or it does not happen at all. It happens in us and around us, in soul and history, in nature and universe.

Reconciliation, reunion, resurrection—this is the New Creation, the New Being, the New state of things. Do we participate in it? The message of Christianity is not Christianity, but a New Reality. A New state of things has appeared, it still appears; it is hidden and visible, it is there and it is here. Accept it, enter into it, let it grasp you.

PART IV
ADDRESSING THE SITUATION

II
Aspects of a Religious
Analysis of Culture

I F WE ABSTRACT the concept of religion from the great commandment, we can say that religion is being ultimately concerned about that which is and should be our ultimate concern. This means that faith is the state of being grasped by an ultimate concern, and God is the name for the content of the concern. Such a concept of religion has little in common with the description of religion as the belief in the existence of a highest being called God, and the theoretical and practical consequences of such a belief. Instead, we are pointing to an existential, not a theoretical, understanding of religion.

Christianity claims that the God who is manifest in Jesus the Christ is the true God, the true subject of an ultimate and unconditional concern. Judged by him, all other gods are less than valid objects of an ultimate concern, and if they are made into one, become idols. Christianity can claim this extraordinary character because of the extraordinary character of the events on which it is based, namely, the creation of a new reality within and under the conditions of man's predicament. Jesus as the bringer of this new reality is subject to those conditions, to finitude and anxiety, to law and tragedy, to conflicts and death. But he victoriously keeps the unity with God, sacrificing himself as Jesus to himself as the Christ. In doing so it creates the new reality of which the Church is the communal and historical embodiment.

From this it follows that the unconditional claim made by Christianity is not related to the Christian Church, but to the event on which the Church is based. If the Church does not subject itself to the judgment which is pronounced by the Church, it becomes idolatrous towards itself. Such idolatry is its permanent temptation, just because it is the bearer of the New Being in history. As such it judges the world by its very presence. But the Church is also of the world and included under the judgment with which it judges the world. A Church which tries to exclude itself from such a judgment loses its right to judge the world and is rightly judged by the world. This is the tragedy of the Roman Catholic Church. Its way of dealing with culture is dependent upon its unwillingness to subject itself to the judgment pronounced by itself. Protestantism, at least in principle, resists this temptation, though actually it falls into it in many ways, again and again.

A second consequence of the existential concept of religion is the disappearance of the gap between the sacred and secular realm. If religion is the state of being grasped by an ultimate concern, this state cannot be restricted to a special realm. The unconditional character of this concern implies that it refers to every moment of our life, to every space and every realm. The universe is God's sanctuary. Every work day is a day of the Lord, every supper a Lord's supper, every work the fulfillment of a divine task, every joy a joy in God. In all preliminary concerns, ultimate concern is present, consecrating them. Essentially the religious and the secular are not separated realms. Rather they are within each other.

But this is not the way things actually are. In actuality, the secular element tends to make itself independent and to establish a realm of its own. And in opposition to this, the religious element tends to establish itself also as a special realm. Man's predicament is determined by this situation. It is the situation of the estrangement of man from his true being. One could rightly say that the existence of religion as a special realm is the most conspicuous proof of man's fallen state. This does not mean that under the conditions of estrangement which determine our destiny the religious should be swallowed by the secular, as secularism desires, nor that the secular should be swallowed by the religious, as ecclesiastic imperialism desires. But it does mean that the inseparable division is a witness to our human predicament.

The third consequence following from the existential concept of religion refers to the relation of religion and culture. Religion as ultimate concern is the meaning-giving substance of culture, and culture is the totality of forms in which the basic concern of religion expresses itself. In abbreviation: religion is the substance of culture, culture is the form of religion. Such a consideration definitely prevents the establishment of a dualism of religion and culture. Every religious act, not only in organized religion, but also in the most intimate movement of the soul, is culturally formed.

The fact that every act of man's spiritual life is carried by language, spoken or silent, is proof enough for this assertion. For language is the basic cultural creation. On the other hand, there is no cultural creation without an ultimate concern expressed in it. This is true of the theoretical functions of man's spiritual life, e.g. artistic intuition and cognitive reception of reality, and it is true of the practical functions of man's spiritual life, e.g. personal and social transformation of reality. In each of these functions in the whole of man's cultural creativity, an ultimate concern is present. Its immediate expression is the style of a culture. He who can read the style of a culture can discover its ultimate concern, its religious substance. This we will now try to do in relation to our present culture.

THE SPECIAL CHARACTER OF CONTEMPORARY CULTURE

Our present culture must be described in terms of one predominant movement and an increasingly powerful protest against this movement. The spirit of the predominant movement is the spirit of industrial society. The spirit of the protest is the spirit of the existentialist analysis of man's actual predicament. The actual style of our life, as it was shaped in the 18th and 19th centuries, expresses the still unbroken power of the spirit of industrial society. There are numerous analyses of this style of thought, life, and artistic expression. One of the difficulties in analyzing it is its dynamic character, its continuous change, and the influence the protest against it has already had upon it. We may nevertheless elaborate two main characteristics of man in industrial society.

The first of these is the concentration of man's activities upon the methodical investigation and technical transformation of his world, including himself, and the consequent loss of the dimension of depth in his encounter with reality. Reality has lost its inner transcendence or, in another metaphor, its transparency for the eternal. The system of finite interrelations which we call the universe has become self-sufficient. It is calculable and manageable and can be improved from the point of view of man's needs and desires. Since the beginning of the eighteenth century God has been removed from the power field of man's activities. He has been put alongside the world without permission to interfere with it because every interference would disturb man's technical and business calculations. The result is that God has become superfluous and the universe left to man as its master. This situation leads to the second characteristic of industrial society.

In order to fulfill his destiny, man must be in possession of creative powers, analogous to those previously attributed to God, and so creativity must become a human quality. The conflict between what man essentially is and what he actually is, his estrangement, or in traditional terms his fallen state, is disregarded. Death and guilt disappear even in the preaching of early industrial society. Their acknowledgment would interfere with man's progressive conquest of nature, outside and inside himself. Man has shortcomings, but there is no sin and certainly no universal sinfulness. The bondage of the will, of which the Reformer spoke, the demonic powers which are central for the New Testament, the structures of destruction in personal and communal life, are ignored or denied. Educational processes are able to adjust the large majority of men to the demands of the system of production and consumption. Man's actual state is hence mistakenly regarded as his essential state, and he is pictured in a position of progressive fulfillment of his potentialities.

This is supposed to be true not only of man as an individual personality, but also of man as community. The scientific and technical conquest of time and space is considered as the road to the reunion of mankind. The demonic structures of history, the conflicts of power in every realization of life are seen as preliminary impediments. Their tragic and inescapable character is denied. As the universe replaces God, as man in the center of the universe replaces the Christ, so the expectation of peace and justice in history replaces the expectation of the Kingdom of God. The dimension of depth in the divine and demonic has disappeared. This is the spirit of industrial society manifest in the style of its creations.

The attitude of the churches toward this situation was contradictory. Partly they defended themselves by retiring to their traditional past in doctrine, cult, and life. But in so doing, they used the categories created by the industrial spirit against which they were fighting. They drew the symbols in which the depth of being expresses itself down to the level of ordinary, so to speak, two-dimensional experiences. They understood them literally and defended their validity by establishing a supranatural above the natural realm. But supranaturalism is only the counterpart of naturalism and vice versa. They produce each other in neverending fights against each other. Neither could live without its opposite.

The impossibility of this kind of defense of the tradition was recognized by the other way in which the churches reacted to the spirit of industrial society. They accepted the new situation and tried to adapt themselves to it by reinterpreting the traditional symbols in contemporary terms. This is the justification and even the glory of what we call today "liberal theology." But it must also be stated that in its theological understanding of God and man, liberal theology paid the price of adjustment by losing the message of the new reality which was preserved by its supra-naturalistic defenders. Both ways in which the churches dealt with the spirit of industrial society proved to be inadequate.

While naturalism and supranaturalism, liberalism and ortho-doxy were involved in undecisive struggles, historical providence prepared another way of relating religion to contemporary culture. This preparation was done in the depth of industrial civilization, sometimes by people who represented it in its most antireligious implications. This is the large movement known as existentialism which started with Pascal, was carried on by a few prophetic minds in the nineteenth century and came to a full victory in the twentieth century.

Existentialism, in the largest sense, is the protest against the spirit of industrial society within the framework of industrial society. The protest is directed against the position of man in the system of production and consumption of our society. Man is supposed to be the master of his world and of himself. But actually he has become a part of the reality he has created, an object among objects, a thing among things, a cog within a universal machine to which he must adapt himself in order not to be smashed by it. But this adaptation makes him a means for ends which are means themselves, and in which an ultimate end is lacking. Out of this predicament of man in the industrial society the experiences of emptiness and meaninglessness, of dehumanization and estrangement have resulted. Man has ceased to encounter reality as meaningful. Reality in its ordinary forms and structures does not speak to him any longer.

One way out is that man restricts himself to a limited section of reality and defends it against the intrusion of the world into his castle. This is the neurotic way out which becomes psychotic if reality disappears completely. It involves subjection to the demands of culture and repression of the question of meaning. Or some may have the strength to take anxiety and meaninglessness courageously upon themselves and live creatively, expressing the predicament of the most sensitive people in our time in cultural production. It is the latter way to which we owe the artistic and philosophical works of culture in the first half of the twentieth century. They are creative expressions of the destructive trends in contemporary culture. The great works of the visual arts, of music, of poetry, of literature, of architecture, of dance, of philosophy, show in their style both the encounter with nonbeing, and the strength which can stand this encounter and shape it creatively. Without this key, contemporary culture is a closed door. With this key, it can be understood as the revelation of man's predicament, both in the present world and in the world universally. This makes the protesting element in contemporary culture theologically significant.

THE CULTURAL FORMS IN WHICH RELIGION ACTUALIZES ITSELF

The form of religion is culture. This is especially obvious in the language used by religion. Every language, including that of the Bible, is the result of innumerable acts of cultural creativity. All functions of man's spiritual life are based on man's power to speak vocally or silently. Language is the expression of man's freedom from the given situation and its concrete demands. It gives him universals in whose power he can create worlds above the given world of technical civilization and spiritual content.

Conversely, the development of these worlds determines the development of language. There is no sacred language which has fallen from a supranatural heaven and been put between the covers of a book. But there is human language, based on man's encounter with reality, changing through the millennia, used for the needs of daily life, for expression and communication, for literature and poetry, and used also for the expression and communication of our ultimate concern. In each of these cases the language is different. Religious language is ordinary language, changed under the power of what it expresses, the ultimate of being and meaning. The expression of it can be narrative (mythological, legendary, historical), or it can be prophetic, poetic, liturgical. It becomes holy for those to whom it expresses their ultimate concern from generation to generation. But there is no holy language in itself, as translations, retranslations and revisions show.

This leads to a second example of the use of cultural creations within religion: religious art. One principle which must be emphasized again and again in religious art is the principle of artistic honesty. There is no sacred artistic style in Protestant, in contrast, for example, to Greek Orthodox doctrine. An artistic style is honest only if it expresses the real situation of the artist and the cultural period to which he belongs. We can participate in the artistic styles of the past in so far as they were honestly expressing the encounter which they had with God, man, and world. But we cannot honestly imitate them and produce for the cult of the Church works which are not the result of a creating ecstasy, but which are learned reproductions of creative ecstasies of the past. It was a religiously significant achievement of modern architecture that it liberated itself from traditional forms which, in the context of our period, were nothing but trimmings without meaning and, therefore, neither aesthetically valuable nor religiously expressive.

A third example is taken from the cognitive realm. It is the question: what elements of the contemporary philosophical consciousness can be used for the theological interpretation of the Christian symbols? If we take the existentialist protest against the spirit of industrial society seriously, we must reject both naturalism and idealism as tools for theological self-expression. Both of them are creations of that spirit against which the protest of our century is directed. Both of them have been used by theology in sharply conflicting methods, but neither of them expresses the contemporary culture.

Instead, theology must use the immense and profound material of the existential analysis in all cultural realms, including therapeutic psychology. But theology cannot use it by simply accepting it. Theology must confront it with the answer implied in the Christian message. The confrontation of the existential analysis with the symbol in which Christianity has expressed its ultimate concern is the method which is adequate both to the message of Jesus as the Christ and to the human predicament as rediscovered in contemporary culture. The answer cannot be derived from the question. It is said to him who asks, but it is not taken *from* him. Existentialism cannot give answers. It can determine the form of the answer, but whenever an existentialist artist or philosopher answers, he does so through the power of another tradition which has revelatory sources. To give such answers is the function of the Church not only to itself, but also to those outside the Church.

THE INFLUENCES OF THE CHURCH ON CONTEMPORARY CULTURE

The Church has the function of answering the question implied in man's very existence, the question of the meaning of this existence. One of the ways in which the Church does this is evangelism. The principle of evangelism must be to show to the people outside the Church that the symbols in which the life of the Church expresses itself are answers to the questions implied in their very existence as human beings. Because the Christian message is the message of salvation and because salvation means healing, the message of healing in every sense of the word is appropriate to our situation. This is the reason why movements at the fringe of the Church, sectarian and evangelistic movements of a most primitive and unsound character, have such great success. Anxiety and despair about existence itself induces millions of people to look out for any kind of healing that promises success.

The Church cannot take this way. But it must understand that the average kind of preaching is unable to reach the people of our time. They must feel that Christianity is not a set of doctrinal or ritual or moral laws, but is rather the good news of the conquest of the law by the appearance of a new healing reality. They must feel that the Christian symbols are not absurdities, unacceptable for the questioning mind of our period, but that they point to that which alone is of ultimate concern, the ground and meaning of our existence and of existence generally.

There remains a last question, namely, the question of how the Church should deal with the spirit of our society which is responsible for much of what must be healed by the Christian message. Has the Church the task and the power to attack and to transform the spirit of industrial society? It certainly cannot try to replace the present social reality by another one, in terms of a progress to the realized Kingdom of God. It cannot sketch perfect social structures or suggest concrete reforms. Cultural changes occur by the inner dynamics of culture itself. The Church participates in them, sometimes in a leading role, but then it is a cultural force beside others and not the representative of the new reality in history.

In its prophetic role the Church is the guardian who reveals dynamic structures in society and undercuts their demonic power by revealing them, even within the Church itself. In so doing the Church listens to prophetic voices outside itself, judging both the culture and the Church in so far as it is a part of the culture. We have referred to such prophetic voices in our culture. Most of them are not active members of the manifest Church. But perhaps one could call them participants of a "latent Church," a Church in which the ultimate concern which drives the manifest Church is hidden under cultural forms and deformations.

Sometimes this latent Church comes into the open. Then the manifest Church should recognize in these voices what its own spirit should be and accept them even if they appear hostile to the Church. But the Church should also stand as a guardian against the demonic distortions into which attacks must fall if they are not grasped by the right subject of our ultimate concern. This was the fate of the communist movement. The Church was

not sufficiently aware of its function as guardian when this movement was still undecided about its way. The Church did not hear
the prophetic voice in communism and therefore did not recognize its demonic possibilities.

Judging means seeing both sides. The Church judges culture,
including the Church's own forms of life. For its forms are created
by culture, as its religious substance makes culture possible. The
Church and culture are within, not alongside, each other. And
the Kingdom of God includes both while transcending both.

12
The Word of Religion

I F RELIGION had no word for us in this time, it would have no word at all worth listening to. And if religion had only the word everybody has—every newspaper, every radio, every speaker —if religion simply followed the general trend of public opinion, it would have no word at all worth listening to. If religion gave only a little more enthusiasm, a little more certainty, a little more dignity to something that would be done anyhow, with or without religion, then religion would have no significance at all for the present situation or for any other situation. If religion ceased to be the spiritual sword, cutting through all human enthusiasms and certainties and dignities, judging them, transforming them, transcending them—then religion would be swallowed up by the general process of civilization and should disappear as soon as possible as a useless and disturbing nuisance.

Religion has very often been nothing more than the superfluous consecration of some situation or action which was neither judged nor transformed by this consecration. Religion has consecrated the feudal order and its own participation in it without transcending it. Religion has consecrated nationalism without transforming it. Religion has consecrated democracy without judging it. Religion has consecrated war and the arms of war without using

From Paul Tillich, *The Protestant Era* (Chicago: University of Chicago Press), 185–191. Reprinted by permission of University of Chicago Press. Copyright © 1957 by Paul Tillich.

its spiritual arms against war. Religion has consecrated peace and the security of peace without disturbing this security with its spiritual threat. Religion has consecrated the bourgeois ideal of family and property without judging it and has consecrated systems of exploitation of men by men without transcending them; on the contrary, it has used them for its own benefit.

The first word, therefore, to be spoken by religion to the people of our time must be a word spoken against religion. It is the word the old Jewish prophets spoke against the priestly and royal and pseudoprophetic guardians of their national religion, who consecrated distorted institutions and distorted politics without judging them. The same word must be spoken today about our religious institutions and politics. Will religion in this country, in this moment of history, simply follow the trend of events, the way public opinion runs, the direction in which the makers of public opinion want us to move? Will religion, after it has consecrated a self-complacent and egoistic enthusiasm for peace, consecrate a self-intoxication with war? Will religion in our situation transcend our situation or not?

A word can be spoken by religion to the people of our time only if it is a transcending and therefore a judging and transforming word. Otherwise, religion would become another contributor to what is accepted anyhow, another servant of public opinion, which in some cases is a tyrant as terrorizing as any personal tyrant. If our religion is able to transcend all this, in which direction must it do so?

There are two lines by which the meaning of human existence can be symbolized: the vertical and the horizontal, the first one pointing to the eternal meaning as such, the second to the temporal realization of the eternal meaning. Every religion necessarily has both directions, although different religions overemphasize the one or the other. The mystical element which belongs to all religion is symbolized by the vertical line; the active element which also belongs to all religion is symbolized by the horizontal line. If religion is to speak a transcending, judging, and transforming word to the people of our time, it must do so in both directions, the vertical as well as the horizontal, and this in mutual interdependence.

The first line, the vertical one, symbolizes the attitude of "in spite of" and points to what we may call the "religious reservation." While the second line, the horizontal one, symbolizes the attitude of "because of" and points to what we may call the "religious obligation." In both directions religion has important things to say with respect to the present situation.

I I

History is the sphere in which man *determines himself* in freedom. And history, at the same time, is the sphere in which man *is determined* by fate against his freedom. Very often the creations of his freedom are the tools used by fate against him; as, for instance, today the technical powers created by him turn against him with irresistible force. There are periods in history in which the element of freedom is predominant; and there are periods in which fate and necessity prevail. The latter is true of our day. In the moment in which (with the wilful help of the ruling classes in all countries) the power of the dictators was firmly established and the decisive step in the catastrophic self-destruction of the liberal system of life was taken, a period of prevailing necessity began.

In a period like this, in which individual destiny no longer counts, in which the value of human life is as low as it was three hundred years ago in the religious wars of self-destruction; in a period like this in which, in practically all countries of the world, insecurity has become as predominant as it was in the most primitive stages of human development and in which the feeling of meaninglessness in millions of people brings about social and personal insanity in ever increasing amounts; in a period like this, in which the law of tragedy turns the attempts to strengthen the good into a strengthening of the evil (as we have experienced with respect to the struggle against war in the Anglo-Saxon countries or with respect to nationalism in the dictatorial countries) —in such a period, the emphasis on the horizontal line, on what we could do and should do, has lost its power because everybody feels that whatever we do, however good it may be, will directly or indirectly confirm a historical destiny which shows us its destructive side and hides from us its constructive power.

But, even if the creative possibilities in the catastrophes of our day were more apparent than they are, they would not concern the victims of these catastrophes in their immediate existence, in their quest for happiness, in their longing for meaning and fulfillment. The people of our day must be enabled to say "in spite of," they must be taught to find for themselves the religious reservation which cannot be conquered by the tragedy of history. It is hard to find it, but it must be found if cynicism and despair are not to prevail as they do now, driving the masses into the hands of agitators, driving the strong to the glorification of heroic self-destruction and the weak to the loss of all meaning of life and to suicide.

The human soul cannot maintain itself without the vertical line, the knowledge of an eternal meaning, however this may be expressed in mythological or theological terms. If the people of our day are no longer able to say "in spite of," they will not resist the terrible impact of the historical catastrophe on their minds. If we no longer understand the words of the psalmist, that the loss of body and life and of earth and heaven cannot deprive him of the ultimate meaning of his life—or if we no longer feel what the poet means when he says that all our running, all our striving, is eternal rest in God the Lord—if all this has become strange and unreal to us, then we have lost the power of facing reality without cynicism and despair.

But are the churches and religious groups prepared to speak this word of the vertical line, the "in spite of," the religious reservation, to the people of our time? Or have they forgotten the vertical line entirely? Looking at the prevailing type of the religious life in this country, we might assume that this is the case, that there is no more pointing to the religious reservation but only moral demand, humanitarian activity, and political partisanship. However this may be—and certainly it is not entirely this way—religion's demand on man stands: namely, that man be not only *in* history but also *above* history. And, since this demand is valid and represents the first word that religion must say to the people of our time, it may transform the methods and institutions of our religious life in a very radical way. The sooner this happens, the better. This country is still in a preliminary stage with respect to our historic tragedy. It still has time. The horizontal line has still much of its splendor and attractiveness. The quest for a religious reservation has not yet force enough to reshape our religious consciousness.

But religious leaders should foresee the coming and prepare themselves for it. *The usual question, "What shall we do?" must be answered with the unusual question, "Whence can we receive?"* People must understand again that one cannot do much without having received much. Religion is, first, an open hand to receive a gift and, second, an acting hand to distribute gifts. Without coming from the religious reservation, carrying with us something eternal, we are of no use in working for the religious obligation to transform the temporal.

III

Of course we are not asked to enter the religious reservation in order to stay in it. The vertical line must become dynamic and actual in the horizontal line; the attitude of "in spite of" must become the driving power in an attitude of "because of." What is the word of religion to the people of our time in this respect? Must it say a word at all? Or is the tremendous trend of activism in the attitude of America today a sufficient guaranty for the fulfillment of the religious obligation? Obviously, after everything

I have said, the answer must be "No." Activism as such cannot overcome the law of tragedy, and especially not if it has the character of escapism, the attempt, namely, to escape the feeling of meaninglessness and emptiness with respect to the eternal. And no keen observer of American religious and secular life can overlook this hidden element of flight from one's self implied in all kinds of humanitarian and political activities. The horizontal line becomes empty and distorted if it is not united continuously with the vertical line. This is manifested in two ways of dealing with the religious obligation toward history: one is a shortsighted opportunism, the other a self-deceiving utopianism. Against both these attitudes religion must speak its word to the people of our time. The present situation provides abundant examples of both attitudes.

Let us start with a very recent instance of what I have called "opportunism." I mean the opportunism of the ruling classes in the democratic countries which made the rise of the dictators possible, kept them in power, sacrificed to them first the democratic minorities in their own countries and then one country after the other, including the struggling democracy in Spain. Everybody knows this today, and it was terribly disturbing when the Englishman, Norman Angell, told us that in the very hour in which he was speaking his countrymen were digging the corpses of their children out of the wreckage of their London houses because they had not cared at all about the corpses of the Chinese children in their wreckages a year earlier. Religious obligation, first of all, includes the practical acknowledgment of the unity of all men, expressed in oriental wisdom by the assertion that the other is thou.

But the point I want to make above all—and the one I think religion must make today in this country—is that America, if she takes responsibility for the present world catastrophe, must take it completely and with the full knowledge of what it means. It does not mean defending America against the dictators, it does not mean defeating Hitler, it does not mean conquering Germany a second time: it means accepting her share of responsibility for the future of Europe and consequently for the whole world. Whatever happens during the later years of the war, any victory will be won on the physical and moral ruins of Europe. It would be a cynical opportunism if America helped to augment those ruins without being ready and able to build something radically new on them. If this country will not look beyond the day of victory, that day will become the birthday of another defeat of all human values and noble aims.

The word that religion has to speak to this nation and to all those who fight with her is the grave question: Are you willing, are you able, to take upon you the full weight of the task before you? If not, keep away from it; do not follow the cause of an easy opportunism, the twin-sister of an easy utopianism. Overcome both of them before you act. Otherwise, the action of this country will increase the destruction of Europe and lead finally to self-destruction. Religion can overcome opportunism because it can overcome utopianism.

The amount of utopianism in this country, as in most countries after the first World War, is even greater than the amount of opportunism. In the crusading slogans of 1917, in the progressive mood of the 1920s, in the humanism and pacifism of the last decades, a disturbing number of illusions were cultivated and destroyed. Religion, perhaps, could have prevented these illusions and disillusionments about human nature and the nature of history. But religion itself had been driven into an illusory attitude.

It had nearly forgotten the religious reservation, the vertical line, and had dedicated its force to the religious obligation, the horizontal line alone. It had consecrated progressivistic utopianism instead of judging and transcending it. Now the time has come when people would despise religion if it had nothing more to say to them than a word of praise and glorification of the greatness and divinity of man and history. They would call it ideology or lie and turn away toward cynicism and despair. This is already true of a large group in the younger generation, and it is the greatest danger for religion as well as for civilization.

Religion must teach youth something they cannot hear anywhere else—to give themselves with an absolute seriousness and a complete devotion to an aim that in itself is fragmentary and ambiguous. Everything we do in history has this fragmentary and ambiguous character; everything is subject to the law of historical tragedy. But religion, although knowing this, does not retire from history; religion, although pronouncing the tragic destiny of all human truth and goodness, works with unrestricted devotion to the good and the true. Such a message is not simple, but, on the other hand, it is not illusory. It is realistic but not pessimistic; it is knowing but not despairing. It breaks utopianism, but it does not break hope. Hope is the opposite of utopianism. Utopianism necessarily will be destroyed. Hope never dies, because it is the application of the venturing "in spite of" to the tragedy of historical action. Hope unites the vertical and the horizontal lines, the religious reservation and the religious obligation. Therefore, the ultimate word that religion must say to the people of our time is the word of hope.

I do not make concrete suggestions about possible political actions in the name of religion. This is impossible, and it never should be tried. Religion as such could not say whether this country should go into war, and religion as such cannot suggest war aims or social reforms. Religion can give and must give the basis of such decisions; it can give and must give the ultimate criteria of such decisions. The word of religion to the people of our time is not the word of political or economic experts, but it is, if it is a religious word, the word of those who know something about man and history; who know the tragedy and the hope involved in the temporal because they know about the eternal . . .

13
The Eternal Now

I am the Alpha and the Omega, the begin-
ning and the end.

—REVELATION 21:6

I T I S our destiny and the destiny of everything in our world
that we must come to an end. Every end that we experience
in nature and mankind speaks to us with a loud voice: you also
will come to an end! It may reveal itself in the farewell to a
place where we have lived for a long time, the separation from
the fellowship of intimate associates, the death of someone near
to us. Or it may become apparent to us in the failure of a work
that gave meaning to us, the end of a whole period of life, the
approach of old age, or even in the melancholy side of nature
visible in autumn. All this tells us: you will also come to an end.

Whenever we are shaken by this voice reminding us of our
end, we ask anxiously—what does it mean that we have a beginning and an end, that we come from the darkness of the "not
yet" and rush ahead toward the darkness of the "no more"? When
Augustine asked this question, he began his attempt to answer
it with a prayer. And it is right to do so, because praying means

From Paul Tillich, *The Eternal Now* (New York: Charles Scribner's Sons),
122–32. Reprinted by permission of Charles Scribner's Sons. Copyright © 1963
by Paul Tillich.

elevating oneself to the eternal. In fact, there is no other way of judging time than to see it in the light of the eternal. In order to judge something, one must be partly within it, partly out of it. If we were totally within time, we would not be able to elevate ourselves in prayer, meditation and thought, to the eternal. We would be children of time like all other creatures and could not ask the question of the meaning of time. But as men we are aware of the eternal to which we belong and from which we are estranged by the bondage of time.

I

We speak of time in three ways or modes—the past, present and future. Every child is aware of them, but no wise man has ever penetrated their mystery. We become aware of them when we hear a voice telling us: you also will come to an end. It is the future that awakens us to the mystery of time. Time runs from the beginning to the end, but our awareness of time goes in the opposite direction. It starts with the anxious anticipation of the end. In the light of the future we see the past and present. So let us first consider our going into the future and toward the end that is the last point that we can anticipate in our future.

The image of the future produces contrasting feelings in man. The expectation of the future gives one a feeling of joy. It is a great thing to have a future in which one can actualize one's possibilities, in which one can experience the abundance of life, in which one can create something new—be it new work, a new living being, a new way of life, or the regeneration of one's own being. Courageously one goes ahead toward the new, especially in the earlier part of one's life. But this feeling struggles with other ones: the anxiety about what is hidden in the future, the ambiguity of everything it will bring us, the shortness of its duration that decreases with every year of our life and becomes shorter the nearer we come to the unavoidable end. And finally the end itself, with its impenetrable darkness and the threat that one's whole existence in time will be judged as a failure.

How do men, how do *you,* react to this image of the future with its hope and threat and inescapable end? Probably most of us react by looking at the immediate future, anticipating it, working for it, hoping for it, being anxious about it, while cutting off from our awareness the future which is farther away, and above all, by cutting off from our consciousness the end, the last moment of our future. Perhaps we could not live without doing so most of our time. But perhaps we will not be able to die if we *always* do so. And if one is not able to die, is he really able to live?

How do we react if we become aware of the inescapable end contained in our future? Are we able to bear it, to take its anxiety into a courage that faces ultimate darkness? Or are we thrown into utter hopelessness? Do we hope against hope, or do we repress our awareness of the end because we cannot stand it? Repressing the consciousness of our end expresses itself in several ways.

Many try to do so by putting the expectation of a long life between now and the end. For them it is decisive that the end be delayed. Even old people who are near the end do this, for they cannot endure the fact that the end will not be delayed much longer.

Many people realize this deception and hope for a continuation of this life after death. They expect an endless future in which they may achieve or possess what has been denied them in this life. This is a prevalent attitude about the future, and also a very simple one. It denies that there *is* an end. It refuses to accept that we are creatures, that we come from the eternal ground of time and return to the eternal ground of time and have received a limited span of time as *our* time. It replaces eternity by endless future.

But endless future is without a final aim; it repeats itself and could well be described as an image of hell. This is not the Christian way of dealing with the end. The Christian message says that the eternal stands above past and future. "I am the Alpha and the Omega, the beginning and the end."

The Christian message acknowledges that time runs toward an end, and that we move towards the end of that time which is our time. Many people—but not the Bible—speak loosely of the "hereafter" or of the "life after death." Even in our liturgies eternity is translated by "world without end." But the world, by its very nature, is that which comes to an end. If we want to speak in truth without foolish, wishful thinking, we should speak about the eternal that is neither timelessness nor endless time. The mystery of the future is answered in the eternal of which we may speak in images taken from time. But if we forget that the images are images, we fall into absurdities and self-deceptions. There is not time *after* time, but there is eternity *above* time.

I I

We go towards something that is not yet, and we come from something that is no more. We are what we are by what we came from. We have a beginning as we have an end. There was a time that was not *our* time. We hear of it from those who are older than we; we read about it in history books; we try to envision the unimaginable billions of years in which neither we nor anyone was who could tell us of them. It is hard for us to imagine our "being-no-more." It is equally difficult to imagine our "being-not-yet." But we usually don't care about our not yet being, about the indefinite time before our birth in which we were not. We think: *now* we are; this is *our* time—and we do not want to lose it. We are not concerned about what lies before our beginning. We ask about life after death, yet seldom do we ask about our being before birth. But is it possible to do one without the other? The fourth gospel does not think so. When it speaks of the eternity of the Christ, it does not only point to his return to eternity, but also to his coming *from* eternity. "Truly, truly, I say to you, before Abraham was, I *am*." He comes from another dimension than that in which the past lies. Those to whom he speaks misunderstand him because they think of the historical past. They believe that he makes himself hundreds of years old and they rightly take offense at this absurdity. Yet he does not say, "I *was*" before Abraham; but he says, "I *am*" before Abraham was. He speaks of his beginning out of eternity. And this is the beginning of everything that is—not the uncounted billions of years—but the eternal as the ultimate point in our past.

The mystery of the past from which we come is that it is and is not in every moment of our lives. It is, insofar as we are what the past has made of us. In every cell of our body, in every trait of our face, in every movement of our soul, our past is the present.

Few periods knew more about the continuous working of the past in the present than ours. We know about the influence of childhood experiences on our character. We know about the scars left by events in early years. We have rediscovered what the Greek tragedians and the Jewish prophets knew, that the past is present in us, both as a curse and as a blessing. For "past" always means both a curse and a blessing, not only for individuals, but also for nations and even continents.

History lives from the past, from its heritage. The glory of the European nations is their long, inexhaustibly rich tradition. But the blessings of this tradition are mixed with curses resulting from early splits into separated nations whose bloody struggles have filled century after century and brought Europe again and again to the edge of self-destruction. Great are the blessings *this* nation has received in the course of its short history. But from earliest days, elements have been at work that have been and will remain a curse for many years to come. I could refer, for instance, to racial consciousness, not only within the nation itself, but also in its dealings with races and nations outside its own boundaries. "The American way of life" is a blessing that comes from the past; but it is also a curse, threatening the future.

Is there a way of getting rid of such curses that threaten the life of nations and continents, and, more and more, of mankind as a whole? Can we banish elements of our past into the past so that they lose their power over the present? In man's individual life this is certainly possible. One has rightly said that the strength of a character is dependent on the amount of things that he has thrown into the past. In spite of the power his past holds over him, a man can separate himself from it, throw it out of the present into the past in which it is condemned to remain ineffective—at least for a time. It may return and conquer the present and destroy the person, but this is not necessarily so. We are not inescapably victims of our past. We can make the past remain nothing but *past*. The act in which we do this has been called repentance. Genuine repentance is not the feeling of sorrow about wrong actions, but it is the act of the whole person in which he separates himself from elements of his being, discarding them into the past as something that no longer has any power over the present.

Can a nation do the same thing? Can a nation or any other social group have genuine repentance? Can it separate itself from curses of the past? On this possibility rests the hope of a nation. The history of Israel and the history of the church show that it is possible and they also show that it is rare and extremely painful. Nobody knows whether it will happen to *this* nation. But we know that its future depends on the way it will deal with its past, and whether it can discard into the past elements which are a curse!

In each human life a struggle is going on about the past. Blessings battle with curses. Often we do not recognize what are blessings and what are curses. Today, in the light of the discovery of our unconscious strivings, we are more inclined to see curses than blessings in our past. The remembrance of our parents, which in the Old Testament is so inseparably connected with their blessings, is now much more connected with the curse they have unconsciously and against their will brought upon us. Many of those who suffer under mental afflictions see their past, especially their childhood, only as the source of curses. We know how often this is true. But we should not forget that we would not be able to live and to face the future if there were not blessings that support us and which come from the same source as the curses. A pathetic struggle over their past is going on almost without interruption in many men and women in our time. No medical healing can solve *this* conflict, because no medical healing can change the past. Only a blessing that lies above the conflict of blessing and curse can heal. It is the blessing that changes what seems to be unchangeable—the past. It cannot change the facts; what has happened has happened and remains so in all eternity! But the *meaning* of the facts can be changed by the eternal, and the name of this change is the experience of "forgiveness." If the meaning of the past is changed by forgiveness, its influence on the future is also changed. The character of curse is taken away from it. It becomes a blessing by the transforming power of forgiveness.

There are not always blessings and curses in the past. There is also emptiness in it. We remember experiences that, at the time, were seemingly filled with an abundant content. Now we remember them, and their abundance has vanished, their ecstasy is gone, their fullness has turned into a void. Pleasures, successes, vanities have this character. We don't feel them as curses; we don't feel them as blessings. They have been swallowed by the past. They did not contribute to the eternal. Let us ask ourselves how little in our lives escapes this judgment.

III

The mystery of the future and the mystery of the past are united in the mystery of the present. Our time, the time we have, is the time in which we have "presence." But how can we have "presence"? Is not the present moment gone when we think of it? Is not the present the ever-moving boundary line between past and future? But a moving boundary is not a place to stand upon. If nothing were given to us except the "no more" of the past and the "not yet" of the future, we would not have anything. We could not speak of the time that is *our* time; we would not have "presence."

The mystery is that we *have* a present; and even more, that we have *our* future also because we anticipate it in the present; and that we have *our* past also, because we remember it in the present. In the present our future and our past are *ours*. But there is no "present" if we think of the never-ending flux of time. The riddle of the present is the deepest of all the riddles of time. Again, there is no answer except from that which comprises all time and lies beyond it—the eternal. Whenever we say "now" or "today," we stop the flux of time for us. We accept the present and do not care that it is gone in the moment that we accept it. We live in it and it is renewed for us in every new "present." This is possible because every moment of time reaches into the eternal. It is the eternal that stops the flux of time for us. It is the eternal "now" which provides for us a temporal "now." We live so long as "it is still today"—in the words of the letter to the Hebrews. Not everybody, and nobody all the time, is aware of this "eternal now" in the temporal "now." But sometimes it breaks powerfully into our consciousness and gives us the certainty of the eternal, of a dimension of time which cuts into time and gives us our time.

People who are never aware of this dimension lose the possibility of resting in the present. As the letter to the Hebrews describes it, they never enter into the divine rest. They are held by the past and cannot separate themselves from it, or they escape toward the future, unable to rest in the present. They have not entered the eternal rest which stops the flux of time and gives us the blessing of the present. Perhaps this is the most conspicuous characteristic of our period, especially in the western world and particularly in this country. It lacks the courage to accept "presence" because it has lost the dimension of the eternal.

"I am the beginning and the end." This is said to us who live in the bondage of time, who have to face the end, who cannot escape the past, who need a present to stand upon. Each of the modes of time has its peculiar mystery, each of them carries its peculiar anxiety. Each of them drives us to an ultimate question. There is *one* answer to these questions—the eternal. There is *one* power that surpasses the all-consuming power of time—the eternal: He Who was and is and is to come, the beginning and the end. He gives us forgiveness for what has passed. He gives us courage for what is to come. He gives us rest in His eternal Presence.

PART V

LOVE, POWER, AND JUSTICE

14
The Shaking of the Foundations

I look out on earth . . . lo, all is chaos;
I look at heaven . . . its light is gone;
I look out on the mountains . . . they
*   are trembling;*
And all the hills are swaying!
I look out . . . lo, no man is to be seen;
All the birds have flown!
I look out . . . lo, the sown land lies a
*   desert;*
And the towns are all razed by the
*   Lord's rage.*
For thus has the Lord said:
The whole land shall be desolate . . .
And for this shall the earth mourn
And the heavens above be black . . .
I have purposed it and will not repent;
Neither will I turn back from it.
At the noise of the horsemen and the
*   archers*
The land is all in flight,
Men taking refuge within woods and
*   caves,*
And climbing upon the rocks.
Every city shall be abandoned,
And not a man dwell therein.
You ruined creature, what will you do!
                                    —JEREMIAH 4:23-30

From Paul Tillich, *The Shaking of the Foundations* (New York: Charles
Scribner's Sons), 2–11. Reprinted by permission of Charles Scribner's Sons. Copyright © 1948 by Paul Tillich.

For the mountains shall depart,
And the hills be removed.
But my kindness shall not depart from
    thee;
Neither shall the covenant of my peace
    be removed,
Saith the Lord that has mercy on thee!
        —ISAIAH 54:10

The foundations of the earth do shake.
Earth breaks to pieces,
Earth is split in pieces,
Earth shakes to pieces,
Earth reels like a drunken man,
Earth rocks like a hammock;
Under the weight of its transgression
    earth falls down
To rise no more!

Lift up your eyes to heaven and look
    upon the earth beneath:
For the heavens shall vanish away like
    smoke.
And the earth shall grow old like a
    robe;
The world itself shall crumble.
But my righteousness shall be forever,
And my salvation knows no end.
        —ISAIAH 24:18-20

T IS HARD to speak after the prophets have spoken as they have in these pronouncements. Every word is like the stroke of a hammer. There was a time when we could listen to such words without much feeling and without understanding. There were decades and even centuries when we did not take them seriously. Those days are gone. Today we must take them seriously. For they describe with visionary power what the majority of human beings in our period have experienced, and what, perhaps in a not too distant future, all mankind will experience abundantly: "The foundations of the earth do shake." The visions of the prophets have become an actual, physical possibility, and might become an historical reality. The phrase, "Earth is split in pieces," is not merely a poetic metaphor for us, but a hard reality. That is the religious meaning of the age into which we have entered.

The Bible has always told us of the beginning and the end of the world. It speaks of eternity before the world was founded; it speaks of the time when God laid the foundations of the earth; it speaks of the shaking of these foundations and of the crumbling of the world. In one of the later books, Second Peter, it says that "the heavens will vanish with a crackling roar, and the elements will melt with fervent heat, the earth also and the works therein shall be burnt up." This is no longer vision; it has become physics. We know that in the ground of our earth, and in the ground of everything in our world that has form and structure, destructive forces are bound. Laying the foundations of the earth means binding these forces. When the unruly power of the smallest parts of our material world was restrained by cohesive structures, a place was provided in which life could grow and history develop, in which words could be heard and love be felt, and in which truth could be discovered and the Eternal adored. All this was possible because the fiery chaos of the beginning was transformed into the fertile soil of the earth.

But out of the fertile soil of the earth a being was generated and nourished, who was able to find the key to the foundation of all beings. That being was man. He has discovered the key which can unlock the forces of the ground, those forces which were bound when the foundations of the earth were laid. He has begun to use this key. He has subjected the basis of life and thought and will to *his* will. And he willed destruction. For the sake of destruction he used the forces of the ground; by his thought and his work he unlocked and untied them. That is why the foundations of the earth rock and shake in our time.

In the language of the prophets, it is the Lord Who shakes

the mountains and melts the rocks. This is a language that modern man can not understand. And so God, Who is not bound to any special language, not even to that of the prophets, spoke to the men of today through the mouths of our greatest scientists, and this is what He said: You yourselves can bring about the end upon yourselves. I give the power to shake the foundations of your earth into your hands. You can use this power for creation or destruction. How will you use it? This is what God said to mankind through the work of the scientists and through their discovery of the key to the foundations of life. But through them He did even more. He forced His Word upon them, as He had forced it upon the prophets, in spite of their attempt ever to resist it. For no prophet likes to say what he has to say. And no scientist who participated in the great and terrible discovery liked to say what he had to say. But he could not but speak; he had to raise his voice, like the prophets, to tell this generation what the prophets told their generations: that earth and man, trees and animals, are threatened by a catastrophe which they can scarcely escape. A tremendous anxiety expresses itself through the words of these men. Not only do they feel the shaking of the foundations, but also that they themselves are largely responsible for it. They tell us that they *despise* what they have done, because they know that we are left with only a slight chance of escape. Wavering between little hope and much despair, they urge us to use this chance.

This is the way in which God had spoken to our generation about the shaking of the foundations. We had forgotten about such shaking. And it was science, more than anything else, which had made us forget it. It was not science as knowledge, but rather science for the purpose of hidden idolatry, for the purpose of persuading us to believe in our earth as the place for the establishment of the Kingdom of God, to believe in ourselves as those through whom this was to be achieved. There were prophets of this idolatry—false prophets, as they were called by Jeremiah— who cried: "Progress, infinite progress! Peace, universal peace! Happiness, happiness for everyone!" And now what has happened? That same science, in the saving power of which these false prophets believed, has utterly destroyed that idolatry. The greatest triumph of science was the power it gave to man to annihilate himself and his world. And those who brought about this triumph are speaking today, like the true prophets of the past—which is to say, not of progress, but of a return to the chaos of the beginning; not of peace, but of disruption; and not of happiness, but of doom. In this way science is atoning for the idolatrous abuse to which it has lent itself for centuries. Science, which has closed our eyes and thrown us into an abyss of ignorance about the few things that really matter, has revealed itself, has opened our eyes, and has pointed, at least, to one fundamental truth—that "the mountains shall depart and the hills shall be removed," that "earth shall fall down to rise no more," because its foundations shall be destroyed.

But still we hear voices—and since the first shock, they have been increasing—which try to comfort us, saying: "Perhaps man will use the power to shake the foundations for creative purposes, for progress, for peace and happiness. The future lies in man's hands, in our hands. If we should decide for constructiveness instead of destruction, why should we not be able to continue the creation? Why should we not become like God, at least in this respect?" Job had to become silent when the Lord spoke to *him* out of the whirlwind, saying, "Where wast thou when I laid the foundations of the earth? Declare if thou hast understanding!" But our false voices continue: "Perhaps *we* can answer where Job could not. Have not our scientific discoveries revealed the mysteries of the ways in which the earth was founded? Are we not, in thought and knowledge, able to be present at this event? Why should we be afraid of the shaking of the foundations?" But man is not God; and whenever he has claimed to be like God, he has been rebuked and brought to self-destruction and despair. When he has rested complacently on his cultural creativity or on his technical progress, on his political institutions or on his religious systems, he has been thrown into disintegration and chaos; all the foundations of his personal, natural and cultural life have been shaken. As long as there has been human history, this is what has happened; in our period it has happened on a larger scale than ever before. Man's claim to be like God has been rejected once more; not one foundation of the life of our civilization has remained unshaken. As we read some of the passages from the prophets, we might easily imagine that we were reading the reports of eye-witnesses from Warsaw or Hiroshima or Berlin. Isaiah says: "Behold, the Lord maketh the earth empty and maketh it waste, and turneth it upside down and scattereth its inhabitants. . . . Towns fall to pieces; each man bolts his door; gladness has gone from the earth and pleasure is no more. The cities are left desolate; their gates are battered down; and few are left. . . . For earth has been polluted by the dwellers on its face . . . breaking the Eternal Covenant. Therefore, a curse is crushing the earth, and the guilty people must atone." Every one of these words describes the experience of the peoples of Europe and Asia. The most primitive and most essential foundations of life have been shaken. The destruction is such that we, who have not experienced it, cannot even imagine it. We have not experienced it; and we cannot believe that we could be caught in such a destruction. And yet, I see American soldiers walking through the ruins of these cities, thinking of their own country, and seeing with visionary clarity the doom of its towns and cities. I know that this has happened, and is still happening. There are soldiers who have become prophets, and their message is not very different from the message of the ancient Hebrew prophets. It is the message of the shaking of the foundations, and not those of their enemies, but rather those of their own country. For the prophetic spirit has not disappeared from the earth. Decades before the world wars, men judged the European civilization and prophesied its end in speech and print. There are among us people like these. They are like the refined instruments which register the shaking of the earth on far-removed sections of its surface. These people register the shaking of their civilization, its self-destructive trends, and its disintegration and fall, decades before the final catastrophe occurs. They have an invisible and almost infallible sensorium in their souls; and they have an irresistible urge to pronounce what they have registered, perhaps against their own wills. For no true prophet has ever prophesied voluntarily. It has been forced upon him by a Divine Voice to which he has not been able to close his ears. No man with a prophetic spirit likes to foresee and foresay the doom of his own period. It exposes him to a terrible anxiety within himself, to severe and often deadly attacks from others, and to the charge of pessimism and defeatism on the part of the majority of the people. Men desire to hear good tidings; and the masses listen to those who bring them. All the prophets of the Old and New Testaments, and others during the history of the Church, had the same experience. They all were contradicted by the false prophets, who announced salvation when there was no salvation. "The prophets prophesy falsely, and my people love to have it so," cries Jeremiah in despair. They called him a defeatist and accused him of being an enemy of his country. But is it a sign of patriotism or of confidence in one's people, its institutions and its way of life, to be silent when the foundations are shaking? Is the expression of optimism, whether or not it is justified, so much more valuable than the expression of truth, even if the truth is deep and dark: Most human beings, of course, are not able to stand the message of the shaking of the foundations. They reject and attack the prophetic minds, not because they really disagree with them, but because they sense the truth of their words and cannot receive it. They repress it in themselves; and they transform it into mockery or fury against those who *know* and dare to say that which they know. In which of these two groups do you consider yourselves to be? Among those who respond to the prophetic spirit, or among those who close their ears and hearts against it? I have always felt that there might be a few who are able to register the shaking of the foundations—who are able to stand this, and who are able, above all, to say what they know, because they are courageous enough to withstand the unavoidable enmity of the many. To those few my words are particularly directed.

Why were the prophets able to face what they knew, and then to pronounce it with such overwhelming power? Their power sprang from the fact that they did not really speak of the foundations of the earth as such, but of Him Who laid the foundations

and would shake them; and that they did not speak of the doom
of the nations as such, but of Him Who brings doom for the sake
of His eternal justice and salvation. As the 102nd Psalm says:
"Thy years are throughout all generations. Of old thou has laid
the foundations of the earth, and the heavens are the work of
thy hands. *They vanish,* but *thou shalt endure;* they wear out
like a robe, thou changest them like garments. But thou art the
same and thy years shall have no end. . . . " When the earth
grows old and wears out, when nations and cultures die, the
Eternal changes the garments of His infinite being. He is the
foundation on which all foundations are laid; and this foundation
cannot be shaken. There is something immovable, unchangeable,
unshakeable, eternal, which becomes manifest in our passing
and in the crumbling of our world. On the boundaries of the finite
the infinite becomes visible; in the light of the Eternal the transitoriness of the temporal appears. The Greeks called themselves
"the mortals" because they experienced that which is immortal.
This is why the prophets were able to face the shaking of the
foundations. It is the only way to look at the shaking without
recoiling from it. Or *is* it possible to be conscious of the approaching doom, and yet to regard it with indifference and cynicism? Is it humanly possible to face the *end* cynically? There
are certainly some among us who are cynical toward most of that
which men create and praise. There are some among us who are
cynical about the present situation of the world and the leaders
of the world. We *may* be cynical, of course, about the true motives
behind all human action; we may be cynical about ourselves, our
inner growth and our outer achievements. We may be cynical
about religion and about our Churches, their doctrines, their
symbols and their representatives. There is scarcely one thing
about which we may not be cynical. But we *can not* be cynical
about the shaking of the foundations of everything! I have never
encountered anyone who seriously was cynical about that. I have
seen much cynicism, particularly among the younger people in
Europe before the war. But I know from abundant witnesses that
this cynicism vanished when the foundations of the world began

to shake at the beginning of the European catastrophe. We can be cynical about the end only so long as we do not have to see it, only so long as we feel safety in the place in which our cynicism can be exercised. But if the foundations of this place and all places begin to crumble, cynicism itself crumbles with them. And only two alternatives remain—despair, which is the certainty of eternal destruction, or faith, which is the certainty of eternal salvation. "The world itself shall crumble, but . . . my salvation knows no end," says the Lord. *This* is the alternative for which the prophets stood. This is what we should call *religion*, or more precisely, the religious ground for all religion.

How could the prophets speak as they did? How could they paint these most terrible pictures of doom and destruction without cynicism or despair? It was because, beyond the sphere of destruction, they saw the sphere of salvation; because, in the doom of the temporal, they saw the manifestation of the Eternal. It was because they were certain that they belonged within the two spheres, the changeable *and* the unchangeable. For only he who is also beyond the changeable, not bound within it alone, can face the end. All others are compelled to escape, to turn away. How much of our lives consists in nothing but attempts to look away from the end! We often succeed in forgetting the end. But ultimately we fail; for we always carry the end with us in our bodies and our souls. And often whole nations and cultures succeed in forgetting the end. But ultimately they fail too, for in their lives and growth they always carry the end with them. Often the whole earth succeeds in making its creatures forget its end, but sometimes these creatures feel that their earth is beginning to grow old, and that its foundations are beginning to shake. For the earth always carries its end within it. We happen to live in a time when very few of us, very few nations, very few sections of the earth, will succeed in forgetting the end. For in these days the foundations of the earth *do* shake. May we *not* turn our eyes away; may we not close our ears and our mouths! But may we rather see, through the crumbling of a world, the rock of eternity and the salvation which has no end!

15
The Socialist
Principle

The roots of political thought must be sought in human being itself. Without some notion of human nature, of its powers and tensions, one cannot make any statements about the foundations of political existence and thought. Without a doctrine of human nature, there can be no theory of political tendencies that is more than a depiction of their external form. A doctrine of human nature, however, cannot be worked out here. It must be presupposed, and at best it can create for itself a favorable hearing by its capacity to illuminate political thought.

Human beings differ from nature in that they are creatures with an internal duality. No matter where nature ends and humanity begins, no matter whether there are gradual transitions or a sudden leap between them, somewhere the difference becomes visible. Nature is a unified life-process, unfolding itself without question or demand, and bound by what it finds in itself and its environment. Humanity is a life-process that questions itself and its environment, placing demands on itself and its environment, which therefore is not one with itself. Rather, it has these two aspects: to exist in itself and simultaneously to stand over against itself, thinking about itself and knowing about itself. Human beings possess self-consciousness, or to contrast this with

From Paul Tillich, *The Socialist Decision* (New York: Harper and Row), 2–6. Reprinted by permission of the Publisher. Copyright © 1977 by Harper and Row Publishers, Inc.

nature, they are beings who are internally dualized by virtue of their self-consciousness. Nature lacks this duality. We are not implying in these statements that human beings are composed of two independent parts, for example, of nature and spirit, or body and soul; rather, there is *one* being but twofold in its unity.

Even these very general definitions have consequences for any investigation of political thought. They make it impossible to derive political thinking from purely mental processes, from religious and moral demands or ideological judgments. Political thinking proceeds from human nature as a whole. It is rooted simultaneously in being and in consciousness, more precisely in the indissoluble unity of the two. *Therefore it is impossible to understand a system of political thought without uncovering the human and social reality in which it is rooted*, that is, the interrelation of drives and interests, of pressures and aspirations, which make up social reality. But it is equally impossible even to conceive of this reality as separate from consciousness, that is, to view consciousness and along with it political thought as mere byproducts of being. *Every element of human and social being, down to the most primitive emotional drive, is shaped by consciousness.* Any effort to dissolve this connection ignores the first and most important characteristic of human nature, and therefore results in distortions in the total picture of that nature.

To point out that there is a consciousness that does not correspond to being, the so-called "false consciousness," proves nothing against the unity of being and consciousness. For the very concept of a "false consciousness" is only possible and such a thing is only knowable if there is a true consciousness. A true consciousness, however, is one that arises out of being and at the same time determines it. It is not one without the other. For human nature is a unity in its duality, and the two roots of all political thinking grow out of this unity.

Human beings find themselves in existence; they find themselves as they find their environment, and as this latter finds them and itself. But to find oneself means that one does not originate from oneself; it means to have an origin that is not oneself, or—in the pregnant phrase of Martin Heidegger—to be "thrown" into the world. The human question concerning the "Whence" of existence arises out of this situation. Only later does it appear as a philosophical question. But it has always been a question; and its first and permanently normative answer is enshrined in myth.

The origin is creative. Something new springs into being, something that did not previously exist and now is something with its own character over against the origin. We experience ourselves as posited, yet also as independent. Our life proceeds in a tension between dependence on the origin and independence. For the origin does not let us go; it is not something that was and is no longer, once we become independent selves. Rather, we are continually dependent on the origin; it bears us, it creates us anew at every moment, and thereby holds us fast. The origin brings us forth as something new and singular; but it takes us, as such, back to the origin again. Just in being born we become involved in having to die. "It is necessary that things should pass away into that from which they are born," declares the first saying handed down to us in Western philosophy. Our life runs its course in terms of birth, development and death. No living thing can transcend the limits set by its birth; development is the growing and passing away of what comes from the origin and returns to it. This has been expressed in myth in infinitely diverse ways, according to the things and events in which a particular group envisages its origin. In all mythology, however, there resounds the cyclical law of birth and death. Every myth is a myth of origin, that is, an answer to the question about the "Whence" of existence and an expression of dependence on the origin and on its power. *The consciousness oriented to the myth of origin is the root of all conservative and romantic thought in politics.*

But human beings not only find themselves in existence; they not only know themselves to be posited and withdrawn in the cycle of birth and death, like all living things. They experience a demand that frees them from being simply bound to what is given, and which compels them to add to the question "Whence?"

[*Woher*] the question "Whither?" [*Wozu*]. With this question the cycle is broken in principle and humankind is elevated beyond the sphere of merely living things. For the demand calls for something that does not yet exist but should exist, should come to fulfillment. A being that experiences a demand is no longer simply bound to the origin. Human life involves more than a mere development of what already is. Through the demand, humanity is directed to what ought to be. And what ought to be does not emerge with the unfolding of what is; if it did, it would be something that is, rather than something that ought to be. This means, however, that the demand that confronts humanity is an unconditional demand. The question "Whither?" is not contained within the limits of the question "Whence?" It is something unconditionally new that transcends what is new and what is old within the sphere of mere development. Through human beings, something unconditionally new is to be realized; this is the meaning of the demand that they experience, and which they are able to experience because in them being is twofold. For the human person is not only an individual, a self, but also has knowledge about himself or herself, and thereby the possibility of transcending what is found within the self and around the self. This is human freedom, not that one has a so-called free will, but that as a human being one is not bound to what one finds in existence, that one is subject to a demand that something unconditionally new should be realized through oneself. Thus the cycle of birth and death is broken; the existence and the actions of human beings are not confined within a mere development of their origin. Wherever this consciousness prevails, the tie to the origin has been dissolved in principle and the myth of origin has been broken in principle. *The breaking of the myth of origin by the unconditional demand is the root of liberal, democratic, and socialist thought in politics.*

Yet we cannot stop with a simple opposition between these two aspects of human existence. The demand that human beings experience is unconditional, but it is not alien to human nature. If it were alien to our nature, it would be of no concern to us and we could not perceive it as a demand upon us. It affects us only because it places before us, in the form of a demand, our own essence. Therein alone is grounded the unconditionality and inescapability with which the demand confronts us and must be affirmed by us. But if the demand is our own essence, it is grounded in our origin. The questions "Whence?" and "Whither?" do not belong to two different worlds. And yet, the demand is something unconditionally new over against the origin. This indicates that *the origin is ambiguous.* There is a split in it between the true and the actual origin. *The actual origin is not the origin in truth.* It is not the fulfillment of what is intended for humanity from the origin. The fulfillment of the origin lies rather in what confronts us as a demand, as an ought. The "Whence" of humanity finds its fulfillment in the "Whither." The actual origin is contradicted by the true origin, not absolutely and in every respect, for the actual origin—in order to be actual at all—must participate in the true origin; it expresses it, but at the same time both obscures it and distorts it. The mentality oriented solely to the myth of origin knows nothing of this ambiguity of the origin. Therefore it clings to the origin and feels that it is a sacrilege to go beyond it. The ambiguity of the origin is first revealed to it when the experience of the unconditional demand frees this consciousness from bondage to the origin.

The demand is directed towards the fulfillment of the true origin. Now a person experiences an unconditional demand only from another person. The demand becomes concrete in the "I-Thou" encounter. The content of the demand is therefore that the "thou" be accorded the same dignity as the "I"; this is the dignity of being free, of being the bearer of the fulfillment implied in the origin. This recognition of the equal dignity of the "Thou" and the "I" is justice. *The demand that separates from the ambiguous origin is the demand of justice.* From the unbroken origin proceed powers that are in tension with one another; they seek dominion and destroy each other. From the unbroken origin there comes the power of being, the rising and perishing of forces that "pay one another the penalty and compensation for their injustice according to the ordinance of time," as is asserted in the already quoted first statement of Greek philosophy. The unconditional demand transcends this tragic cycle of existence. It confronts the power and impotence of being with justice, arising from the demand. And yet, the contrast is not absolute, for the ought is the fulfillment of the is. *Justice is the true power of being.* In it the intention of the origin is fulfilled.

16
The Unity of Love, Power, and Justice

NO DISCUSSION of concepts like love, power, and justice is possible without touching the dimension of ultimate concern, the dimension of the holy.

But there is a profounder reason for the necessity of reaching into this dimension. It was our task to show that essentially, in their created nature, love, power, and justice are united. This, however, was not possible without showing that in existence they are separated and conflicting. This leads to the question: How can their essential unity be reestablished? The answer is obvious: Through the manifestation of the ground in which they are united. Love, power, and justice are one in the divine ground, and shall become one in human existence. The holy in which they are united shall become holy reality in time and space. How and in which sense is this possible?

GOD AS THE SOURCE OF LOVE, POWER, AND JUSTICE

The basic assertion about the relation of God to love, power, and justice is made, if one says that God is being itself. For being

From Paul Tillich, *Love, Power, and Justice* (London: Oxford University Press), 108–125. Reprinted by permission of Oxford University Press. Copyright © 1954 by Paul Tillich.

itself, according to our ontological analysis, implies love as well as power and justice. God is the basic and universal symbol for what concerns us ultimately. As being-itself He is ultimate reality, the really real, the ground and abyss of everything that is real. As the God, with whom I have a person-to-person encounter, He is the subject of all the symbolic statements in which I express my ultimate concern. Everything we say about being-itself, the ground and abyss of being, must be symbolic. It is taken out of the material of our finite reality and applied to that which transcends the finite infinitely. Therefore it cannot be used in its literal sense. To say anything about God in the literal sense of the words used means to say something false about Him. The symbolic in relation to God is not less true than the literal, but it is the only true way of speaking about God.

This refers also to the three ideas we are discussing. If we speak of God as loving or, more emphatically, of God as being love, we use our experience of love and our analysis of life as the material which alone we can use. But we also know that if we apply it to God we throw it into the mystery of the divine depth, where it is transformed without being lost. It is still love, but it is now divine love. This does not mean that a higher being has in a fuller sense what we call love, but it does mean that our love is rooted in the divine life, i.e., in something which transcends our life infinitely in being and meaning.

The same we must say of the divine power. It is applied to God symbolically. We experience power in physical acts as well as in the ability to carry through our will against contradicting wills. This experience is the material we use when we speak of the divine power. We speak of His omnipotence and we address Him as the Almighty. Literally taken, this would mean that God is a highest being, who can do what He wants to do, the implication being that there are a lot of things which He does not want to do, a concept which leads into a fog of absurd imaginations. The real meaning of almightiness is that God is the power of being in everything that is, transcending every special power infinitely but acting at the same time as its creative ground. In the religious experience the power of God provokes the feeling of being in the hand of a power which cannot be conquered by any other power, in ontological terms, which is the infinite resistance against nonbeing and the eternal victory over it. To participate in this resistance and this victory is felt as the way to overcome the threat of nonbeing which is the destiny of everything finite. In every prayer to the almighty God, power is seen in the light of the divine power. It is seen as ultimate reality.

Justice is applied to God equally in an ultimate and therefore symbolic sense. God is symbolized as the righteous judge who judges according to the law He has given. This is the material taken out of our experience. It also must be thrown into the mystery of the divine life and in it both preserved and transformed. It has become a true symbol of the relation of the ground of being to that which is grounded in it, especially to man. The divine law is beyond the alternative of natural and positive law. It is the structure of reality and of everything in it, including the structure of the human mind. In so far as it is this, it is natural law, the law of continuous creation, the justice of being in everything. At the same time it is positive law, posited by God in His freedom which is not dependent on any given structure outside Him. In so far as it is natural law, we can understand the law in nature and mankind and formulate it deductively. In so far as it is positive law we have to accept what is given to us empirically and we have to observe it inductively. Both sides are rooted in God's relation to the justice in things.

To see love, power, and justice as true symbols of the divine life, means to see their ultimate unity. Unity is not identity. An element of separation is presupposed when we speak of unity. There are present, in the symbolic application of our three concepts to God, also some symbols of tension.

The first is the tension between love and power. The exclamation has been and will be repeated innumerably: How can an all-powerful God who is, at the same time the God of love, allow such misery? Either He has not sufficient love or He has not sufficient power. As an emotional outburst this question is very understandable. As a theoretical formulation it is rather poor. If God had produced a world in which physical and moral evil were impossible, the creatures would not have had the independence of God which is presupposed in the experience of reuniting love. The world would have become a paradise of dreaming innocence, an infant's paradise, but neither love nor power nor justice would have become real. Actualization of one's potentialities includes, unavoidably, estrangement; estrangement from one's essential being, so that we may find it again in maturity. Only a God who is like a foolish mother, who is so afraid about the well-being of her child that she keeps him in a state of enforced innocence and enforced participation in her own life, could have kept the creatures in the prison of a dreaming paradise. And, as in the case of the mother, this would have been hidden hostility and not love. And it would not have been power either. The power of God is that He overcomes estrangement, not that He prevents it; that He takes it, symbolically speaking, upon Himself, not that He remains in a dead identity with Himself. This is the meaning of the age-old symbol of the god participating in creaturely suffering, a symbol which in Christianity was applied to the interpretation of the Cross of Him who was said to be the Christ. This is the unity of love and power in the depth of reality itself, power not only in its creative element but also in its compulsory element and the destruction and suffering connected with it. These considerations give theology a key to the eternal problem of theodicy, the problem of the relation of the divine love and the divine power to nonbeing, namely to death, guilt, and meaninglessness. The ontological unity of love and power is this key which certainly does not open up the mystery of being but which can replace some rusty keys to misleading doors.

While the tension between love and power refers basically to creation, the tension between love and justice refers basically to salvation. The analysis of transforming justice as an expression of creative love makes it unnecessary for me to reject the ordinary contrast between proportional justice and super-added love. In this sense, there can be no conflict between justice and love in

God. But in another sense there could be, in a sense which is very similar to that in which love and power have been contrasted. Love destroys, as its strange work, what is against love. It does so according to the justice without which it would be chaotic surrender of the power of being. Love, at the same time, as its own work, saves through forgiveness that which is against love. It does so according to the justifying paradox without which it would be a legal mechanism. How can these two works of love be one? They are one because love does not enforce salvation. If it did it would commit a double injustice. It would disregard the claim of every person to be treated not as a thing but as a centered, deciding, free, and responsible self. Since God is love and His love is one with His power, He has not the power to force somebody into His salvation. He would contradict Himself. And this God cannot do. At the same time such an act would disregard the strange work of love, namely the destruction of what destroys love. It would violate the unconditioned character of love and with it the divine majesty. Love must destroy what is against love, but not him who is the bearer of that which is against love. For as a creature, he remains a power of being or a creation of love. But the unity of his will is destroyed, he is thrown into a conflict with himself, the name of which is despair, mythologically speaking, hell. Dante was right when he called even Hell a creation of the divine love. The hell of despair is the strange work that love does within us in order to open us up for its own work, justification of him who is unjust. But even despair does not make us into a mechanism. It is a test of our freedom and personal dignity, even in relation to God. The Cross of Christ is the symbol of the divine love, participating in the destruction into which it throws him who acts against love: This is the meaning of atonement.

Love, power, and justice are one in God. But we must ask: What do love, power, and justice do within an estranged world?

LOVE, POWER, AND JUSTICE IN THE HOLY COMMUNITY

Love, power, and justice are united in God and they are united in the new creation of God in the world. Man is estranged from the ground of his being, from himself and from his world. But he is still man. He cannot completely cut the tie with his creative ground, he is still a centered person and in this sense united with himself. He still participates in his world. In other words: The reuniting love, the power of resisting nonbeing, and the creative justice are still alive in him. Life is not unambiguously good. Then it would not be life but only the possibility of life. And life is not unambiguously evil. Then nonbeing would have conquered being. But life is unambiguous in all its expressions. It is ambiguous also with respect to love, power, and justice. We have touched on this fact in many places in our previous discussions. We must now consider it in the light of the new creation within the world of estrangement, which I suggest calling the holy community.

In an anticipating summary I would say: in the holy community the *agape* quality of love cuts into the *libido, eros,* and *philia* qualities of love and elevates them beyond the ambiguities of their self-centeredness. In the holy community the spiritual power, by surrendering compulsion, elevates power beyond the ambiguities of its dynamic realization. In the holy community justification by grace elevates justice beyond the ambiguities of its abstract and calculating nature. This means that in the holy community love, power, and justice in their ontological structure are affirmed but that their estranged and ambiguous reality is transformed into a manifestation of their unity within the divine life.

Let us first consider the ambiguities of love and the work of love as *agape* in the holy community. Libido is good in itself! We have defended it against Freud's depreciation of what he described as the infinite libidinous drive with its ensuing dissatisfaction and death instinct. We have accepted this as the description of estrangement, but not of libido in its creative meaning. Without libido life would not move beyond itself. The Bible knows this as well as recent depth psychology, and we should be grateful that our new insights into the deeper levels of human nature have rediscovered the Biblical realism which was covered by several strata of idealistic and moralistic self-deception about man. Biblical realism knows both that libido belongs to man's created goodness and that it is distorted and ambiguous in the state of man's estrangement. Libido has become unlimited and has fallen under the tyranny of the pleasure principle. It uses the other being not as an object of reunion but as a tool for gaining pleasure out of him. Sexual desire is not evil as desire, and the breaking of conventional laws is not evil as the breaking of conventional laws, but sexual desire and sexual autonomy are evil if they bypass the center of the other person—in other words, if they are not united with the two other qualities of love, and if they are not under the ultimate criterion of the *agape* quality of love. *Agape* seeks the other one in his center. *Agape* sees him as God sees him. *Agape* elevates libido into the divine unity of love, power, and justice.

The same is true of *eros*. We have, following Plato, defined *eros* as the driving force in all cultural creativity and in all mysticism. As such *eros* has the greatness of a divine-human power. It participates in creation and in the natural goodness of everything created. But it also participates in the ambiguities of life. The *eros* quality of love can be confused with the libido quality and be drawn into its ambiguities. Witness for this is the fact that the New Testament could not use the word *eros* any more because of its predominantly sexual connotations. And even the mystical *eros* can express itself in symbols which are not only taken from the sexual life but which draw the love to God to an openly ascetic, hiddenly sexual level. But more is involved when we speak of the ambiguity of the *eros* quality of love. It is the aesthetic detachment which can take hold of our relation to culture and makes *eros* ambiguous. We have learned this especially

from Kierkegaard. His aesthetic stage of man's spiritual development is not a stage but a universal quality of love exposed to
the dangers Kierkegaard describes. The ambiguity of cultural
eros is its detachment from the realities which it expresses and
consequently the disappearing of existential participation and
ultimate responsibility. The wings of *eros* become wings of escape. Culture is irresponsibly enjoyed. It has not received the
justice which it can demand. *Agape* cuts into the detached safety
of a merely aesthetic *eros*. It does not deny the longing toward
the good and the true and its divine source, but it prevents it
from becoming an aesthetic enjoyment without ultimate seriousness. *Agape* makes the cultural *eros* responsible and the mystical *eros* personal.

The ambiguities of the *philia* quality of love appeared already
in its first description as person-to-person love between equals.
However large the group of equals may be, the *philia* quality of
love establishes preferential love. Some are preferred, the majority are excluded. This is obvious not only in intimate relations
as family and friendship, but also in the innumerable forms of
sympathetic person-to-person encounters. The implicit or explicit
rejection of all those who are not admitted to such a preferential
relation is negative compulsion and can be as cruel as any compulsion. But such a rejection of others is tragically unavoidable.
Nobody can escape the necessity to exercise it. There are special
forms of love with *philia* quality which the psychoanalyst Erich
Fromm has called symbiotic relation and which make this tragic
necessity rather clear. If the one partner of a *philia*-relation is
used by the other one either for the sake of masochistic dependence or of sadistic domination or of both in interdependence,
something which seemed to be friendship of highest quality is
in reality compulsion without justice. Again, *agape* does not deny
the preferential love of the *philia* quality, but it purifies it from
a subpersonal bondage, and it elevates the preferential love into
universal love. The preferences of friendship are not negated, but
they do not exclude, in a kind of aristocratic self-separation, all
the others. Not everybody is a friend, but everybody is affirmed

as a person. *Agape* cuts through the separation of equals and unequals, of sympathy and antipathy, of friendship and indifference, of desire and disgust. It needs no sympathy in order to love; it loves what it has to reject in terms of *philia*. *Agape* loves in everybody and through everybody love itself.

What *agape* does to the ambiguities of love, Spiritual power does to the ambiguities of natural power. The ambiguities of power are rooted in the dynamic character and the compulsory implications of power. Spiritual power is not the conquest of these ambiguities by resignation of power, because this would mean resignation of being. It would be the attempt to annihilate oneself in order to escape guilt. Spiritual power is not the denial of power dynamics. In many stories about the working of the Spiritual power bodily effects are mentioned, like elevation, removal from one place to the other, shock, and horror. There are always psychological effects visible. Spirit is power, grasping and moving out of the dimension of the ultimate. It is not identical with the realm of ideas or meanings. It is dynamic power, overcoming resistance. Then what is its difference from the other forms of power? The Spiritual power works neither through bodily nor through psychological compulsion. It works through man's total personality, and this means, through him as finite freedom. It does not remove his freedom, but it makes his freedom free from the compulsory elements which limit it. The Spiritual power gives a center to the whole personality, a center which transcends the whole personality and, consequently, is independent of any of its elements. And this is ultimately the only way of uniting the personality with itself. If this happens man's natural or social power of being becomes irrelevant. He may keep them, he may resign some of them or even all of them. The Spiritual power works through them or it works through the surrender of them. He may exercise Spiritual power through words or thought, through what he is and what he does, or through the surrender of them or through the sacrifice of himself. In all these forms he can change reality by attaining levels of being which are ordinarily hidden.

This is the power which elevates the holy community above the ambiguities of power.

I do not need to say much about the relation of grace and justice. The act of forgiving has been mentioned in connection with the encounter of person and person. Mutual forgiveness is the fulfillment of creative justice. But mutual forgiveness is justice only if it based on reuniting love, in justification by grace. Only God can forgive, because in Him alone love and justice are completely united. The ethics of forgiveness are rooted in the message of divine forgiveness. Otherwise they are delivered to the ambiguities of justice, oscillating between legalism and sentimentality. In the holy community this ambiguity is conquered.

Agape conquers the ambiguities of love, Spiritual power conquers the ambiguities of power, grace conquers the ambiguities of justice. This is true not only of the encounters of man with man, but also in the encounter of man with himself. Man can love himself in terms of self-acceptance only if he is certain that he is accepted. Otherwise his self-acceptance is self-complacency and arbitrariness. Only in the light and in the power of the "love from above" can he love himself. This implies the answer to the question of man's justice toward himself. He can be just toward himself only in so far as ultimate justice is done to him, namely the condemning, forgiving, and giving judgement of "justification." The condemning element in justification makes self-complacency impossible, the forgiving element saves from self-condemnation and despair, the giving element provides for a Spiritual center which unites the elements of our personal self and makes power over oneself possible.

Justice, power, and love toward oneself is rooted in the justice, power, and love which we receive from that which transcends us and affirms us. The relation to ourselves is a function of our relation to God. . . .

It is the merit of pacifism that, in spite of its theological shortcomings, it has kept this question alive in modern Christianity. Without it the Churches probably would have forgotten the torturing seriousness of any religious affirmation of war. On the other hand, pacifism has usually restricted a much larger problem of human existence to the question of war. But there are other questions of equal seriousness in the same sphere. One of them is the question of armed conflicts within a power group, always going on potentially in the use of police and armed forces for the preservation of order, sometimes coming into the open in revolutionary wars. If successful, they are later on called "glorious revolutions." Does the union of mankind mean that not only national but also revolutionary wars are excluded? And if so, has the dynamics of life come to an end; and does this mean that life itself has come to an end?

One can ask the same question with respect to the dynamics of the economic life. Even in a static society such as that of the Middle Ages, the economic dynamics were important and had tremendous historical consequences. One should remain aware of the fact that often more destruction and suffering is produced by economic than by military battles. Should the economic dynamics be stopped and a static world system of production and consumption be introduced? If this were so the whole technical process would also have to be stopped, life in most realms would have to be organized in ever-repeated processes. Every disturbance would have to be avoided. Again the dynamics of life and with it life itself would have come to an end.

Let us assume for a moment that this were possible. Under an unchangeable central authority all encounters of power with power are regulated. Nothing is risked, everything decided. Life has ceased to transcend itself. Creativity has come to an end. The history of man would be finished, posthistory would have started. Mankind would be a flock of blessed animals without dissatisfaction, without drive into the future. The horrors and sufferings of the historical period would be remembered as the dark ages of mankind. And then it might happen that one or the other of these blessed men would feel a longing for these past ages, their misery and their greatness, and would force a new beginning of history upon the rest.

This image will show that a world without the dynamics of power and the tragedy of life and history is not the Kingdom of God, is not the fulfillment of man and his world. Fulfillment is bound to eternity and no imagination can reach the eternal. But fragmentary anticipations are possible. The Church itself is such a fragmentary anticipation. And there are groups and movements, which although they do not belong to the manifest Church, represent something we may call a "latent Church." But neither the manifest nor the latent Church is the Kingdom of God. . . .

The problems of love, power, and justice categorically demand an ontological foundation and a theological view in order to be saved from the vague talk, idealism, and cynicism with which they are usually treated. Man cannot solve any of his great problems if he does not see them in the light of his own being and of being-itself.

17
Love Is Stronger than Death

We know that we have passed out of death into life, because we love the brethren. He who does not love remains in death.

I JOHN 3:14

IN OUR TIME, as in every age, we need to see something which is stronger than death. Death has become powerful in our time, in individual human beings, in families, in nations and in mankind as a whole. Death has become powerful—that is to say that the End, the finite, and the limitations and decay of our being have become visible. For nearly a century this was concealed in Western civilization. We had become masters in our earthly household. Our control over nature and our social planning had widened the boundaries of our being; the affirmation of life had drowned out its negation which no longer dared make itself heard, and which fled into the hidden anxiety of our hearts, becoming fainter and fainter. We forgot that we are finite, and we forgot the abyss of nothingness surrounding us. We had gathered into our barns the fruits of thousands of years of toil. All generations of men had labored so that we, the generation of fulfillment, might tread death under our feet. It was not death in the sense of the natural end of life which we thought to have

From Paul Tillich, *The New Being* (New York: Charles Scribner's Sons), 170–174. Reprinted by permission of Charles Scribner's Sons. Copyright © 1955 by Paul Tillich.

destroyed, but death as a power in and over life, as the Lord and master of the soul. We kept the picture of death from our children and when here and there, in our neighborhood and in the world, mortal convulsions and the End became visible, our security was not disturbed. For us these events were merely accidental and unavoidable, but they were not enough to tear off the lid which we had fastened down over the abyss of our being.

And suddenly the lid was torn off. The picture of Death appeared, unveiled, in a thousand forms. As in the late Middle Ages the figure of Death appeared in pictures and poetry, and the Dance of Death with every living being was painted and sung, so our generation—the generation of world wars, revolutions, and mass migrations—rediscovered the reality of death. We have seen millions die in war, hundreds of thousands in revolutions, tens of thousands in persecutions and systematic purges of minorities. Multitudes as numerous as whole nations still wander over the face of the earth or perish when artificial walls put an end to their wanderings. All those who are called refugees or immigrants belong to this wandering; in them is embodied a part of these tremendous events in which Death has again grasped the reins which we believed it had relinquished forever. Such people carry in their souls, and often in their bodies, the traces of death, and they will never completely lose them. You who have never taken part yourselves in this great migration must receive these others as symbols of a death which is a component element of life. Receive them as people who, by their destiny, shall remind us of the presence of the End in every moment of life and history. Receive them as symbols of the finiteness and transitoriness of every human concern, of every human life, and of every created thing.

We have become a generation of the End and those of us who have been refugees and exiles should not forget this when we have found a new beginning here or in another land. The End is nothing external. It is not exhausted by the loss of that which we can never regain: our childhood homes, the people with whom we grew up, the country, the things, the language which formed us, the goods, both spiritual and material, which we inherited or earned, the friends who were torn away from us by sudden death. The End is more than all this; it is in us, it has become our very being. We are a generation of the End and we should know that we are. Perhaps there are some who think that what has happened to them and to the whole world should now be forgotten. Is it not more dignified, truer and stronger to say "yes" to that which is our destiny, to refuse to cover the signs of the End in our lives and in our souls, to let the voice of Death be heard? Amid all the new possibilities offered to us, must we not acknowledge ourselves to be that which destiny has made us? Must we not confess that we are symbols of the End? And this End is of an age which was both great and a lie. It is the End for all finitude which always becomes a lie when it forgets that it is finite and seeks to veil the picture of death.

But who can bear to look at this picture? Only he who can look at another picture behind and beyond it—the picture of Love. For love is stronger than death. Every death means parting, separation, isolation, opposition and not participation. So it is, too, with the death of nations, the end of generations, and the atrophy of souls. Our souls become poor and disintegrate insofar as we want to be alone, insofar as we bemoan our misfortunes, nurse our despair and enjoy our bitterness, and yet turn coldly away from the physical and spiritual need of others. Love overcomes separation and creates participation in which there is more than that which the individuals involved can bring to it. Love is the infinite which is given to the finite. Therefore we love in others, for we do not merely love others, but we love the Love that is in them and which is more than their or our love. In mutual assistance what is most important is not the alleviation of need but the actualization of love. Of course, there is no love which does not want to make the other's need its own. But there is also no true help which does not spring from love and create love. Those who fight against death and disintegration through all kinds of relief agencies know this. Often very little external help is possible. And the gratitude of those who receive help is first and always gratitude for love and only afterwards gratitude for help. Love, not help, is stronger than death. But there is no love which does not become help. Where help is given without love, there new suffering grows from the help.

It is love, human and divine, which overcomes death in nations and generations and in all the horror of our time. Help has become almost impossible in the face of the monstrous powers which we are experiencing. Death is given power over everything finite, especially in our period of history. But death is given no power over love. Love is stronger. It creates something new out of the destruction caused by death; it bears everything and overcomes everything. It is at work where the power of death is strongest, in war and persecution and homelessness and hunger and physical death itself. It is omnipresent and here and there, in the smallest and most hidden ways as in the greatest and most visible ones, it rescues life from death. It rescues each of us, for love is stronger than death.

PART VI

THE COURAGE
TO BE

18
Estrangement and Sin

THE STATE OF EXISTENCE is the state of estrangement. Man is estranged from the ground of his being, from other beings, and from himself. The transition from essence to existence results in personal guilt and universal tragedy. . . .

"Estrangement" as a philosophical term was created and applied by Hegel, especially in his doctrine of nature as estranged mind (*Geist*). But his discovery of estrangement happened long before he developed his philosophy of nature. In his early fragments he described life-processes as possessing an original unity which is disrupted by the split into subjectivity and objectivity and by the replacement of love by law. . . . The individual is estranged and not reconciled; society is estranged and not reconciled; existence is estrangement. In the strength of this insight, they become revolutionaries against the world as it existed and were existentialists long before the beginning of the twentieth century.

In the sense in which it was used by the anti-Hegelians, estrangement points to the basic characteristic of man's predicament. Man as he exists is not what he essentially is and ought to be. He is estranged from his true being. The profundity of the term "estrangement" lies in the implication that one belongs

From Paul Tillich, *Systematic Theology*, Vol. 2 (Chicago: University of Chicago Press), 44–47. Reprinted by permission of University of Chicago Press. Copyright © 1975 by Paul Tillich.

essentially to that from which one is estranged. Man is not a stranger to his true being, for he belongs to it. He is judged by it but cannot be completely separated, even if he is hostile to it. Man's hostility to God proves indisputably that he belongs to him. Where there is the possibility of hate, there and there alone is the possibility of love.

Estrangement is not a biblical term but is implied in most of the biblical descriptions of man's predicament. It is implied in the symbols of the expulsion from paradise, in the hostility between man and nature, in the deadly hostility of brother against brother, in the estrangement of nation from nation through the confusion of language, and in the continuous complaints of the prophets against their kings and people who turn to alien gods. Estrangement is implied in Paul's statement that man perverted the image of God into that of idols, in his classical description of "man against himself," in his vision of man's hostility against man as combined with his distorted desires. In all these interpretations of man's predicament, estrangement is implicitly asserted. Therefore, it is certainly not unbiblical to use the term "estrangement" in describing man's existential situation.

Nevertheless, "estrangement" cannot replace "sin." Yet the reasons for attempts to replace the word "sin" with another word are obvious. The term has been used in a way which has little to do with its genuine biblical meaning. Paul often spoke of "Sin" in the singular and without an article. He saw it as a quasi-personal power which ruled this world. But in the Christian churches, both Catholic and Protestant, sin has been used predominantly in the plural, and "sins" are deviations from moral laws. This has little to do with "sin" as the state of estrangement from that to which one belongs—God, one's self, one's world. Therefore, the characteristics of sin are here considered under the heading of "estrangement." And the word "estrangement" itself implies a reinterpretation of sin from a religious point of view.

Nevertheless, the word "sin" cannot be overlooked. It expresses what is not implied in the term "estrangement," namely, the personal act of turning away from that to which one belongs. Sin expresses most sharply the personal character of estrangement over against its tragic side. It expresses personal freedom and guilt in contrast to tragic guilt and the universal destiny of estrangement. The word "sin" can and must be saved, not only because classical literature and liturgy continuously employ it but more particularly because the word has a sharpness which accusingly points to the element of personal responsibility in one's estrangement. Man's predicament is estrangement, but his estrangement is sin. It is not a state of things, like the laws of nature, but a matter of both personal freedom and universal destiny. For this reason the term "sin" must be used after it has been reinterpreted religiously. An important tool for this reinterpretation is the term "estrangement."

Reinterpretation is also needed for the terms "original" or "hereditary" with respect to sin. But in this case reinterpretation may demand the rejection of the terms. Both point to the universal character of estrangement, expressing the element of destiny in estrangement. But both words are so much burdened with literalistic absurdities that it is practically impossible to use them any longer.

If one speaks of "sins" and refers to special acts which are considered as sinful, one should always be conscious of the fact that "sins" are the expressions of "sin." It is not the disobedience to a law which makes an act sinful but the fact that it is an expression of man's estrangement from God, from men, from himself. Therefore, Paul calls everything sin which does not result from faith, from the unity with God. And in another context (following Jesus) all laws are summed up in the law of love by which estrangement is conquered. Love as the striving for the reunion of the separated is the opposite of estrangement. In faith and love, sin is conquered because estrangement is overcome by reunion.

19
Courage and Transcendence

COURAGE is the self-affirmation of being in spite of the fact of nonbeing. It is the act of the individual self in taking the anxiety of nonbeing upon itself by affirming itself either as part of an embracing whole or in its individual selfhood. Courage always includes a risk, it is always threatened by nonbeing, whether the risk of losing oneself and becoming a thing within the whole of things or of losing one's world in an empty self-relatedness. Courage needs the power of being, a power transcending the nonbeing which is experienced in the anxiety of fate and death, which is present in the anxiety of emptiness and meaninglessness, which is effective in the anxiety of guilt and condemnation. The courage which takes this threefold anxiety into itself must be rooted in a power of being that is greater than the power of oneself and the power of one's world. Neither self-affirmation as a part nor self-affirmation as oneself is beyond the manifold threat of nonbeing. Those who are mentioned as representatives of these forms of courage try to transcend themselves and the world in which they participate in order to find the power of being-itself and a courage to be which is beyond the threat of nonbeing. There are no exceptions to this rule; and this means that every courage to be has an open or hidden religious root. For religion is the state of being grasped

From Paul Tillich, *The Courage to Be* (New Haven: Yale University Press), 155–190. Reprinted by permission of Yale University Press. Copyright ©1952 by Paul Tillich.

by the power of being-itself. In some cases the religious root is carefully covered, in others it is passionately denied; in some it is deeply hidden and in others superficially. But it is never completely absent. For everything that is participates in being-itself, and everybody has some awareness of this participation, especially in the moments in which he experiences the threat of nonbeing. This leads us to a final consideration, the double question: How is the courage to be rooted in being-itself, and how must we understand being-itself in the light of the courage to be? The first question deals with the ground of being as source of the courage to be, the second with courage to be as key to the ground of being.

THE POWER OF BEING AS SOURCE OF THE COURAGE TO BE

THE MYSTICAL EXPERIENCE AND THE COURAGE TO BE

Since the relation of man to the ground of his being must be expressed in symbols taken from the structure of being, the polarity of participation and individualization determines the special character of this relation as it determines the special character of the courage to be. If participation is dominant, the relation to being-itself has a mystical character, if individualization prevails the relation to being-itself has a personal character, if both poles are accepted and transcended the relation to being-itself has the character of faith.

In mysticism the individual self strives for a participation in the ground of being which approaches identification. Our question is not whether this goal can ever be reached by a finite being but whether and how mysticism can be the source of the courage to be. . . . All mystics draw their power of self-affirmation from the experience of the power of being-itself with which they are united. But one may ask, can courage be united with mysticism in any way? It seems that in India, for example, courage is considered the virtue of the *kshatriya* (knight), to be found below the levels of the Brahman or the ascetic saint. Mystical identification transcends the aristocratic virtue of courageous self-sacrifice. It is self-surrender in a higher, more complete, and more radical form. It is the perfect form of self-affirmation. But if this so, it is courage in the larger though not in the narrower sense of the word. The ascetic and ecstatic mystic affirms his own essential being over against the elements of nonbeing which are present in the finite world, the realm of Maya. It takes tremendous courage to resist the lure of appearances. The power of being which is manifest in such courage is so great that the gods tremble in fear of it. The mystic seeks to penetrate the ground of being, the all-present and all-pervasive power of the Brahman. In doing so he affirms his essential self which is identical with the power of the Brahman, while all those who affirm themselves in the bondage of Maya affirm what is not their true self, be they animals, men, or gods. This elevates the mystic's self-affirmation above the courage as a special virtue possessed by the aristocratic-soldiery. But he is not above courage altogether. That which from the point of view of the finite world appears as self-negation is from the point of view of ultimate being the most perfect self-affirmation, the most radical form of courage.

In the strength of this courage the mystic conquers the anxiety of fate and death. Since being in time and space and under the categories of finitude is ultimately unreal, the vicissitudes arising from it and the final nonbeing ending it are equally unreal. Nonbeing is no threat because finite being is, in the last analysis, nonbeing. Death is the negation of that which is negative and the affirmation of that which is positive. In the same way the anxiety of doubt and meaninglessness is taken into the mystical courage to be. Doubt is directed toward everything that is and that, according to its Maya character, is doubtful. Doubt dissolves the veil of Maya, it undermines the defense of mere opinions against ultimate reality. And this manifestation is not exposed to doubt because it is the presupposition of every act of doubt. Without a consciousness of truth itself doubt of truth would be impossible. The anxiety of meaninglessness is conquered where the ultimate meaning is not something definite but the abyss of every definite meaning. The mystic experiences step after step the lack of meaning in the different levels of reality which he enters, works through, and leaves. As long as he walks ahead on this road the anxieties of guilt and condemnation are also conquered. They are not absent. Guilt can be acquired on every level, partly through a failure to fulfill its intrinsic demands, partly through a failure to proceed beyond the level. But as long as the certainty of final fulfillment is given, the anxiety of guilt does not become anxiety of condemnation. There is automatic punishment according to the law of karma, but there is no condemnation in Asiatic mysticism.

The mystical courage to be lasts as long as the mystical situation. Its limit is the state of emptiness of being and meaning, with its horror and despair, which the mystics have described. In these moments the courage to be is reduced to the acceptance of even this state as a way to prepare through darkness for light, through emptiness for abundance. As long as the absence of the power of being is felt as despair, it is the power of being which makes itself felt through despair. To experience this and to endure it is the courage to be of the mystic in the state of emptiness. Although mysticism in its extreme positive and extreme negative aspects is a comparatively rare event, the basic attitude, the striving for union with ultimate reality, and the corresponding courage to take the nonbeing which is implied in finitude upon oneself are a way of life which is accepted by and has shaped large sections of mankind.

But mysticism is more than a special form of the relation to the ground of being. It is an element of every form of this relation. Since everything that is participates in the power of being, the element of identity on which mysticism is based cannot be absent in any religious experience. There is no self-affirmation of a finite being, and there is no courage to be in which the ground of being and its power of conquering nonbeing is not effective. And the experience of the presence of this power is the mystical element even in the person-to-person encounter with God.

THE DIVINE-HUMAN ENCOUNTER AND THE COURAGE TO BE   The pole of individualization expresses itself in the religious experience as a personal encounter with God. And the courage derived from it is the courage of confidence in the personal reality which is manifest in the religious experience. In contradistinction to the mystical union one can call this relation a personal communion with the source of courage. Although the two types are in contrast they do not exclude each other. For they are united by the polar interdependence of individualization and participation. The courage of confidence has often, especially in Protestantism, been identified with the courage of faith. But this is not adequate, because confidence is only one element in faith. Faith embraces both mystical participation and personal confidence. Most parts of the Bible describe the religious encounter in strongly personalist terms. Biblicism, notably that of the Reformers, follows this emphasis. Luther directed his attack against the objective, quantitative, and impersonal elements in the Roman system. He fought for an immediate person-to-person relationship between God and man. In him the courage of confidence reached its highest point in the history of Christian thought. Every work of Luther, especially in his earlier years, is filled with such courage. Again and again he uses the word *trotz,* "in spite of." In spite of all the negativities which he had experienced, in spite of the anxiety which dominated that period, he derived the power of self-affirmation from his unshakable confidence in God and from the personal encounter with him. According to the expressions of anxiety in his period, the negativity his courage had to conquer was symbolized in the figures of death and the devil. It has rightly been said that Albrecht Dürer's engraving, "Knight, Death, and the Devil," is a classic expression of the spirit of the Lutheran Reformation and—it might be added—of Luther's courage of confidence, of his form of the courage to be. A knight in full armor is riding through a valley, accompanied by the figure of death on one side, the devil on the other. Fearlessly, concentrated, confident he looks ahead. He is alone but he is not lonely. In his solitude he participates in the power which gives him the courage to affirm himself in spite of the presence of the negativities of existence. His courage is certainly not the courage to be as a part. The Reformation broke away from the semicollectivism of the Middle Ages. Luther's courage of confidence is personal confidence, derived from a person-to-person encounter with God. Neither popes nor councils could give him this confidence. Therefore he had to reject them just because they relied on a doctrine which blocked off the courage of confidence. They sanctioned a system in which the anxiety of death and guilt never was completely conquered. There were many assurances but no certainty, many supports for the courage of confidence but no unquestionable foundation. The collective offered different ways of resisting anxiety but no way in which the individual could take his anxiety upon himself. He never was certain; he never could affirm his being with unconditional confidence. For he never could encounter the unconditional directly with his total being, in an immediate personal relation. There was, except in mysticism, always mediation through the Church, an indirect and partial meeting between God and the soul. When the Reformation removed the mediation and opened up a direct, total, and personal approach to God, a new nonmystical courage to be was possible. It is manifest in the heroic representatives of fighting Protestantism, in the Calvinist as well as in the Lutheran Reformation, and in Calvinism even more conspicuously. It is not the heroism of risking martyrdom, of resisting the authorities, of transforming the structure of Church and society, but it is the courage of confidence which makes these men heroic and which is the basis of the other expressions of their courage. One could say—and liberal Protestantism often has said—that the courage of the Reformers is the beginning of the individualistic type of the courage to be as oneself. But such an interpretation confuses a possible historical effect with the matter itself. In the courage of the Reformers the courage to be as oneself is both affirmed and transcended. In comparison with the mystical form of courageous self-affirmation the Protestant courage of confidence affirms the individual self as an individual self in its encounter with God as person. This radically distinguishes the personalism of the Reformation from all the later forms of individualism and Existentialism. The courage of the Reformers is not the courage to be oneself—as it is not the courage to be as a part. It transcends and unites both of them. For the courage of confidence is not rooted in confidence about oneself. The Reformation pronounces the opposite: one can become confident about one's existence only after ceasing to base one's confidence on oneself. On the other hand the courage of confidence is in no way based on anything finite besides oneself, not even on the Church. It is based on God and solely on God, who is experienced in a unique and personal encounter. The courage of the Reformation transcends both the courage to be as a part and the courage to be as oneself. It is threatened neither by the loss of oneself nor by the loss of one's world.

GUILT AND THE COURAGE TO ACCEPT ACCEPTANCE   In the center of the Protestant courage of confidence stands the courage to accept acceptance in spite of the consciousness of guilt. Luther, and in fact the whole period, experienced the anxiety of guilt and condemnation as the main form of their anxiety. The courage to affirm oneself in spite of this anxiety is the courage which we have called the courage of confidence. It is rooted in the personal, total, and immediate certainty of divine forgiveness. There is belief in forgiveness in all forms of man's courage to be, even in neocollectivism. But there is no interpretation of human existence in which it is so predominant as in genuine Protestantism. And there is no movement in history in which it is equally profound and equally paradoxical. In the Lutheran formula that "he who is unjust is just" (in the view of the divine forgiveness) or in the more modern phrasing that "he who is unacceptable is accepted" the victory over the anxiety of guilt and condemnation is sharply expressed. One could say that the courage to be is the courage to accept oneself as accepted in spite of being unacceptable. One does not need to remind the theologians of the fact that this is the genuine meaning of the Pauline-Lutheran doctrine of "justification by faith" (a doctrine which in its original phrasing has become incomprehensible even for students of theology). But one must remind theologians and ministers that in the fight against the anxiety of guilt by psychotherapy the idea of acceptance has received the attention and gained the significance which in the Reformation period was to be seen in phrases like "forgiveness of sins" or "justification through faith." Accepting acceptance though being unacceptable is the basis for the courage of confidence.

Decisive for this self-affirmation is its being independent of any moral, intellectual, or religious precondition: it is not the good or the wise or the pious who are entitled to the courage to accept acceptance but those who are lacking in all these qualities and are aware of being unacceptable. This, however, does not mean acceptance by oneself as oneself. It is not a justification of one's accidental individuality. It is not the Existentialist courage to be as oneself. It is the paradoxical act in which one is accepted by that which infinitely transcends one's individual self. It is in the experience of the Reformers the acceptance of the unacceptable sinner into judging and transforming communion with God.

The courage to be in this respect is the courage to accept the forgiveness of sins, not as an abstract assertion but as the fundamental experience in the encounter with God. Self-affirmation in spite of the anxiety of guilt and condemnation presupposes participation in something which transcends the self. In the communion of healing, for example the psychoanalytic situation, the patient participates in the healing power of the helper by whom he is accepted although he feels himself unacceptable. The healer, in this relationship, does not stand for himself as an individual but represents the objective power of acceptance and self-affirmation. This objective power works through the healer in the patient. Of course, it must be embodied in a person who can realize guilt, who can judge, and who can accept in spite of the judgment. Acceptance by something which is less than personal could never overcome personal self-rejection. A wall to which I confess cannot forgive me. No self-acceptance is possible if one is not accepted in a person-to-person relation. But even if one is personally accepted it needs a self-transcending courage to accept this acceptance, it needs the courage of confidence. For being accepted does not mean that guilt is denied. The healing helper who tried to convince his patient that he was not really guilty would do him a great disservice. He would prevent him from taking his guilt into his self-affirmation. He may help him to transform displaced, neurotic guilt feelings into genuine ones which are, so to speak, put on the right place, but he cannot tell him that there is no guilt in him. He accepts the patient into his communion without condemning anything and without covering up anything.

Here, however, is the point where the religious "acceptance as being accepted" transcends medical healing. Religion asks for the ultimate source of the power which heals by accepting the unacceptable, it asks for God. The acceptance by God, his forgiving or justifying act, is the only and ultimate source of a courage to be which is able to take the anxiety of guilt and condemnation into itself. For the ultimate power of self-affirmation can only be the power of being-itself. Everything less than this, one's own or anybody else's finite power of being, cannot overcome the radical, infinite threat of nonbeing which is experienced in the despair of self-condemnation. This is why the courage of confidence, as it is expressed in a man like Luther, emphasizes unceasingly exclusive trust in God and rejects any other foundation for his courage to be, not only as insufficient but as driving him into more guilt and deeper anxiety. The immense liberation brought to the people of the sixteenth century by the message of the Reformers and the creation of their indomitable courage to accept acceptance was due to the *sola fide* doctrine, namely to the message that the courage of confidence is conditioned not by anything finite but solely by that which is unconditional itself and which we experience as unconditional in a person-to-person encounter.

FATE AND THE COURAGE TO ACCEPT ACCEPTANCE   As the symbolic figures of death and the devil show, the anxiety of this period was not restricted to the anxiety of guilt. It was also an anxiety of death and fate. The astrological ideas of the later ancient world had been revived by the Renaissance and had influenced even those humanists who joined the Reformation. We have already referred to the Neo-Stoic courage, expressed in some Renaissance pictures, where man directs the vessel of his life although it is driven by the winds of fate. Luther faced the anxiety of fate on another level. He experienced the connection between the anxiety of guilt and the anxiety of fate. It is the uneasy conscience which produces innumerable irrational fears in daily life. The rustling of a dry leaf horrifies him who is plagued by guilt. Therefore conquest of the anxiety of guilt is also conquest of the anxiety of fate. The courage of confidence takes the anxiety of fate as well as the anxiety of guilt into itself. It says "in spite of" to both of them. This is the genuine meaning of the doctrine of providence. Providence is not a theory about some activities of God; it is the religious symbol of the courage of confidence with respect to fate and death. For the courage of confidence says "in spite of" even to death.

Like Paul, Luther was well aware of the connection of the anxiety of guilt with the anxiety of death. In Stoicism and Neo-Stoicism the essential self is not threatened by death, because it belongs to being-itself and transcends nonbeing. Socrates, who in the power of his essential self conquered the anxiety of death, has become the symbol for the courage to take death upon oneself. This is the true meaning of Plato's so-called doctrine of immortality of the soul. In discussing this doctrine we should neglect the arguments for immortality, even those in Plato's *Phaedon*, and concentrate on the image of the dying Socrates. All the arguments, skeptically treated by Plato himself, are attempts to interpret the courage of Socrates, the courage to take one's death into one's self-affirmation. Socrates is certain that the self which the executioners will destroy is not the self which affirms itself in his courage to be. He does not say much about the relation of the two selves, and he could not because they are not numerically two, but one in two aspects. But he makes it clear that the courage to die is the test of the courage to be. A self-affirmation which omits taking the affirmation of one's death into itself tries to escape the test of courage, the facing of nonbeing in the most radical way.

The popular belief in immortality which in the Western world has largely replaced the Christian symbol of resurrection is a mixture of courage and escape. It tries to maintain one's self-affirmation even in the face of one's having to die. But it does this by continuing one's finitude, that is one's having to die, infinitely, so that the actual death never will occur. This, however, is an illusion and, logically speaking, a contradiction in terms. It makes endless what, by definition, must come to an end. The "immortality of the soul" is a poor symbol for the courage to be in the face of one's having to die.

The courage of Socrates (in Plato's picture) was based not on a doctrine of the immortality of the soul but on the affirmation of himself in his essential, indestructible being. He knows that he belongs to two orders of reality and that the one order is transtemporal. It was the courage of Socrates which more than any philosophical reflection revealed to the ancient world that everyone belongs to two orders.

But there was one presupposition in the Socratic (Stoic and Neo-Stoic) courage to take death upon oneself, namely the ability of every individual to participate in both orders, the temporal and the eternal. This presupposition is not accepted by Christianity. According to Christianity we are estranged from our essential being. We are not free to realize our essential being, we are bound to contradict it. Therefore death can be accepted only through a state of confidence in which death has ceased to be the "wages of sin." This, however, is the state of being accepted in spite of being unacceptable. Here is the point in which the ancient world was transformed by Christianity and in which Luther's courage to face death was rooted. It is the being accepted into communion with God that underlies this courage, not a questionable theory of immortality. The encounter with God in Luther is not merely the basis for the courage to take upon oneself sin and condemnation, it is also the basis for taking upon oneself fate and death. For encountering God means encountering transcendent security and transcendent eternity. He who participates in God participates in eternity. But in order to participate in him you must be accepted by him and you must have accepted his acceptance of you.

Luther had experiences which he describes as attacks of utter despair (*Anfechtung*), as the frightful threat of a complete meaninglessness. He felt these moments as satanic attacks in which everything was menaced: his Christian faith, the confidence in his work, the Reformation, the forgiveness of sins. Everything broke down in the extreme moments of this despair, nothing was left of the courage to be. Luther in these moments, and in the descriptions he gives of them, anticipated the descriptions of them by modern Existentialism. But for him this was not the last word. The last word was the first commandment, the statement that God is God. It reminded him of the unconditional element in human experience of which one can be aware even in the abyss of meaninglessness. And this awareness saved him.

It should not be forgotten that the great adversary of Luther, Thomas Münzer, the Anabaptist and religious socialist, describes similar experiences. He speaks of the ultimate situation in which everything finite reveals its finitude, in which the finite has come to its end, in which anxiety grips the heart and all previous meanings fall apart, and in which just for this reason the Divine Spirit can make itself felt and can turn the whole situation into a courage to be whose expression is revolutionary action. While Luther represents ecclesiastical Protestantism, Münzer represents evangelical radicalism. Both men have shaped history, and actually Münzer's views had even more influence in America than Luther's. Both men experienced the anxiety of meaninglessness and described it in terms which had been created by Christian mystics. But in doing so they transcended the courage of confidence which is based on a personal encounter with God. They had to receive elements from the courage to be which is based on mystical union. This leads to a last question: whether the two types of the courage to accept acceptance can be united in view of the all-pervasive presence of the anxiety of doubt and meaninglessness in our own period.

ABSOLUTE FAITH AND THE COURAGE TO BE We have avoided the concept of faith in our description of the courage to be which is based on mystical union with the ground of being as well as in our description of the courage to be which is based on the personal encounter with God. This is partly because the concept of faith has lost its genuine meaning and has received the connotation of "belief in something unbelievable." But this is not the only reason for the use of terms other than faith. The decisive reason is that I do not think either mystical union or personal encounter fulfills the idea of faith. Certainly there is faith in the elevation of the soul above the finite to the infinite, leading to its union with the ground of being. But more than this is included in the concept of faith. And there is faith in the personal encounter with the personal God. But more than this is included in the concept of faith. Faith is the state of being grasped by the power of being-itself. The courage to be is an expression of faith and what "faith" means must be understood through the courage to be. We have defined courage as the self-affirmation of being in spite of nonbeing. The power of this self-affirmation is the power of being which is effective in every act of courage. Faith is the experience of this power.

But it is an experience which has a paradoxical character, the character of accepting acceptance. Being-itself transcends every finite being infinitely; God in the divine-human encounter transcends man unconditionally. Faith bridges this infinite gap by accepting the fact that in spite of it the power of being is present, that he who is separated is accepted. Faith accepts "in spite of"; and out of the "in spite of" of faith the "in spite of" of courage is born. Faith is not a theoretical affirmation of something uncertain, it is the existential acceptance of something transcending ordinary experience. Faith is not an opinion but a state. It is the state of being grasped by the power of being which transcends everything that is and in which everything that is participates. He who is grasped by this power is able to affirm himself because he knows that he is affirmed by the power of being-itself. In this point mystical experience and personal encounter are identical. In both of them faith is the basis of the courage to be.

This is decisive for a period in which, as in our own, the anxiety of doubt and meaninglessness is dominant. Certainly the anxiety of fate and death is not lacking in our time. The anxiety of fate has increased with the degree to which the schizophrenic split of our world has removed the last remnants of former security. And the anxiety of guilt and condemnation is not lacking either. It is surprising how much anxiety of guilt comes to the surface in psychoanalysis and personal counseling. The centuries of puritan and bourgeois repression of vital strivings have produced almost as many guilt feelings as the preaching of hell and purgatory in the Middle Ages.

But in spite of these restricting considerations one must say that the anxiety which determines our period is the anxiety of doubt and meaninglessness. One is afraid of having lost or of having to lose the meaning of one's existence. The expression of this situation is the Existentialism of today.

Which courage is able to take nonbeing into itself in the form of doubt and meaninglessness? This is the most important and most disturbing question in the quest for the courage to be. For the anxiety of meaninglessness undermines what is still unshaken in the anxiety of fate and death and of guilt and condemnation. In the anxiety of guilt and condemnation doubt has not yet undermined the certainty of an ultimate responsibility. We are threatened but we are not destroyed. If, however, doubt and meaninglessness prevail one experiences an abyss in which the meaning of life and the truth of ultimate responsibility disappear. Both the Stoic who conquers the anxiety of fate with the Socratic courage of wisdom and the Christian who conquers the anxiety of guilt with the Protestant courage of accepting forgiveness are in a different situation. Even in the despair of having to die and the despair of self-condemnation meaning is affirmed and certitude preserved. But in the despair of doubt and meaninglessness both are swallowed by nonbeing.

The question then is this: Is there a courage which can conquer the anxiety of meaninglessness and doubt? Or in other words, can the faith which accepts acceptance resist the power of nonbeing in its most radical form? Can faith resist meaninglessness? Is there a kind of faith which can exist together with doubt and meaninglessness? These questions lead to the last aspect of the problem discussed in these lectures and the one most relevant to our time: How is the courage to be possible if all the ways to create it are barred by the experience of their ultimate insufficiency? If life is as meaningless as death, if guilt is as questionable as perfection, if being is no more meaningful than nonbeing, on what can one base the courage to be?

There is an inclination in some Existentialists to answer these questions by a leap from doubt to dogmatic certitude, from meaninglessness to a set of symbols in which the meaning of a special ecclesiastical or political group is embodied. This leap can be interpreted in different ways. It may be the expression of a desire for safety; it may be as arbitrary as, according to Existentialist principles, every decision is; it may be the feeling that the Christian message is the answer to the questions raised by an analysis of human existence; it may be a genuine conversion, independent of the theoretical situation. In any case it is not a solution of the problem of radical doubt. It gives the courage to be to those who are converted but it does not answer the question as to how such a courage is possible in itself. The answer must accept, as its precondition, the state of meaninglessness. It is not an answer if it demands the removal of this state; for that is just what cannot be done. He who is in the grip of doubt and meaninglessness cannot liberate himself from this grip; but he asks for an answer which is valid within and not outside the situation of his despair. He asks for the ultimate foundation of what we have called the "courage of despair." There is only one possible answer, if one does not try to escape the question: namely that the acceptance of despair is in itself faith and on the boundary line of the courage to be. In this situation the meaning of life is reduced to despair about the meaning of life. But as long as this despair is an act of life it is positive in its negativity. Cynically speaking, one could say that it is true to life to be cynical about it. Religiously speaking, one would say that one accepts oneself as accepted in spite of one's despair about the meaning of this acceptance. The paradox of every radical negativity, as long as it is an active negativity, is that it must affirm itself in order to be able to negate itself. No actual negation can be without an implicit affirmation. The hidden pleasure produced by despair witnesses to the paradoxical character of self-negation. The negative lives from the positive it negates.

The faith which makes the courage of despair possible is the acceptance of the power of being, even in the grip of nonbeing. Even in the despair about meaning being affirms itself through us. The act of accepting meaninglessness is in itself a meaningful act. It is an act of faith. We have seen that he who has the courage to affirm his being in spite of fate and guilt has not removed them. He remains threatened and hit by them. But he accepts his acceptance by the power of being-itself in which he participates and which gives him the courage to take the anxieties of fate and guilt upon himself. The same is true of doubt and meaninglessness. The faith which creates the courage to take them into itself has no special content. It is simply faith, undirected, absolute. It is undefinable, since everything defined is dissolved by doubt and meaninglessness. Nevertheless, even absolute faith is not an eruption of subjective emotions or a mood without objective foundation.

An analysis of the nature of absolute faith reveals the following elements in it. The first is the experience of the power of being which is present even in face of the most radical manifestation of nonbeing. If one says that in this experience vitality resists despair one must add that vitality in man is proportional to intentionality. The vitality that can stand the abyss of meaninglessness is aware of a hidden meaning within the destruction of meaning. The second element in absolute faith is the dependence of the experience of nonbeing on the experience of being and the dependence of the experience of meaninglessness on the experience of meaning. Even in the state of despair one has enough being to make despair possible. There is a third element in absolute faith, the acceptance of being accepted. Of course, in the state of despair there is nobody and nothing that accepts. But there is the power of acceptance itself which is experienced. Meaninglessness, as long as it is experienced, includes an experience of the "power of acceptance." To accept this power of acceptance consciously is the religious answer of absolute faith, of a faith which has been deprived by doubt of any concrete content, which nevertheless is faith and the source of the most paradoxical manifestation of the courage to be.

This faith transcends both the mystical experience and the divine-human encounter. The mystical experience seems to be nearer to absolute faith but it is not. Absolute faith includes an element of skepticism which one cannot find in the mystical experience. Certainly mysticism also transcends all specific contents, but not because it doubts them or has found them meaningless; rather it deems them to be preliminary. Mysticism uses the specific contents as grades, stepping on them after having used them. The experience of meaninglessness, however, denies them (and everything that goes with them) without having used them. The experience of meaninglessness is more radical than mysticism. Therefore it transcends the mystical experience.

Absolute faith also transcends the divine-human encounter. In this encounter the subject-object scheme is valid: a definite subject (man) meets a definite object (God). One can reverse this statement and say that a definite subject (God) meets a definite object (man). But in both cases the attack of doubt undercuts the subject-object structure. The theologians who speak so strongly and with such self-certainty about the divine-human encounter should be aware of a situation in which this encounter is prevented by radical doubt and nothing is left but absolute faith. The acceptance of such a situation as religiously valid has, however, the consequence that the concrete contents of ordinary faith must be subjected to criticism and transformation. The courage to be in its radical form is a key to an idea of God which transcends both mysticism and the person-to-person encounter.

THE COURAGE TO BE AS THE KEY
TO BEING-ITSELF

NONBEING OPENING UP BEING   The courage to be in all its forms has, by itself, revelatory character. It shows the nature of being, it shows that the self-affirmation of being is an affirmation that overcomes negation. In a metaphorical statement (and every assertion about being-itself is either metaphorical or symbolic) one could say that being includes nonbeing but nonbeing does not prevail against it. "Including" is a spatial metaphor which indicates that being embraces itself and that which is opposed to it, nonbeing. Nonbeing belongs to being, it cannot be separated from it. We could not even think "being" without a double negation: being must be thought as the negation of the negation of being. This is why we describe being best by the metaphor "power of being." Power is the possibility a being has to actualize itself against the resistance of other beings. If we speak of the power of being-itself we indicate that being affirms itself against nonbeing. In our discussion of courage and life we have mentioned the dynamic understanding of reality by the philosophers of life. Such an understanding is possible only if one accepts the view that nonbeing belongs to being, that being could not be the ground of life without nonbeing. The self-affirmation of being without nonbeing would not even be self-affirmation but an immovable self-identity. Nothing would be manifest, nothing expressed, nothing revealed. But nonbeing drives being out of its seclusion, it forces it to affirm itself dynamically. Philosophy has dealt with the dynamic self-affirmation of being-itself wherever it spoke dialectically, notably in Neoplatonism, Hegel, and the philosophers of life and process. Theology has done the same whenever it took the idea of the living God seriously, most obviously in the trinitarian symbolization of the inner life of God. Spinoza, in spite of his static definition of substance (which is his name for the ultimate power of being), unites philosophical and mystical tendencies when he speaks of the love and knowledge with which God loves and knows himself through the love and knowledge of finite beings. Nonbeing (that in God which makes his self-affirmation dynamic) opens up the divine self-seclusion and reveals him as power and love. Nonbeing makes God a living God. Without the No he has to overcome in himself and in his creature, the divine Yes to himself would be lifeless. There would be no revelation of the ground of being, there would be no life.

But where there is nonbeing there is finitude and anxiety. If we say that nonbeing belongs to being-itself, we say that finitude and anxiety belong to being-itself. Wherever philosophers or theologians have spoken of the divine blessedness they have implicitly (and sometimes explicitly) spoken of the anxiety of finitude which is eternally taken into the blessedness of the divine infinity. The infinite embraces itself and the finite, the Yes includes itself and the No which it takes into itself, blessedness comprises itself and the anxiety of which it is the conquest. All this is implied if one says that being includes nonbeing and that through nonbeing it reveals itself. It is a highly symbolic language which must be used at this point. But its symbolic character does not diminish its truth; on the contrary, it is a condition of its truth. To speak unsymbolically about being-itself is untrue.

The divine self-affirmation is the power that makes the self-affirmation of the finite being, the courage to be, possible. Only because being-itself has the character of self-affirmation in spite of nonbeing is courage possible. Courage participates in the self-affirmation of being-itself, it participates in the power of being which prevails against nonbeing. He who receives this power in an act of mystical or personal or absolute faith is aware of the source of his courage to be.

Man is not necessarily aware of this source. In situations of cynicism and indifference he is not aware of it. But it works in him as long as he maintains the courage to take his anxiety upon himself. In the act of the courage to be the power of being is effective in us, whether we recognize it or not. Every act of courage is a manifestation of the ground of being, however questionable the content of the act may be. The content may hide or distort true being, the courage in it reveals true being. Not arguments but the courage to be reveals the true nature of being-itself. By affirming our being we participate in the self-affirmation of being-itself. There are no valid arguments for the "existence" of God, but there are acts of courage in which we affirm the power of being, whether we know it or not. If we know it, we accept acceptance consciously. If we do not know it, we nevertheless accept it and participate in it. And in our acceptance of that which we do not know the power of being is manifest to us. Courage has revealing power, the courage to be is the key to being-itself.

THEISM TRANSCENDED   The courage to take meaninglessness into itself presupposes a relation to the ground of being which we have called "absolute faith." It is without a *special* content, yet it is not without content. The content of absolute faith is the "God above God." Absolute faith and its consequence, the courage that takes the radical doubt, the doubt about God, into itself, transcends the theistic idea of God.

Theism can mean the unspecified affirmation of God. Theism in this sense does not say what it means if it uses the name of God. Because of the traditional and psychological connotations of the word God such an empty theism can produce a reverent mood if it speaks of God. Politicians, dictators, and other people who wish to use rhetoric to make an impression on their audience like to use the word God in this sense. It produces the feeling in their listeners that the speaker is serious and morally trustworthy. This is especially successful if they can brand their foes as atheistic. On a higher level people without a definite religious commitment like to call themselves theistic, not for special purposes but because they cannot stand a world without God, whatever this God may be. They need some of the connotations of the word God and they are afraid of what they call atheism. On the highest level of this kind of theism the name of God is used as a poetic or practical symbol, expressing a profound emotional state or the highest ethical idea. It is a theism which stands on the boundary line between the second type of theism and what we call "theism transcended." But it is still too indefinite to cross this boundary line. The atheistic negation of this whole type of theism is as vague as the theism itself. It may produce an irreverent mood and angry reaction of those who take their theistic affirmation seriously. It may even be felt as justified against the rhetorical-political abuse of the name God, but it is ultimately as irrelevant as the theism which it negates. It cannot reach the state of despair any more than the theism against which it fights can reach the state of faith.

Theism can have another meaning, quite contrary to the first one: it can be the name of what we have called the divine-human encounter. In this case it points to those elements in the Jewish-Christian tradition which emphasize the person-to-person relationship with God. Theism in this sense emphasizes the personalistic passages in the Bible and the Protestant creeds, the personalistic image of God, the word as the tool of creation and revelation, the ethical and social character of the kingdom of God, the personal nature of human faith and divine forgiveness, the historical vision of the universe, the idea of a divine purpose, the infinite distance between creator and creature, the absolute separation between God and the world, the conflict between holy God and sinful man, the person-to-person character of prayer and practical devotion. Theism in this sense is the nonmystical side of biblical religion and historical Christianity. Atheism from the point of view of this theism is the human attempt to escape the divine-human encounter. It is an existential—not a theoretical —problem.

Theism has a third meaning, a strictly theological one.

Theological theism is, like every theology, dependent on the religious substance which it conceptualizes. It is dependent on theism in the first sense insofar as it tries to prove the necessity of affirming God in some way; it usually develops the so-called arguments for the "existence" of God. But it is more dependent on theism in the second sense insofar as it tries to establish a doctrine of God which transforms the person-to-person encounter with God into a doctrine about two persons who may or may not meet but who have a reality independent of each other.

Now theism in the first sense must be transcended because it is irrelevant, and theism in the second sense must be transcended because it is one-sided. But theism in the third sense must be transcended because it is wrong. It is bad theology. This can be shown by a more penetrating analysis. The God of theological theism is a being beside others and as such a part of the whole of reality. He certainly is considered its most important part, but as a part and therefore as subjected to the structure of the whole. He is supposed to be beyond the ontological elements and categories which constitute reality. But every statement subjects him to them. He is seen as a self which has a world, as an ego which is related to a thou, as a cause which is separated from its effect, as having a definite space and an endless time. He is being, not being-itself. As such he is bound to the subject-object structure of reality, he is an object for us as subjects. At the same time we are objects for him as a subject. And this is decisive for the necessity of transcending theological theism. For God as a subject makes me into an object which is nothing more than an object. He deprives me of my subjectivity because he is all-powerful and all-knowing. I revolt and try to make *him* into an object, but the revolt fails and becomes desperate. God appears as the invincible tyrant, the being in contrast with whom all other beings are without freedom and subjectivity. He is equated with the recent tyrants who with the help of terror try to transform everything into a mere object, a thing among things, a cog in the machine they control. He becomes the model of everything against which Existentialism revolted. This is the God Nietzsche said had to be killed because nobody can tolerate being made into a mere object of absolute knowledge and absolute control. This is the deepest root of atheism. It is an atheism which is justified as the reaction against theological theism and its disturbing implications. It is also the deepest root of the Existentialist despair and the widespread anxiety of meaninglessness in our period.

Theism in all its forms is transcended in the experience we have called absolute faith. It is the accepting of the acceptance without somebody or something that accepts. It is the power of being-itself that accepts and gives the courage to be. This is the highest point to which our analysis has brought us. It cannot be described in the way the God of all forms of theism can be described. It cannot be described in mystical terms either. It transcends both mysticism and personal encounter, as it transcends both the courage to be as a part and the courage to be as oneself.

THE GOD ABOVE GOD AND THE COURAGE TO BE The ultimate source of the courage to be is the "God above God"; this is the result of our demand to transcend theism. Only if the God of theism is transcended can the anxiety of doubt and meaninglessness be taken into the courage to be. The God above God is the object of all mystical longing, but mysticism also must be transcended in order to reach him. Mysticism does not take seriously the concrete and the doubt concerning the concrete. It plunges directly into the ground of being and meaning, and leaves the concrete, the world of finite values and meanings, behind. Therefore it does not solve the problem of meaninglessness. In terms of the present religious situation this means that Eastern mysticism is not the solution of the problems of Western Existentialism, although many people attempt this solution. The God above the God of theism is not the devaluation of the meanings which doubt has thrown into the abyss of meaninglessness; he is their potential restitution. Nevertheless absolute faith agrees with the faith implied in mysticism in that both transcend the theistic objectivation of a God who is a being. For mysticism such a God is not more real than any finite being, for the courage to be such a God has disappeared in the abyss of meaninglessness with every other value and meaning.

The God above the God of theism is present, although hidden, in every divine-human encounter. Biblical religion as well as Protestant theology are aware of the paradoxical character of this encounter. They are aware that if God encounters man God is neither object nor subject and is therefore above the scheme into which theism has forced him. They are aware that personalism with respect to God is balanced by a transpersonal presence of the divine. They are aware that forgiveness can be accepted only if the power of acceptance is effective in man—biblically speaking, if the power of grace is effective in man. They are aware of the paradoxical character of every prayer, of speaking to somebody to whom you cannot speak because he is not "somebody," of asking somebody of whom you cannot ask anything because he gives or gives not before you ask, of saying "thou" to somebody who is nearer to the I than the I is to itself. Each of these paradoxes drives the religious consciousness toward a God above the God of theism.

The courage to be which is rooted in the experience of the God above the God of theism unites and transcends the courage to be as a part and the courage to be as oneself. It avoids both the loss of oneself by participation and the loss of one's world by individualization. The acceptance of the God above the God of theism makes us a part of that which is not also a part but is the ground of the whole. Therefore our self is not lost in a larger whole, which submerges it in the life of a limited group. If the self participates in the power of being-itself it receives itself back. For the power of being acts through the power of the individual selves. It does not swallow them as every limited whole, every collectivism, and every conformism does. This is why the Church, which stands for the power of being-itself or for the God who transcends the God of the religions, claims to be the mediator of the courage to be. A church which is based on the authority of the God of theism cannot make such a claim. It inescapably develops into a collectivist or semicollectivist system itself.

But a church which raises itself in its message and its devotion to the God above the God of theism without sacrificing its concrete symbols can mediate a courage which takes doubt and meaninglessness into itself. It is the Church under the Cross which alone can do this, the Church which preaches the Crucified who cried to God who remained his God after the God of confidence had left him in the darkness of doubt and meaninglessness. To be as a part in such a church is to receive a courage to be in which one cannot lose one's self and in which one receives one's world.

Absolute faith, or the state of being grasped by the God beyond God, is not a state which appears beside other states of the mind. It never is something separated and definite, an event which could be isolated and described. It is always a movement in, with, and under other states of the mind. It is the situation on the boundary of man's possibilities. It *is* this boundary. Therefore it is both the courage of despair and the courage in and above every courage. It is not a place where one can live, it is without the safety of words and concepts, it is without a name, a church, a cult, a theology. But it is moving in the depth of all of them. It is the power of being, in which they participate and of which they are fragmentary expressions.

One can become aware of it in the anxiety of fate and death when the traditional symbols, which enable men to stand the vicissitudes of fate and the horror of death have lost their power. When "providence" has become a superstition and "immortality" something imaginary that which once was the power in these symbols can still be present and create the courage to be in spite of the experience of a chaotic world and a finite existence. The Stoic courage returns but not as the faith in universal reason. It returns as the absolute faith which says Yes to being without seeing anything concrete which could conquer the nonbeing in fate and death.

And one can become aware of the God above the God of theism in the anxiety of guilt and condemnation when the traditional symbols that enable men to withstand the anxiety of guilt and condemnation have lost their power. When "divine judgment" is interpreted as a psychological complex and forgiveness as a remnant of the "father-image," what once was the power in those symbols can still be present and create the courage to be in spite of the experience of an infinite gap between what we are and what we ought to be. The Lutheran courage returns, but not supported by the faith in a judging and forgiving God. It returns in terms of the absolute faith which says Yes although there is no special power that conquers guilt. The courage to take the anxiety of meaninglessness upon oneself is the boundary line up to which the courage to be can go. Beyond it is mere non-being. Within it all forms of courage are reestablished in the power of the God above the God of theism. *The courage to be is rooted in the God who appears when God has disappeared in the anxiety of doubt.*

20
You Are
Accepted

Moreover the law entered, that the of-
fence might abound. But where sin
abounded, grace did much more abound.
—ROMANS 5:20

THESE WORDS of Paul summarize his apostolic experience, his religious message as a whole, and the Christian understanding of life. To discuss these words, or
to make them the text of even several sermons, has
always seemed impossible to me. I have never dared to use them
before. But something has driven me to consider them during
the past few months, a desire to give witness to the two facts
which appeared to me, in hours of retrospection, as the all-
determining facts of our life: the abounding of sin and the greater
abounding of grace.

There are few words more strange to most of us than "sin"
and "grace." They are strange, just because they are so well-
known. During the centuries they have received distorting connotations, and have lost so much of their genuine power that we
must seriously ask ourselves whether we should use them at all,
or whether we should discard them as useless tools. But there is
a mysterious fact about the great words of our religious tradition:

From Paul Tillich, *The Shaking of the Foundations* (New York: Charles
Scribner's Sons), 153—163. Reprinted by permission of Charles Scribner's Sons.
Copyright © 1948 by Paul Tillich.

they cannot be replaced. All attempts to make substitutions, including those I have tried myself, have failed to convey the reality that was to be expressed; they have led to shallow and impotent talk. There are no substitutes for words like "sin" and "grace." But there *is* a way of rediscovering their meaning, the same way that leads us down into the depth of our human existence. In that depth these words were conceived; and *there* they gained power for all ages; *there* they must be found again by each generation, and by each of us for himself. Let us therefore try to penetrate the deeper levels of our life, in order to see whether we can discover in them the realities of which our text speaks.

Have the men of our time still a feeling of the meaning of sin? Do they, and do we, still realize that sin does *not* mean an immoral act, that "sin" should never be used in the plural, and that not our sins, but rather our *sin* is the great, all-pervading problem of our life? Do we still know that it is arrogant and erroneous to divide men by calling some "sinners" and others "righteous"? For by way of such a division, we can usually discover that we ourselves do not *quite* belong to the "sinners," since we have avoided heavy sins, have made some progress in the control of this or that sin, and have been even humble enough not to call ourselves "righteous." Are we still able to realize that this kind of thinking and feeling about sin is far removed from what the great religious tradition, both within and outside the Bible, has meant when it speaks of sin?

I should like to suggest another work to you, not as a substitute for the word "sin," but as a useful clue in the interpretation of the word "sin": "separation." Separation is an aspect of the experience of everyone. Perhaps the word "sin" has the same root as the word "asunder." In any case, *sin is separation.* To be in the state of sin is to be in the state of separation. And separation is threefold: there is separation among individual lives, separation of a man from himself, and separation of all men from the Ground of Being. This three-fold separation constitutes the state of everything that exists; it is a universal fact; it is the fate of every life. And it is our human fate in a very special sense. For *we* as men know that we are separated. We not only suffer with all other creatures because of the self-destructive consequences of our separation, but also know *why* we suffer. We know that we are estranged from something to which we really belong, and with which we *should* be united. We know that the fate of separation is not merely a natural event like a flash of sudden lightning, but that it is an experience in which we actively participate, in which our whole personality is involved, and that, as fate, it is also *guilt*. Separation which is fate *and* guilt constitutes the meaning of the word "sin." It is *this* which is the state of our entire existence, from its very beginning to its very end. Such separation is prepared in the mother's womb, and before that time in every preceding generation. It is manifest in the special actions of our conscious life. It reaches beyond our graves into all the succeeding generations. It is our existence itself. *Existence is separation!* Before sin is an act, it is a state.

We can say the same things about grace. For the sin and grace are bound to each other. We do not even have a knowledge of sin unless we have already experienced the unity of life, which is grace. And conversely, we could not grasp the meaning of grace without having experienced the separation of life, which is sin. Grace is just as difficult to describe as sin. For some people, grace is the willingness of a divine king and father to forgive over and again the foolishness and weakness of his subjects and children. We must reject such a concept of grace; for it is a merely childish destruction of a human dignity. For others, grace is a magic power in the dark places of the soul, but a power without any significance for practical life, a quickly vanishing and useless idea. For others, grace is the benevolence that we may find beside the cruelty and destructiveness in life. But then, it does not matter whether we say "life goes on," or whether we say "there is grace in life"; if grace means no more than this, the word should, and will, disappear. For other people, grace indicates the gifts that one has received from nature or society, and the power to do good things with the help of those gifts. But grace is more than gifts. In grace something is overcome; grace occurs "in spite of" something; grace occurs in spite of separation and estrangement. Grace is the *re*union of life with life, the *re*conciliation of the self with itself. Grace is the acceptance of that which is rejected. Grace transforms fate into a meaningful destiny; it changes guilt into confidence and courage. There is something triumphant in the word "grace": in spite of the abounding of sin grace abounds much more.

And now let us look down into ourselves to discover there the struggle between separation and reunion, between sin and grace, in our relation to others, in our relation to ourselves, and in our relation to the Ground and aim of our being. If our souls respond to the description that I intend to give, words like "sin" and "separation," "grace" and "reunion," may have a new meaning for us. But the words themselves are not important. It is the response of the deepest levels of our being that is important. If such a response were to occur among us this moment, we could say that we have known grace.

Who has not, at some time, been lonely in the midst of a social event? The feeling of our separation from the rest of life is most acute when we are surrounded by it in noise and talk. We realize then much more than in moments of solitude how strange we are to each other, how estranged life is from life. Each one of us draws back into himself. We cannot penetrate the hidden center of another individual; nor can that individual pass beyond the shroud that covers our own being. Even the greatest love cannot break through the walls of the self. Who has not experienced that disillusionment of all great love? If one were to hurl away his self in complete self-surrender, he would become a nothing, without form or strength, a self without self, merely an object of contempt and abuse. Our generation knows more than the generation of our fathers about the hidden hostility in the ground of our souls. Today we know much about the profusive aggressiveness in every being. Today we can confirm what Immanuel Kant, the prophet of human reason and dignity, was honest enough to say: there is something in the misfortune of our best friends which does not displease us. Who amongst us is dishonest enough to deny that this is true also of him? Are we not almost always ready to abuse everybody and everything, although often in a very refined way, for the pleasure of self-elevation, for an occasion for boasting, for a moment of lust? To know that we are ready is to know the meaning of the separation of life from life, and of "sin abounding."

The most irrevocable expression of the separation of life from life today is the attitude of social groups within nations towards each other, and the attitude of nations themselves towards other nations. The walls of distance, in time and space, have been removed by technical progress; but the walls of estrangement between heart and heart have been incredibly strengthened. The madness of the German Nazis and the cruelty of the lynching mobs in the South provide too easy an excuse for us to turn our thoughts from our own selves. But let us just consider ourselves and what we feel, when we read, this morning and tonight, that in some sections of Europe all children under the age of three are sick and dying, or that in some sections of Asia millions without homes are freezing and starving to death. The strangeness of life to life is evident in the strange fact that we can know all this, and yet can live today, this morning, tonight, as though we were completely ignorant. And I refer to the most sensitive people amongst us. In both mankind and nature, life is separated from life. Estrangement prevails among all things that live. Sin abounds.

It is important to remember that we are not merely separated from each other. For we are also separated from ourselves. *Man Against Himself* is not merely the title of a book, but rather also indicates the rediscovery of an age-old insight. Man is split within himself. Life moves against itself through aggression, hate, and despair. We are wont to condemn self-love; but what we really mean to condemn is contrary to self-love. It is that mixture of selfishness and self-hate that permanently pursues us, that prevents us from loving others, and that prohibits us from losing ourselves in the love with which we are loved eternally. He who is able to love himself is able to love others also; he who has learned to overcome self-contempt has overcome his contempt for others. But the depth of our separation lies in just the fact that we are not capable of a great and merciful divine love towards ourselves. On the contrary, in each of us there is an instinct of self-destruction, which is as strong as our instinct of self-preservation. In our tendency to abuse and destroy others, there is an open or hidden tendency to abuse and to destroy ourselves. Cruelty towards others is always also cruelty towards ourselves. Nothing is more obvious than the split in both our unconscious life and conscious personality. Without the help of modern psychology, Paul expressed the fact in his famous words, "For I do not do the good I desire, but rather the evil that I do not desire." And then he continued in words that might well be the motto of all depth psychology: "Now if I should do what I do not wish to do, it is not I that do it, but rather sin which dwells within me." The apostle sensed a split between his conscious will and his real will, between himself and something strange within and alien to him. He was estranged from himself; and that estrangement he called "sin." He also called it a strange "law in his limbs," an irresistible compulsion. How often we commit certain acts in perfect consciousness, yet with the shocking sense that we are being controlled by an alien power! That is the experience of the separation of ourselves from ourselves, which is to say "sin," whether or not we like to use that word.

Thus, the state of our whole life is estrangement from others and ourselves, because we are estranged from the Ground of our being, because we are estranged from the origin and aim of our life. And we do not know where we have come from, or where we are going. We are separated from the mystery, the depth, and the greatness of our existence. We hear the voice of that depth; but our ears are closed. We feel that something radical, total, and unconditioned is demanded of us; but we rebel against it, try to escape its urgency, and will not accept its promise.

We cannot escape, however. If that something is the Ground of our being, we are bound to it for all eternity, just as we are bound to ourselves and to all other life. We always remain in the power of that from which we are estranged. That fact brings us to the ultimate depth of sin: separated and yet bound, estranged and yet belonging, destroyed and yet preserved, the state which is called despair. Despair means that there is no escape. Despair is "the sickness unto death." But the terrible thing about the sickness of despair is that we cannot be released, not even through open or hidden suicide. For we all know that we are bound eternally and inescapably to the Ground of our being. The abyss of separation is not always visible. But it has become more visible to our generation than to the preceding generations, because of our feeling of meaninglessness, emptiness, doubt, and cynicism—all expressions of despair, of our separation from the roots and the meaning of our life. Sin in its most profound sense, sin, as despair, abounds amongst us.

"Where sin abounded, grace did much more abound," says Paul in the same letter in which he describes the unimaginable power of separation and self-destruction within society and the individual soul. He does not say these words because sentimental interests demand a happy ending for everything tragic. He says them because they describe the most overwhelming and determining experience of his life. In the picture of Jesus as the Christ, which appeared to him at the moment of his greatest separation from other men, from himself and God, he found himself accepted in spite of his being rejected. And when he found that he was accepted, he was able to accept himself and to be reconciled to others. The moment in which grace struck him and overwhelmed him, he was reunited with that to which he belonged, and from which he was estranged in utter strangeness. Do we know what it means to be struck by grace? It does *not* mean that we suddenly believe that God exists, or that Jesus is the Saviour, or that the Bible contains the truth. To believe that something *is*, is almost contrary to the meaning of grace. Furthermore, grace does not mean simply that we making progress in our moral self-control, in our fight against special faults, and in our relationships to men and to society. Moral progress may be a fruit of grace; but it is not grace itself, and it can even prevent us from receiving grace.

For there is too often a graceless acceptance of Christian doctrines and a graceless battle against the structures of evil in our personalities. Such a graceless relation to God may lead us by necessity either to arrogance or to despair. It would be better to refuse God and the Christ and the Bible than to accept Them without grace. For if we accept without gracé, we do so in the state of separation, and can only succeed in deepening the separation. We cannot transform our lives, unless we allow them to be transformed by that stroke of grace. It happens; or it does not happen. And certainly it does *not* happen if we try to force it upon ourselves, just as it shall not happen so long as we think, in our self-complacency, that we have no need of it. Grace strikes us when we are in great pain and restlessness. It strikes us when we walk through the dark valley of a meaningless and empty life. It strikes us when we feel that our separation is deeper than usual, because we have violated another life, a life which we loved, or from which we were estranged. It strikes us when our disgust for our own being, our indifference, our weakness, our hostility, and our lack of direction and composure have become intolerable to us. It strikes us when, year after year, the longed-for perfection of life does not appear, when the old compulsions reign within us as they have for decades, when despair destroys all joy and courage. Sometimes at that moment a wave of light breaks into our darkness, and it is as though a voice were saying: "You are accepted. *You are accepted,* accepted by that which is greater than you, and the name of which you do not know. Do not ask for the name now; pehaps you will find it later. Do not try to do anything now; perhaps later you will do much. Do not seek for anything; do not perform anything; do not intend anything. *Simply accept the fact that you are accepted!*" If that happens to us, we experience grace. After such an experience we may not be better than before, and we may not believe more than before. But everything is transformed. In that moment, grace conquers sin, and reconciliation bridges the gulf of estrangement. And nothing is demanded of this experience, no religious or moral or intellectual presupposition, nothing but *acceptance.*

In the light of this grace we perceive the power of grace in our relation to others and to ourselves. We experience the grace of being able to look frankly into the eyes of another, the miraculous grace of reunion of life with life. We experience the grace of understanding each other's words. We understand not merely the literal meaning of the words, but also that which lies behind them, even when they are harsh and angry. For even then there is a longing to break through the walls of separation. We experience the grace of being able to accept the life of another, even if it be hostile and harmful to us, for, through grace, we know that it belongs to the same Ground to which we belong, and by which we have been accepted. We experience the grace which is able to overcome the tragic separation of the sexes, of the generations, of the nations, of the races, and even the utter strangeness between man and nature. Sometimes grace appears in all these separations to reunite us with those to whom we belong. For life belongs to life.

And in the light of this grace we perceive the power of grace in our relation to ourselves. We experience moments in which we accept ourselves, because we feel that we have been accepted by that which is greater than we. If only more such moments were given to us! For it is such moments that make us love our life, that make us accept ourselves, not in our goodness and self-complacency, but in our certainty of the eternal meaning of our life. We cannot force ourselves to accept ourselves. We cannot compel anyone to accept himself. But sometimes it happens that we receive the power to say "yes" to ourselves, that peace enters into us and makes us whole, that self-hate and self-contempt disappear, and that our self is reunited with itself. Then we can say that grace has come upon us.

"Sin" and "grace" are strange words; but they are not strange things. We find them whenever we look into ourselves with searching eyes and longing hearts. They determine our life. They abound within us and in all of life. May grace more abound within us!

PART VII
THE FUTURE OF RELIGIONS

21
The Personal Character
of the Experience of
the Holy

THERE IS no type of religion which does not personify the holy which is encountered by man in his religious experience. In every religion the experience of the holy is mediated by some piece of finite reality. Everything can become a medium of revelation, a bearer of divine power. "Everything" not only includes all things in nature and culture, in soul and history; it also includes principles, categories, essences, and values. Through stars and stones, trees and animals, growth and catastrophe; through tools and houses, sculpture and melody, poems and prose, laws and customs; through parts of the body and functions of the mind, family relations and voluntary communities, historical leaders and national elevation; through time and space, being and nonbeing, ideals and virtues, the holy can encounter us. Everything that is, really or ideally, has become a medium of the divine mystery sometime in the course of the history of religion. But, in the moment in which something took on this role, it also received a personal face. Even tools and stones and categories became personal in the religious encounter, the encounter with the holy. *Persona*, like the Greek *prosopon*, points to the individual and at the same time universally meaningful

From Paul Tillich, *Biblical Religion and the Search for Ultimate Reality* (Chicago: University of Chicago Press), 22–28. Reprinted by permission of University of Chicago Press. Copyright © 1964 by Paul Tillich.

character of the actor on the stage. For person is more than individuality. "Person" is individuality on the human level, with self-relatedness and world-relatedness and therefore with rationality, freedom, and responsibility. It is established in the encounter of an ego-self with another self, often called the "I-thou" relationship, and it exists only in community with other persons. These basic characteristics of personal being include others, such as the possibility of asking and receiving answers, as previously described. When we speak of "personification" in the religious experience, we attribute all these characteristics to the bearers of the holy, although they do not actually have them. Neither a stone nor a virtue is self-related and has freedom and responsibility. In what sense, then, can we attribute personal qualities to a-personal beings? We can do this if we consider them not objects of a cognitive approach but elements of an encounter, namely, the encounter with the holy. They are parts of this encounter, not as things or values, but as bearers of something beyond themselves. This something beyond themselves is the holy, the numinous presence of that which concerns us ultimately. Man can experience the holy in and through everything, but, as the holy, it cannot be less than he is; it cannot be a-personal. Nothing that is less than we, nothing that encounters less than the center of our personality, can be of ultimate concern for us. It is meaningless to ask whether the holy *is* personal or whether its bearers *are* personal. If "is" and "are" express an objective, cognitive assertion, they certainly are *not* personal. But this is not the question. The question is what becomes of them as elements of the religious encounter? And then the answer is clearly that they become personal. Perhaps one should not speak of "personification," literally "making personal," because this seems to imply the fabrication of something untrue and artificial as a necessary concession to the primitive mind. The personal encounter in religious experience is as real as the encounter of subject and object in the cognitive experience or the encounter of vision and meaning in the artistic experience. In this sense religious personalism expresses reality, namely, reality within the religious encounter.

Wherever the holy is experienced, the person-to-person character of this experience is obvious. It is easy to show that this is the case in the so-called "primitive religions" and their personal divinities, however subhuman they may be. One deals with them as one deals with persons. It is equally easy to show the personal character of the encounter with the holy in the great mythological religions. All the gods of the myths are personal; they all are "thou's" for a human ego. Man can pray to them and influence them by sacrifice or moral behavior. Mysticism tries to transcend the ego-thou relation between God and man and does so successfully in the great mystics, at least in ecstatic moments. But the religions out of which mysticism has arisen, in India, China, Persia, and Europe, are personalistic. They have personal gods who are adored, even if one knows that beyond them there is the transpersonal *One,* the ground and abyss of everything personal. An Indian Brahman with whom I had a conversation about this point made it very clear to me that he stood in the transpersonalistic thinking of India's classical tradition but that, as a religious Hindu, he would say that the Brahman power makes itself personal for us. He did not attribute the personal element in religion only to man's subjectivity. He did not call it illusion; he described it as an inner quality of the transpersonal Brahman power. In every religion the holy is encountered in personal images.

THE SPECIAL CHARACTER OF BIBLICAL PERSONALISM

The personalism of biblical religion must be seen against the background of universal religion, representing it and, at the same time, denying it in a unique way. In the I-thou structure of the religious encounter the personalism of the Bible is like the personalism of any other religion. But it is different from the personalism of any other religion in its creation of an idea of personal relationship which is exclusive and complete. Every religion calls its God "thou," for instance, in a prayer. Biblical religion does the same, but it excludes elements from the prayer which would transform it into a person-thing relation; for instance, the "do-ut-des" or bargain relationship which makes of the divine "thou" a means for one's ends. In fighting against such an attitude, biblical religion has discovered the full meaning of the personal. It is the unconditional character of the biblical God that makes the relation to him radically personal. For only that which concerns us in the center of our personal existence concerns us unconditionally. The God who is unconditional in power, demand, and promise is the God who makes us completely personal and who, consequently, is completely personal in our encounter with him. It is not that we first know what person is and then apply the concept of God to this. But, in the encounter with God, we first experience what person should mean and how it is distinguished from, and must be protected from, everything a-personal.

If biblical religion is not only personal but the source of the full meaning of *person,* how can the a-personal concept "being" be of ultimate concern and a matter of infinite passion? Is this first confrontation not also the last, namely, the end of all attempts to achieve a synthesis between ontology and biblical religion? Is not God in the religious encounter *a* person among others, related to them as an *I* to a *thou,* and vice versa? And, if so, is he not *a* being, while the ontological question asks the question of being-itself, of the power of being in and above all beings? In the ontological question, is not God himself transcended?

22
On the Boundary Line

I T I S highly improbable that any dramatic change occurs in the mind of a man between his sixty-fourth and seventy-fourth years of age. In any case, no such change has happened to me. But since the writers of articles for this series are asked to report even subtle changes, I will try to say something about mine, hoping that they may be of more than merely autobiographical interest.

In the years between 1950 and 1960 my external situation underwent considerable change: my retirement from Union Theological Seminary, my appointment as university professor at Harvard, my increased lecturing activities at institutions of higher learning in America and Europe, and finally—though only recently—my encounter with the East through a lecture trip to Japan. The experiences produced by these events had a definite influence on my thinking, especially when they converged with the inner dialectics of my thought.

I

If one's whole life were dedicated to the fascination and the discipline of thought, one could easily forget the fact that reality

From Paul Tillich, "On the Boundary Line," *The Christian Century* (December 7, 1960): 1435—37. Reprinted by permission of *The Christian Century*. Copyright © 1960 by Christian Century Foundation.

opens itself up to us only by existential participation, by entering the situation about which one makes conceptual statements. The situation changes when life gives reality to what is for mere thought only possibility. Then the flavor of actual experience, a flavor which is lacking even in indisputable abstract statements, appears in one's thinking and writing. I hope that I have been involved in this process in the last ten years, to the advantage of my teaching and writing.

Perhaps the most significant experience in this respect was my visit to Japan from May to July of this year. Although the trip took place at the end of the ten-year period about which I have been asked to write, the picture would be incomplete if I did not mention it. The encounter served to bring to full awareness elements of thought which had been present for a long time. A friend of mine in whose political judgment I have an almost unlimited confidence asked me years ago, "Why don't you take the Eastern world into consideration within your religious-political thought?" This concern has been a thorn in my intellectual flesh ever since; I expressed it in some of my addresses in Japan as the desire to overcome Western provincialism. I cannot judge at this moment to what degree I have succeeded in overcoming it, but I have felt an immense enrichment of substance ever since my trip. "Substance" in this context means more than new insights and certainly more than a better knowledge of another section of the world. It means being somehow transformed through participation.

In Japan there was no question of my being "converted" to Zen or any other form of Buddhism, but there were many opportunities for me to be introduced existentially into what were to me strange forms of religious life, forms which showed unconditional seriousness and ultimate concern apart from any Christian influence. This experience was nothing new in terms of the sort of knowledge to be gained through books and conversations. But it was new in terms of existential encounter and community with persons having non-Western attitudes. And these opportunities I grasped—or more precisely, I was grasped by them and drawn into their spiritual atmosphere.

II

It is easy to perceive and to describe these experiences, but it is very difficult to formulate their theoretical implications. In my case, they have confirmed my theological conviction that one cannot divide the religions of mankind into one true and many false religions. Rather, one must subject all religions, including Christianity, to the ultimate criteria of religion: the criterion of a faith which transcends every finite symbol of faith and the criterion of a love which unconditionally affirms, judges and receives the other person. In light of these criteria two realities of the religious situation were confirmed in each of the many discussions I had not only with Christian ministers and missionaries but with Buddhist scholars and priests. The first: Christianity, in encounter with the East, must rid itself of all elements of a Jesu-logical (as opposed to a Christo-logical) theology. It must understand that it cannot appear in Asia as one religion among the many others already there, but as the bearer of a judgment and a promise that transcends religion and nonreligion.

To such a message the leading groups in the Eastern world are open on the basis of their own most profound religious experiences. The small but influential Non-Church movement in Japan is a definite example of this attitude. Such observations have strengthened my theological conviction that within the narrower concept of religion, describing it in its concrete existence, a larger concept is implied which transcends the concrete existence of any religion, as God transcends each of his manifestations. On the basis of such an assertion—which neither denies the concrete religions nor demands their mixture—a conversation with the East is possible, while it is impossible if every concrete religion claims absoluteness for itself in its particular forms of life.

The situation is different with respect to the second criterion, that of *agape*, a love which unconditionally affirms, judges and receives the other. It was in reference to *agape* that the differences between East and West became most evident to me. The evaluation of the individual person in his temporal rights and his eternal significance, the attitude toward a social transformation and toward history as a medium of revelatory events—these are fundamentally different in the two types of religion, Eastern and Western, and this difference has largely determined the destiny of the two cultures based on them. Certainly there is a strong emphasis on compassion in Buddhism, and the expression of it in my encounter with Buddhist friends was often overwhelming. It is ultimately rooted in the feeling for the identity of the substance in every being, while in *agape* the experience of participation in that which remains "other" is decisive. Although I was confirmed in my conviction of the superiority of the principle of participation, I felt that the principle of identity has produced a relation to nature in the East which is superior to that in the West. The controlling attitude in the West—rooted in the conquest of technology over nature—has brought about an estrangement between man and nature the depth of which one can hardly realize without having experienced the opposite attitude in the East. In encountering the immense religious significance of nature in Japan I felt the inadequacy of theological attempts, my own as well as those of others, to regain some of the positive religious experience of nature, an element which was not lacking in Christianity before the rise of modern industrial society.

III

The Zen Buddhist *propaganda-fidei* in America and Europe is a very ambitious matter. Genuine Zen, and not some aesthetically watered-down version, is a path of stern discipline and immense concentration. Little of this is shown in the manifestations of Zen in the West. But the fact that so many highly educated people prefer Zen to Christianity seems to me to stem from their aversion to the "objectified" and literally interpreted Christian symbols. The necessity of "demythologizing" in the sense of "deliteraliz-ing" or "deobjectifying" has become more urgent for me in light of these observations and of the whole impact of Eastern wisdom on me. And Eastern wisdom, like every other wisdom, certainly belongs to the self-manifestations of the Logos and must be in-cluded in the interpretation of Jesus as the Christ, if he is rightly to be called the incarnation of the Logos. The encounter with world religions puts a task before Christian theology which is very similar to that of the early church in its encounter with Hellenistic culture.

One aspect of this problem came to my attention when I visited the Brussels world's fair more than two years ago and saw the exhibitions of the Asian and African nations. The works dis-played were up to a certain period—about the middle of the nineteenth century—the treasurers of their ancient cultures. But for the period since then they showed only their attempts to compete successfully with the industrialized nations in producing tools and gadgets. In Japan the problem is intensified, because this is a nation which is not only equal to but in some respects ahead of the old industrial nations, yet which is in the process of losing its traditional symbols, and with them a meaning of life. The West has not been able to provide a substitute for this loss. Can we give them more than scientific knowledge and technical skills? This is the question they keep asking, and it is one which we must ask ourselves from the religious as well as from the cultural point of view.

23

Christian Principles of Judging Non-Christian Religions

I

I want to ask the question: what has Christianity, in the course of its history, thought about other religions in general and certain religions in particular? How did it meet them? To what degree will this determine the encounter of Christianity with the world religions today? And above all: what has been and what will be the attitude of Christianity to the powerful quasi-religions which are, in their modern form, something new for Christianity?

Before going into this problem empirically I want to introduce a rather general consideration concerning all religions and, even more generally, all social groups. If a group—like an individual—is convinced that it possesses a truth, it implicitly denies those claims to truth which conflict with that truth. I would call this the natural self-affirmation in the realm of knowledge; it is only another word for personal certainty. This is so natural and so inescapable that I have never found even a sceptic who did not affirm

From Paul Tillich, *Christianity and the Encounter of the World Religions* (New York: Columbia University Press), 28–51. Reprinted by permission of Columbia University Press. Copyright © 1963 by Columbia University Press.

his scepticism while contradicting everybody who denied its validity. If even the sceptic claims the right to affirm his scepticism
(if he makes a statement at all), and to contradict those who
doubt it, why should the member of a religious group be deprived
of his "civil right," so to speak, of affirming the fundamental
assertion of his group and of contradicting those who deny this
assertion? It is natural and unavoidable that Christians affirm
the fundamental assertion of Christianity that Jesus is the Christ
and reject what denies this assertion. What is permitted to the
sceptic cannot be forbidden to the Christian—or, for that matter,
to the adherent of any other religion.

Consequently the encounter of Christianity with other religions, as well as with quasi-religions, implies the rejection of
their claims insofar as they contradict the Christian principle,
implicitly or explicitly. But the problem is not the right of rejecting
that which rejects us; rather it is the nature of this rejection. It
can be the rejection of everything for which the opposite group
stands; it can be a partial rejection together with a partial acceptance of assertions of the opposite group; or it can be a dialectical union of rejection and acceptance in the relation of the
two groups. In the first case the rejected religion is considered
false, so that no communication between the two contradictory
positions is possible. The negation is complete and under certain
circumstances deadly for the one or the other side. In the second
case some assertions and actions of the one or the other side are
considered false, others true. This is more tolerant than the attitude of total negation, and it is certainly an adequate response
to a statement of facts or ideas some of which may be true, some
false, but it is not possible to judge works of art or philosophy or
the complex reality of religions in this way. The third way of
rejecting other religions is a dialectical union of acceptance and
rejection, with all the tensions, uncertainties, and changes which
such dialectic implies. If we look at the history of Christianity as
a whole, we can point to a decisive predominance of this latter
response in the attitude of Christian thinking and acting towards
the non-Christian religions. But it is almost impossible to discover

a consistent line of thought about this problem. And even less consistent is the attitude of Christianity to the contemporary quasi-religions. This observation contradicts the popular assumption that Christianity had an exclusively negative attitude toward other faiths. Indeed, nothing is farther from the truth. In this assumption a confusion frequently takes place between the attitude of the Christian churches toward Christian heretics, especially in the late Middle Ages, and their attitude toward members of other religions. The demonic cruelty of the former is in contrast with the comparative mildness of the latter.

The indefiniteness of the attitude toward strange religions starts in the Old Testament. In the earlier prophets, the pagan gods are treated as powers inferior to the power of Jahweh, particularly in foreseeing and determining the future, in hearing prayers, and in executing justice, but they are regarded as competing realities. Of course, in the long run, their loss of power led to their loss of being; a god without ultimate power is a "nothing," as they were later called. Jahweh has superior power because he is the God of justice. Since Amos, prophecy threatened Israel, the nation of Jahweh, with destruction by Jahweh because of its injustice. The covenant between Jahweh and the nation does not give the nation a claim to Jahweh's championship; he will turn against them if they violate justice. The exclusive monotheism of the prophetic religion is not due to the absoluteness of one particular god as against others, but it is the universal validity of justice which produces the exclusive monotheism of the God of justice. This, of course, implies that justice is a principle which transcends every particular religion and makes the exclusiveness of any particular religion conditional. It is this principle of conditional exclusiveness which will guide our further inquiry into the attitude of Christianity to the world religions.

Jesus' words are the basic confirmation of this principle. In the grand scene of the ultimate judgment (Matt. 25; 31ff.), the Christ puts on his right the people from all nations who have acted with righteousness and with that agape—love which is the substance of every moral law. Elsewhere Jesus illustrates this principle by the story of the Good Samaritan, the representative of a rejected religion who practices love, while the representatives of the accepted religion pass by. And when the disciples complain about people who perform works similar to theirs, but outside their circle, he defends them against the disciples. Although the Fourth Gospel speaks more clearly than the others of the uniqueness of the Christ, it interprets him at the same time in the light of the most universal of all concepts used in this period, the concept of the Logos, the universal principle of the divine self-manifestation, thus freeing the interpretation of Jesus from a particularism through which he would become the property of a particular religious group. Further, in the talk with the Samaritan woman, Jesus denies the significance of any particular place of adoration and demands an adoration "in Spirit and in Truth."

Paul is in a situation which is typical of all later developments. He has to fight on two fronts—against the legalism of Christianized Jews and against the libertinism of Christianized pagans. He has to defend the new principle revealed in the appearance of the Christ. But, as always, defense narrows down. So his first condemnations are uttered against Christian distorters of his message; anathemas are always directed against Christians, not against other religions or their members. With respect to other religions he makes the assertion, unheard of for a Jew, that Jews and pagans are equally under the bondage of sin and equally in need of salvation—a salvation which comes not from a new religion, the Christian, but from an event in history which judges all religions, including Christianity.

In early Christianity the judgment of other religions was determined by the idea of the Logos. The Church Fathers emphasized the universal presence of the Logos, the Word, the principle of divine self-manifestation, in all religions and cultures. The Logos is present everywhere, like the seed on the land, and this presence is a preparation for the central appearance of the Logos in a historical person, the Christ. In the light of these ideas Augustine could say that the true religion had existed always and was called Christian only after the appearance of the Christ.

Accordingly, his dealing with other religions was dialectical, as was that of his predecessors. They did not reject them unambiguously and, of course, they did not accept them unambiguously. But in their apologetic writings they acknowledged the preparatory character of these religions and tried to show how their inner dynamics drives them toward questions whose answer is given in the central event on which Christianity is based. They tried to show the convergent lines between the Christian message and the intrinsic quests of the pagan religions. In doing so they used not only the large body of literature in which the pagans had criticized their own religions (for example, the Greek philosophers), but also made free use of the positive creations from the soil of the pagan religions. On the level of theological thought they took into Christianity some of the highest conceptualizations of the Hellenistic and, more indirectly, of the classical Greek feeling toward life—terms like physis (natura), hypostasis (substance), ousia (power of being), prosopon (persona, not person in our sense), and above all logos (word and rational structure in the later Stoic sense). They were not afraid to call the God to whom they prayed as the Father of Jesus, the Christ, the unchangeable One.

All these are well-known facts, but it is important to see them in the new light of the present encounter of the world religions, for then they show that early Christianity did not consider itself as a radical-exclusive, but as the all-inclusive religion in the sense of the saying: "All that is true anywhere in the world belongs to us, the Christians." And it is significant that the famous words of Jesus, "You, therefore, must be perfect, as your heavenly Father is perfect" (which was always an exegetic riddle), would, according to recent research, be better translated, "You must be all-inclusive as your heavenly Father is all-inclusive."

Besides the reception of basic concepts from pagan metaphysical thought, which always means implicitly religious thought, early Christianity adopted moral principles from the Stoics, who represented both a philosophy and a way of life—a process which is already present in the Pauline letters. The early Church shaped its ritual structure in analogy with that of the mystery religions, some of which were its serious competitors, and used the Roman legal and the Germanic feudal forms for its social and political self-realization, while on the more popular, but officially accepted, level it has, through the veneration of saints, appropriated and transformed many genuine pagan motifs and symbols.

I I

This astonishing universalism, however, was always balanced by a criterion which was never questioned, either by the orthodox or by the heretical groups: the image of Jesus as the Christ, as documented in the New, and prepared for in the Old Testament. Christian universalism was not syncretistic; it did not mix, but rather subjected whatever it received to an ultimate criterion. In the power of this polarity between universality and concreteness it entered the Medieval period, having to compete with no religion equal to it in either of these respects. In both the Mediterranean and the northern half of Western civilization the one all-embracing religion and the one all-embracing culture were amalgamated into a unity of life and thought. All conflicts, however severe, occurred within this unity. No external encounters disturbed it.

But in the seventh century something happened which slowly changed the whole situation. The first outside encounter took place with the rise of Islam, a new and passionate faith, fanatically carried over the known world, invading, subjecting, and reducing Eastern Christianity and threatening all Christendom. Based on Old Testament, pagan, and Christian sources, and created by a prophetic personality, it was not only adapted to the needs of primitive tribes, but also capable of absorbing large elements of the ancient culture, and soon surpassed Western Christianity in culture and civilization. The shock produced by these events can be compared only with the shock produced by the establishment of the Communist quasi-religion in Eastern Europe, Russia, and China, threatening Western Christianity and its liberal-humanist quasi-religious transformation.

The victorious wars of the Islamic tribes and nations forced Christianity to become aware of itself as one religion confronted with another against which it had to defend itself. According to the law that defense narrows down the defender, Christianity became at this point radically exclusive. The Crusades were the expression of this new self-consciousness. They were the result of the first encounter of Christianity with a new world religion. (This analogy, to leap to the present for a moment, makes understandable the crusading spirit of this country against the two radicalized types of quasi-religions—Fascism on the one hand, Communism on the other. The often irrational and almost obsessive character of this crusading spirit shows that here expressions of ultimate concern are at work, though deeply ambiguous ones. Their ambiguity shows itself also in the fact that, just as in the period of the Crusades, they conflict with sober political judgment and profounder religious insight.)

The irrational character of the crusading spirit was confirmed by the fact that the narrowed self-consciousness, created by the encounter of Christianity with Islam, produced also a changed self-consciousness with respect to the Jews. Since the period of the New Testament, and expressed most clearly in the Johannine literature, a Christian anti-Judaism has existed, based, of course, on the rejection of Jesus as the Messiah by the vast majority of the Jews. Nevertheless, they were tolerated and often welcomed in the earlier period; the Church waited for their conversion. But after the shock of the encounter with Islam the Church became conscious of Judaism as another religion and anti-Judaism became fanatical. Only after this was it possible for governments to use the Jews as political scapegoats to cover up their own political and economic failures, and only since the end of the nineteenth century did religious anti-Judaism become racial anti-

Semitism, which was—and still is—one of the many ingredients in the radicalized nationalistic quasi-religion.

III

But the encounter of Christianity with a new and an old world religion in the period of the Crusades worked not only for a fanatical exclusiveness; it also worked slowly in the direction of a tolerant relativism. In the same early thirteenth century in which Pope Innocent III gave the model for Hitler's Nürnberg laws against the Jews, there was created by Christian, Islamic, and Jewish forces the near-miracle of a tolerant humanism on the basis of current traditions at the court of Emperor Frederick II in Sicily. It took one to two centuries for similar ideas to come again to the surface, changing the Christian judgment of non-Christian religions in a radical way.

The great Cardinal and member of the Papal Court, Nicholas Cusanus, was able in the middle of the fifteenth century, in spite of his being an acknowledged pillar of the Roman Church, to write his book, *De Pace Fidei* (The Peace between the Different Forms of Faith). He tells how representatives of the great religions had a sacred conversation in heaven. The divine Logos explained their unity by saying: "There is only one religion, only one cult of all who are living according to the principles of Reason [the Logos-Reason], which underlies the different rites. . . . The cult of the gods everywhere witnesses to Divinity. . . . So in the heaven of [Logos-] Reason the concord of the religions was established."

The vision of Cusanus was an anticipation of later developments. Ideas appeared which renewed and even transcended the early Christian universalism, but without falling into relativism. People like Erasmus, the Christian humanist, or Zwingli, the Protestant Reformer, acknowledged the work of the Divine Spirit beyond the boundaries of the Christian Church. The Socinians, predecessors of the Unitarians and of much liberal Protestant theology, taught a universal revelation in all periods. The leaders of the Enlightenment, Locke, Hume, and Kant, measured Christianity by its reasonableness and judged all other religions by the same criterion. They wanted to remain Christians, but on a universalist, all-inclusive basis. These ideas inspired a large group of Protestant theologians in the nineteenth and early twentieth centuries. A symptom of this situation is the rise of philosophies of religion, the very term implying that Christianity has been subsumed under the universal concept of religion. This seems harmless enough, but it is not. In the periods in which the concrete element dominated and repressed the universalist element, the theologians were aware of this danger and they maintained a unique claim for Christianity by contrasting revelation—restricted to Christianity—with religion as designating every non-Christian religion. Or they called Christianity the true religion, all other religions "false religions." With the disappearance of this distinction, however, Christianity, while still claiming some superiority, stepped down from the throne of exclusiveness to which these theologians had raised it and became no more than the exemplar of the species religion. Thus Christian universalism was transformed into humanist relativism.

This situation is reflected in the way in which both philosophers and theologians, in their philosophies of religion, dealt with Christianity in relation to other religions. Kant, in his book on *Religion within the Limits of Pure Reason*, gives Christianity an exalted standing by interpreting its symbols in terms of his *Critique of Practical Reason*. Fichte uses the Fourth Gospel to exalt Christianity as a representative of mysticism; Schelling and Hegel consider it, in spite of Islam, as the fulfillment of all that is positive in the other religions and cultures; Schleiermacher gives a construction of the history of religions in which Christianity takes the highest place in the highest type of religion. My own teacher, Ernst Troeltsch, in his famous essay, "The Absoluteness of Christianity," asks most radically the question of the standing of Christianity among the world religions. He, like all the other Christian theologians and philosophers, who subsume Christianity under the concept of religion, construes Christianity as the most adequate realization of the potentialities implied in that concept. But since the concept of religion is itself derived from the Christian-humanist tradition, the procedure is circular. Troeltsch was aware of this situation and drew the consequences in his interpretation of history, in which he states no universal aim of history, but restricts himself to his own tradition, of which Christianity is an element. He calls it "Europeism"; today we would probably call it "The West." A consequence of this withdrawal was his advocation of the replacement of missionary attacks on the other world religions by "cross-fertilization," which was meant more as cultural exchange than as interreligious unity of acceptance and rejection. The resignation implied in this solution followed a general trend of nineteenth century thought, positivism in the original sense of the word, as acceptance of the empirically given without a superior criterion.

There was, however, always a majority of theologians and church people who interpreted Christianity in a particularistic and absolutistic way. They emphasized the exclusiveness of the salvation through Christ, following the main line of the theology of the Reformers, their orthodox systematizers and their pietistic transformers. In several waves the antiuniversalist movements attacked the universalist trends which had become powerful in the last centuries. Every relativistic attitude towards the world religions was denounced as a negation of the absolute truth of Christianity. Out of this tradition (which is not necessarily fundamentalist in the ordinary sense) a strong particularistic turn of theology has grown. It was called in Europe crisis-theology; in America it is being called neo-orthodoxy. Its founder and outstanding representative is Karl Barth. This theology can be summed up from the point of view of our problem as the rejection of the concept of religion if applied to Christianity. According to him, the Christian Church, the embodiment of Christianity, is based on the only revelation that has ever occurred, namely, that in Jesus Christ. All human religions are fascinating, but futile attempts of man to reach God, and the relation to them, therefore, is no problem; the Christian judgment of them is unambiguous rejection of their claim to be based on revelation. Consequently, the problem which is the subject of this book—the encounter of Christianity with the world religions—may be an interesting historical problem, but is not a theological one. Yet history itself forced the problem on Barth, not through an encounter with a non-Christian religion in the proper sense, but through a highly dramatic encounter with one of the radicalized and demoniacal quasi-religions—Nazism. Under Barth's leadership the European Christian churches were able to resist its onslaught; the radical self-affirmation of Christianity in his theology made any compromise with Nazism impossible. But, according to the law mentioned above, the price paid for this successful defense was a theological and ecclesiastical narrowness which blinded the majority of Protestant leaders in Europe to the new situation arising out of the encounters of religions and quasi-religions all over the world. The missionary question was treated in a way which contradicted not only Troeltsch's idea of a cross-fertilization of the high religions, but also early Christian universalism, and it deserves mention that Barth and his whole school gave up the classical doctrine of the Logos in which this universalism was most clearly expressed.

The present attitude of Christianity to the world religions is as indefinite as that in most of its history. The extreme contrast between men like Barth and the theologian of missions, Kraemer, on the one side, and Troeltsch and the philosophical historian, Toynbee, with his program of a synthesis of the world religions, on the other, is symbolic for the intrinsic dialects of the relation of Christianity to the religions proper.

I V

We must still ask the question, at least in general terms, of what the attitude of Christianity to the quasi-religions is. The answer presupposes a discussion of the attitude of Christianity to the secular realm in general. I do not say to secularism, for there is no problem in this. Secularism, i.e., the affirmation of secular culture in contrast to, and to the exclusion of, religion can only be rejected by Christianity as well as by every other religion. But the secular realm does not necessarily affirm itself in the form of secularism; it can affirm itself as an element within an over-arching religious system, as was the case in the Middle Ages. Under such conditions Christianity has used the creations of the secular realm, wherever found—in Egypt or Greece or Rome—for the building of its own life. In our own period Christianity has been able to accept the different technical and economic revolutions and, after some brief reactions, the scientific affir-mations which underlie these transformations of our historical existence. The relation of Protestantism to the secular realm is the most positive, due to the Protestant principle that the sacred sphere is not nearer to the Ultimate than the secular sphere. It denies that either of them has a greater claim to grace than the other; both are infinitely distant from and infinitely near to the Divine. This stems from the fact that Protestantism was largely a lay movement, like the Renaissance, and that in its later de-velopment a synthesis between the Enlightenment and Protes-tantism was possible, while in Catholic countries, even today, Christianity and the Enlightenment are still struggling with each other. The danger of the Protestant idea, of course, is that the acceptance of secularism can lead to a slow elimination of the religious dimension altogether, even within the Protestant churches. The general attitude of the Christian churches to the secular realm determines their judgment about the quasi-religions which have arisen on the basis of secularism.

First of all, it is obvious that Protestantism is more open to and, consequently, a more easy prey of the quasi-religions. The Roman Church has denied to all three types of quasi-religion—the nationalist, the socialist, and the liberal-humanist—any *religious* significance. It did not reject the nationalist or socialist idea as such; the social ethics of the Catholic Church could deal positively with both ideas under the criterion of the church tradition. More complex, and on the whole negative, is the Catholic attitude to the liberal-humanist quasi-religion, for it is hardly possible to purge this movement of its religious implications. Totally opposed, however, is the Catholic Church to the quasi-religious radicalizations of nationalism and socialism, namely Fascism and Communism. The religious element of neither can be denied—even if this element is a dogmatic "atheism." This leads to the uncompromising rejection of Communism, and to the less passionate, but equally unambiguous, rejection of Fascism by the Catholic Church.

Its positive valuation of the secular makes the relation of Protestantism to the quasi-religions much more dialectical and even ambiguous. Protestantism can receive and transform the religious elements of the quasi-religions. It has done so in different ways with all three of them, but it has also partly—though never totally—succumbed to their radicalized forms. The Catholic Church has not been open to such reception of and subjection to the quasi-religions.

A few facts may show the ambiguous character of Protestantism in relation to the quasi-religions. The national idea was, since the reform councils of the fifteenth and the Reformation of the sixteenth centuries, a decisive tool in the fight of Christian groups against Rome. This was seen more clearly in England than anywhere else; Holland followed later, while in Germany Luther used national protests against Rome in defense of the Reformation without having a German nation behind him. Only in the late nineteenth century did the nationalism of the newly founded German Empire come into conflict with the Roman Church. When Nazism radicalized the nationalistic faith, certain Protestant groups succumbed to it, while the majority repulsed the demonic attack of the nationalistic quasi-religion. In the United States there is a kind of conservative Protestantism (religiously as well as politically) which supports, often fanatically, the nationalist quasi-religion. It is a symptom of the openness of Protestantism to the danger of what one could call nationalist apostasy.

Protestantism had, in its earlier stages, less affinity to movements for social justice than Catholicism. Its negative judgment about the human predicament made it conservative and authoritarian. Nevertheless, there were the spiritually strong (though politically weak) movements of Social Gospel and Christian Socialism, which tried to discuss and transform the religious element in the Socialist faith and to use it for Protestant social ethics. Against the Communist radicalization and demonization of Socialism, the Protestant churches were as uncompromising as the Catholic church, but there is a strong desire in many Protestant groups not only to reject, but also to understand, what is going on in one-half of the inhabited world.

Protestantism has its most intimate relation with the liberal-humanist quasi-religion. In many cases, as in all forms of liberal Protestantism, a full amalgamation has taken place. . . . Both Protestantism and liberal humanism [are] spiritual but fragile. . . .

One thing should have become clear through the preceding descriptions and analyses: that Christianity is not based on a simple negation of the religions or quasi-religions it encounters. The relation is profoundly dialectical, and that is not a weakness, but the greatness of Christianity, especially in its self-critical, Protestant form.

24
Martin Buber

The following statement is an address
by Paul Tillich at a memorial meeting held
on July 13 at the Park Avenue Synagogue
under the auspices of the American Friends
of the Hebrew University in Jerusalem,
where Martin Buber served as Professor
of Social Philosophy until his retirement
in 1951.

T WOULD BE inadequate for this occasion if I tried to give a detached evaluation of Martin Buber's work. We are asked to speak here about what he meant to us as a person, as well as in his work. We were asked because one knew that our evaluation of his thought would be, at the same time, a witness and a confession. In this sense I want to speak. And it is in this sense that I shall start with my image of him as a partner in a dialogue which lasted with many interruptions for forty years. It was a dialogue on the basis of our own religious encounters, and it included philosophical as well as theological questions. But first let me tell you about some personal memories.

When less than two years ago I left his home in Jerusalem after a great evening of reminiscences and exchanges, I asked him whether he would come again to Europe or America. He answered with a clear "No," and he looked at me with an expression in his eyes which said unmistakably: "This is a final farewell." It was.

From Paul Tillich, "Martin Buber—1878–1965," *Pastoral Psychology* (September 1965): 52–54, 66. Reprinted by permission of *Pastoral Psychology*. Copyright © 1965 by *Pastoral Psychology*.

Going back through four decades from this last to our first meeting, I remember the conference of Religious Socialists in Germany in the year 1924. Our movement, founded after the First World War, tried to heal the catastrophic split between the churches and labor in most European countries. It was my task to elaborate adequate concepts from the theological, philosophical, and sociological sides. This meant that I had to replace traditional religious terms, including the word "God," with words which could be accepted by the religious humanists who belonged to our movement. After I had finished, Martin Buber arose and attacked what he called the "abstract facade" I had built. With great passion, he said that there are some aboriginal words like "God," which cannot be replaced at all. He was right and I learned the lesson. I don't believe that concepts like "ultimate reality" or "unconditional concern," which are much used in my systematic writing, appear in the three volumes of my sermons. This awareness, produced by Martin Buber, enabled me, I believe, to preach at all.

Behind this attack on the conceptual facade of my presentation lay a deeper problem. It came out in two unforgettable evenings of dialogue in the house of mutual friends in New York. At that time both of us were refugees from Nazi Germany. This dialogue was one of the most important I ever had. It dealt with the question of how far Buber's I-Thou encounter, contrasted to the I-It relation, is an exact description of what really happens in the encounter of person with person. I asked (in a hidden defense of my conceptual facade many years ago) whether one can say that there is a *"pure* I," related to a *"pure* Thou." Or whether there is a particular "I" with qualities, able to be conceptualized, and a particular "Thou" with qualities, different or opposed, but equally able to be conceptualized; for instance as a male, a European, a Jew of the twentieth century, an intellectual, et cetera. This question becomes especially important if one asks for the difference between the encounter between man and man, and the encounter between man and God. In order to make this distinction, concepts must be used which are more than facade, and describe the structure of the building itself. But again, what I learned and used later in my ethical writings is the insight that the moral imperative and its unconditional character are identical with the demand that I acknowledged every person as person, every "thou" as a "thou," and that I am acknowledged in the same way.

In these dialogues, as in almost all encounters with Martin Buber, something happened which transcended for me in importance the dialogue itself. It was the experience of a man whose whole being was impregnated by the experience of the divine presence. He was, as one could say, "God-possessed." God never could become an "object" in Martin Buber's presence. The certainty of God always preceded the certainty of himself and his world. God, for him, was not an object of doubt, but the presupposition— even of doubt. This is the only way, I believe, which makes a dialogue with those who doubt and even with those who deny God, possible. But this presupposes a universalism like that of Martin Buber.

It is characteristic that we never discussed the Jewish-Christian contrast directly. This was not the existential question today for either of us. It was not denied, but our real problems could not be discussed in terms of unity and trinity, not even in terms of law and gospel. The reason was that Buber's universalism transcended any particular religion, although it was derived from his interpretation of Judaism, just as I derived my universalism from what I think to be the true nature of Christianity. This is the reason why our dialogues never were Jewish-Christian dialogues but dialogues about the relation of God, man, and nature. They were dialogues between a Jew and a Protestant who had transcended the limits of Judaism as well as of Protestantism, while remaining a Jew the one, and a Protestant the other. This concrete universalism seems to me to be the only justifiable form of universalism.

Martin Buber has been called religiously a prophet, philo-

sophically an existentialist. There is truth and untruth in both
statements. He himself resented it to be called a prophet, because
he knew that a prophet who calls himself a prophet, proves that
he is not a prophet. But for those who encountered him, he had
prophetic passion and prophetic words. Prophetic means: expressing the divine presence in a particular situation. And that
he did. Perhaps he also disliked to be called an existentialist
philosopher, but again, he was, even in a very radical sense, as
his abstinence from conceptual formulations shows. The exis-
tentalist element in his thought was in unity with the prophetic
element in his whole being. It was not psychological or sociological existentialism, it was an existentialism rooted in the divine
human encounter. It could be called theonomous, God-determined
existentialism.

The intensity of the God-experience in Martin Buber had another
equally important consequence. He could, without visible conflict,
unite the prophetic with the mystical element in the God-man
relationship. I consider this union to be the inner aim, the telos
of the movement of religion and of theological thought. The way
he did it was determined by his acquaintance with, and his interpretation of, the Hassidic mystics. This is different from the
way in which the main line of Jewish and Christian mysticism
tried to create the union of both elements in dependence on
Philonic and neo-Platonic mysticism. It was a mystical experience
of the divine presence in the encounter and activities of the daily
life. Buber knew that the prophetic, without the mystical element,
degenerates into legalism and moralism, while the mystical element alone leads to an escape from reality and from the demands
of the here and now.

The prophetic as well as the mystical way transcends religion
in the narrower sense of the word, without necessarily denying
it. This gave Martin Buber his freedom from ritualism and his
freedom for the secular world. But, of course, it brought him also
suspicion and hostility from those who make a true relation to

God dependent on the belonging to a particular religion with particular ritual and doctrinal norms. Buber was open for the cultural creations of past and present, in philosophy as well as the arts, in the social as well as in the political realm. For him, God was present and could be found in the universe of nature and of history. This openness for the secular—in which I always agreed in the name of which I call the Protestant Principle—anticipated an emphasis which has appeared in the latest phase of Protestant theology: the freedom from religion, including the institutions of religion, in the name of that to which religion points. This attitude is a reason for Martin Buber's far-reaching influence on the secular world, and particularly on the younger generation for which the traditional activities and assertions of churches and synagogues have become largely irrelevant. He knew that we cannot produce new symbols at will, but he also knew that we cannot use them as if nothing had happened in history. This makes him a genuine theologian.

As long as I have known Martin Buber, I felt his reality as something which transcends bodily presence or intellectual influence. He was there in the midst of the Western world, a part of it, a power in it, through his person, but also independent of him as an individual being, as a spiritual reality impossible to be overlooked, provoking Yes or No or both. This spiritual reality which was in the man Martin Buber will last for a long time in future history and open up for many that which is above history.

25

The Significance of the History of Religions for the Systematic Theologian

A THEOLOGIAN who accepts the subject, "The Significance of the History of Religions for the Systematic Theologian," and takes this subject seriously, has already made, explicitly or implicitly, two basic decisions. On the one hand he has separated himself from a theology which rejects all religions other than that of which he is a theologian. On the other hand if one accepts the subject affirmatively and seriously, he has rejected the paradox of a religion of nonreligion, or a theology without theos, also called a theology of the secular. . . .

In order to reject both this old and new orthodox attitude one must accept the following systematic presuppositions. First one must say that revelatory experiences are universally human. Religions are based on something that is given to a man wherever he lives. He is given a revelation, a particular kind of experience which always implies saving powers. One never can separate revelation and salvation. There are revealing and saving powers in all religions. God has not left himself unwitnessed. This is the first presupposition.

From Paul Tillich, *The Future of Religions* (New York: Harper and Row), 81–82, 94. Reprinted by permission of Harper & Row Publishers, Inc. Copyright © 1966 by Hannah Tillich.

The second assumption states that revelation is received by man in terms of his finite human situation. Man is biologically, psychologically, and sociologically limited. Revelation is received under the conditions of man's estranged character. It is received always in a distorted form, especially if religion is used as a means to an end and not as an end in itself.

There is a third presupposition that one must accept. When systematic theologians assume the significance of the history of religions, it involves the belief that there are not only particular revelatory experiences throughout human history, but that there is a revelatory process in which the limits of adaptation and the failures of distortion are subjected to criticism. Such criticism takes three forms: the mystical, the prophetic, and the secular.

A fourth assumption is that there may be—and I stress this there *may* be—a central event in the history of religions which unites the positive results of those critical developments in the history of religion in and under which revelatory experiences are going on—an event which, therefore, makes possible a concrete theology that has universalistic significance.

There is also a fifth presupposition. The history of religions in its essential nature does not exist alongside the history of culture. The sacred does not lie beside the secular, but it is its depths. The sacred is the creative ground and at the same time a critical judgment of the secular. But the religious can be this only if it is at the same time a judgment on itself, a judgment which must use the secular as a tool of one's own religious self-criticism.

Only if the theologian is willing to accept these five presuppositions can he seriously and fully affirm the significance of the history of religions for theology against those who reject such significance in the name of a new or of an old absolutism. . . .

But now my last word. What does this mean for our relationship to the religion of which one is a theologian? Such a theology remains rooted in its experiential basis. Without this, no theology at all is possible. But it tries to formulate the basic experiences which are universally valid in universally valid statements. The universality of a religious statement does not lie in an all-embracing abstraction which would destroy religion as such, but it lies in the depths of every concrete religion. Above all it lies in the openness to spiritual freedom both from one's own foundation and for one's own foundation.

PART VIII
LIVING ON THE BOUNDARY

26
Frontiers

I

Existence on the frontier, in the boundary situation, is full of tension and movement. It is in truth not standing still, but rather a crossing and return, a repetition of return and crossing, a back-and-forth—the aim of which is to create a third area beyond the bounded territories, an area where one can stand for a time without being enclosed in something tightly bounded. The frontier situation is not yet what one can call "peace"; and yet it is the portal through which every individual must pass, and through which the nations must pass, in order to achieve peace. For peace is to stand in the Comprehensive (*Übergreifenden*) which is sought in crossing and recrossing the frontiers. Only he who participates on both sides of a boundary line can serve the Comprehensive and thereby peace—not the one who feels secure in the voluntary calm of something tightly bounded. Peace appears where—in personal as well as in political life—an old boundary has lost its importance and thereby its power to occasion disturbance, even if it still continues as a partial boundary. Peace is not side-by-side existence without tension. It is unity within that which comprehends, where there is no lack of opposition of living forces and conflicts between the Old and the sometimes New—but in which they do not break out destructively, but are held in the peace of the Comprehensive.

From Paul Tillich, *The Future of Religions* (New York: Harper and Row), 53–63. Reprinted by permission of Harper & Row Publishers, Inc. Copyright © 1966 by Hannah Tillich.

If crossing and reversing the frontiers is the way to peace, then the root of disturbance and of war is the anxiety for that which lies on the other side, and the will to eliminate that which arises from it.

I I

When destiny leads one to the frontier of his being, it makes him personally conscious that he stands before the decision either to fall back upon that which he already is or else to transcend himself. Every person is at that point led to the frontier of his being. He perceives the Other over beyond himself, and it appears to him as a possibility and awakens in him the anxiety of the potential. He sees in the mirror of the other his own limitedness, and he recoils; for at the same time this limitedness was his security, and now it is threatened. The anxiety of the potential draws him back into his bounded reality and its momentary calm. But the situation into which he will return is no longer the same. His experience of the potential and his failure toward it leaves a thorn behind, which cannot be eliminated, which can only be driven out of the consciousness by suppression. And where that occurs, there arises that spiritual phenomenon which we call fanaticism. The original meaning of the word is "divinely inspired." That is what the fanatic feels. But the word itself has changed its meaning, and one could rather say, "demoniacally inspired"—that is, born out of a distraught spiritual structure and thereby destructively fulfilled. That can appear in smaller, greater, or enormous measure, in persons and in groups.

I think of young students, theologians or perhaps natural scientists, who come to the universities from the security of tightly bounded thinking and belief; who are led there to the frontier of other thinking and belief; who realize what they themselves are like in the mirror of the other; who experience the potential but are not mature enough for it; who fall back on the old certainties, but now affirm them fanatically with the aim of eliminating the frontiers which they cannot cross over, of bringing all spiritual possibilities into subjection to their own, of dissolving them in their own identity. The aggression of the fanatic is the result of his weakness, his anxiety to cross over his own boundary, and his incapacity to see that realized in the other which he has suppressed in himself. It happens too that, in doubt toward his own spiritual world, one may cross the frontier, find in the new belief a new tightly bounded security, never go back again, and develop a counter-aggression—the often especially strong fanaticism of the renegade, the religious as well as the antireligious. That is the ground out of which the wars of religion proceed. And if today they are no longer bloody wars, they are still battles that shatter the souls, in which the weapons of hate are used— namely, lies, distortion, exclusion, suppression—in order to eliminate the frontiers which one was too weak to cross over. Religious groups and whole churches can be driven into this posture. And it may be appropriate here to say a word about the German Protestant churches.

Perhaps before the church struggle there were groups among them who had indeed crossed the frontier, but who had not found their way back, and who exchanged the narrowness where they went—a critically emptied Christianity, for the narrowness from which they came—a traditionally calcified Christianity. Against the radically anti-Christian attacks of Nazism the churches had to draw back on the tradition and defend their identity at the cost of narrowing the boundary of their life. But their task today is to return to the frontier, to cross over it and wrestle for the Beyond in the to-and-fro between church and culture. If the churches do not risk this crossing of the frontier of their own identity, they will be irrelevant for unnumbered persons who, essentially, belong to them. And the thorn of having failed can produce a fanatical self-approval, which tries to incorporate culture into itself and remove the boundary against it.

Another example of the call to border-crossing may be given. It also begins with the individual and leads on to the situation of groups, here and now. I think of people who are confronted by the possibility of going out of their national or cultural boundaries, either for study or by personal encounters in one's own or a foreign land. For a moment the limits of their own cultural existence, their national or continental limitedness, are visible to them. But they cannot bear the sight. They cannot cross over the frontiers and seek for something Beyond.

The anxiety of the potential seizes them and drives them back. And the encounter with the stranger, which is a challenge to cross the frontier, becomes the occasion of a foreign-hating fanaticism. The boundary which he is unable to cross over, man purposes to wipe out by destroying what is strange.

There is a social class among all industrial people which is admirably characterized by this conceptual framework: the lower middle class, the petit bourgeois, or—in a sociologically comprehensive symbol—the Philistine. Regardless of what social class he appears in, he can be exactly characterized as someone who—because of his anxiety at reaching his own frontier and seeing himself in the mirror of the different—can never risk rising above the habitual, the recognized, the established. He leaves unrealized the possibilities which are given every person from time to time to rise up out of himself—whether it is a person—who could have drawn him out of his narrowness, or an unusual work of art—which could have brought his security based on self into an upheaval. But all about him he sees people who have gone over the frontiers which he is unable to cross. And the secret envy becomes hate.

And, when in the Germany of the Hitler-period hate received unlimited power to fulfill itself, the frontiers were closed—so that a whole nation was unable to see beyond itself. And then the attempt was made to eliminate the frontiers by conquest or by destruction of that which lay on the other side of the boundary —whether they were other races or neighboring peoples, opposing political systems or new artistic styles, higher or lower social classes, or personalities developed through the crossing of borders. That is the demonic urge, perhaps in every person, to wipe out one's frontiers in order to be the whole thing by one's self.

Therefore I feel that I would not fulfill my task as a theologian did I not add a second point: first, that there are elements in all lands, and also in the United States, which correspond to the type of Philistine described. They raise their heads ever and again, not without success, but today in new forms and with numerous followers. And the second thing which I say only with trembling, as one for whom for years of his life Berlin was not only homeland but also a religious concept: everything which I have said about crossing the frontier is true too for crossing the line which is today hardest for the Western world to cross, the frontier toward the East. It is wrong when the Western peoples are prevented by education, literature and propaganda from crossing this frontier which is erected not only in Berlin. We must also see what is going on in depth over there, and seek to understand it from a human standpoint—not just polemically. And I wish I were capable of saying that to those on the other side of the line, too.

The politically and spiritually responsible people of the West should fight for the point that the education of the peoples serves not only the inculcation and deepening of that which is their own, however great it may be, but that it lead out across the boundary—in knowledge, in understanding, in encounter, even if what I encountered seems to be only something standing in opposition. Encouragement to cross over from what is merely one's own—that is what education can contribute toward the achievement of peace. And more important than anything else at this point is education in a consciousness of history, which writes historical knowledge with historical understanding and is in no sense limited to class work in history.

I I I

Up to now we have spoken of crossing the frontier. But frontier is not only something to be crossed: it is also something which must be brought to fruition. Boundary is a dimension of form, and form makes everything what it is. The boundary between man and animal makes it possible to require and express things from men which can neither be required nor expected of an animal. The frontier between England and France made possible the development of two great—substantially different—cultures. The frontier between religion and philosophy makes possible the freedom of philosophical thought and the passion of religious submission. Definition is *ab-grenzung*, and without it there is no possibility of grasping or recognizing reality.

No culture was so aware of the significance of the boundary line as the Greeks. Plato and his Pythagorean predecessors attributed everything positive to the bounded and everything negative to the unbounded. Space, even self itself, is bounded. The figures of the gods, and the temple in which they are sculptured, remain measured by the standard of the human. Limiting thought must bound the passion which drives toward the unbounded. The tragic hero, who breaks out of the essential limit, is driven back by the gods—the protectors of frontiers—and destroyed. The essential limits of man are the subject of oracles and seers, tragedians and philosophers. They want to call back to them from the false, too narrow or too wide factual limits. For the essential limit and the factual limit do not coincide. The essential limit stands demanding, judging, giving goals beyond the factual limit.

In the younger generation, in the United States and outside as well, there has appeared a problem in recent years which is treated again and again in literature and discussion: "the search for identity." It is the expression of a period in which many are incapable of finding the essential limit in and beyond their passing factual limits, and not just alone as individuals, but also as members of society—national, cultural, religious. How can persons, how can peoples find their identity and thereby their true limits—when they lose their final meaning in the actual limits? That is the point where the question of the frontier and the question of peace merge with each other. For the one who has found his identity and thereby the frontier of his nature does not need to lock himself in or to break out. He will bring to fruition what his nature is. Of course, in that realization all the questions of the border crossings come back—but accompanied now by a consciousness of himself and his own potential. At all times and in all places mankind has undertaken something beyond its essential nature and its limits. The communicators of these insights, upon whom religious experiences, basic revelations as well as creative cultures depend, have expressed through laws and ordinances in various ways the essential limits for all that is human. They have given voice to the conscience of the individual, the voice of this essential nature, and they have shaped the ethos of the groups for long periods. But no life process is exhausted in the law alone. The essential nature also contains the goal, and words for frontier often also express the end toward which a life process strives—such as the Latin "finis," the Greek "telos."

For Socrates, the consciousness of this goal was the voice of his daemon, which showed to him his essential limit in difficult decisions. In Christianity it is the consciousness of being religiously guided—or, more dynamically, being driven by the Spirit. Among peoples it is the consciousness of calling, in which the identity—and with it the essential limit—of a nation expresses itself. The world-historical results of the consciousness of calling are extraordinary. They have been vastly decisive for the manner of peace and disturbance in the world of nations. The Greeks' consciousness of calling, to represent the humane against barbarism, saved Europe from the Persian invasion. Rome's consciousness of calling, to be the carrier of the idea of Law, created the unity of Mediterranean culture. Israel's consciousness of calling is the foundation for the three prophetic religions of the West. The German imperial consciousness of calling created the religio-political unity of the Middle Ages. The Italian consciousness of calling of the Renaissance courts achieved the renaissance of the Western world out of Roman and Christian antiquity, the French consciousness of calling—the civilization of the upper classes and the emancipation of the citizenry, the English consciousness of calling—the opening of the world in the spirit of Christian humanism, the Russian consciousness of calling before *and* after the Bolshevik revolution—hope for the salvation of the West from its individualistic corruption through a unity founded in religion or ideology. And the American consciousness of calling has created faith in a new beginning and the spirit of a crusade for its universal accomplishment. In all of these cases of consciousness of calling a people found its essential limits and sought to make them into factual limits.

But thereby there occurred that which is responsible for the lack of peace and the tragedy of world history. The power which is necessary for every bringing to fruition of something alive has the tendency—in the political just as in the personal dimension—to cut loose from the goal which it should serve, that is, the realization of that calling, to become independent and then to develop a reality destructive of frontiers and contrary to nature. It is not power that is evil but the power which is cut loose from its essential limit. It is most violent when the consciousness of calling has lost its creative force, sometimes too, when the consciousness of calling is totally lacking.

And that seems to be the case with the Germany of the nineteenth and twentieth centuries. The failure of Germany, from the middle of the nineteenth century on, lay in the fact that it developed power without this power's being put at the service of a calling. What Bismarck called *Realpolitik* was power politics without a guiding consciousness of calling. And thereby Hitler could, with demoniacal ease, suggest the absurd racial consciousness of calling to broad circles of the German people—a facade, but an effective facade, for a development of power led by no true consciousness of calling.

Peace is possible where power stands in the service of a genuine consciousness of calling and knowledge of the essential limit, limits the importance of the factual limits. The fact that this foundation of politics was not admitted is the source of the

German lack of peace in the twentieth century. The goal of all peaceful efforts in literature and politics should be that it be again accepted. Let peace speeches be avoided which, because they cannot help, do damage, since world history is so deeply rooted in the demonic. Pacifistic legalism demands the unconditional holding fast to frontiers as they are in fact drawn today, here and now. It forgets the dynamics of world history and the creative and correcting effect of the essential frontier.

From this there is derived a second challenge to German political education, and finally to politics itself. The first was this: to lead to a crossing of the frontier, that is, the factual limit, and to conquer anxiety toward that which lies on the other side. The second challenge is this: to lead to acceptance of one's own essential limit and in its light to judge the greater or lesser weight of factual limits. In this light, narrow political boundaries could be more appropriate for a people than broader. Differing frontiers could represent the parts of a human group, linguistically but not politically united, in the group's historical essence. The acceptance of narrow boundaries could be more comprehensive in advancing the essential frontier and also the way along which a people discovers and maintains its identity. That has been demonstrated repeatedly in the course of history, and today we are in an historical moment, where the realization of the essential frontiers for most lands, at least in the Western world, depends upon their devoting themselves to more comprehensive factual frontiers.

Could there be totally comprehensive boundaries? In principle, yes! For the essential limits of all human groups are contained in the essential frontiers of humanity. The identity of every single group is a manifestation of the identity of humanity and of the nature of human existence. But the situation is different today for the factual frontiers. They are marked by one of the deepest divisions in world history, between East and West in the political sense, which includes both will to power and consciousness of calling—a consciousness of calling, indeed, which on both sides

has the character of exclusiveness and therefore, given the circumstances of contemporary technology, threatens humanity with
self-destruction.

I V

This leads to the deepest and most decisive of boundary line
problems: all life is subject to a common frontier, finitude. The
Latin, "finis," means both "frontier" and "end."

The final frontier stands behind every other frontier and gives
every other the color of transitoriness. We always stand on this
boundary line, but no one can cross over it. There is only one
stance toward it, namely that of acceptance. That is true of individuals and of groups, families, races, nations. But nothing is
more difficult than to accept the last impassable border. Everything finite would like to extend itself into infinity. The individual
wants to continue his life indefinitely, and in many Christian
lands a superstition has developed inside and outside the churches
which misinterprets eternal life as endless duration, and does not
perceive that an infinity of the finite could be a symbol for hell.
In the same way, families resist their finitude in time and in
space and destroy each other in a reciprocal battle to eliminate
the frontier. But most important for the possibility of peace is the
acceptance of their own finitude by the nations—of their time,
of their space, and of the finitude of their worth.

The temptation not to accept it, to lift one's self to the level
of the Unconditioned, the Divine, runs through all history. Whoever
falls for this seduction destroys his world and himself. Hence the
condemnations of the prophets against the peoples, above all
against their own. Hence the warnings in the threnodies of the
Greek choruses against the pride of the whole race. Hence the
characterization which we must give the system of political absolutism of our day: namely, that they are the most terrible manifestations of the demonic-destructive powers in the depths of

man. All of the Moloch-powers of the past put together do not have the sum total of sacrifices to show what have been made for them.

And again humanity stands before a devilish temptation—i.e., to turn back in one historical moment the act of creation which, across millions of years, has brought man into being. There is no human group which has the right to begin something for the sake of its frontiers whose continuation must lead to the destruction of itself and of all other human reality. To reverse the divine act of creation is a demoniacal border crossing and a revolt against the divine foundation and God-fixed goal of our being. Resistance to the attempt to set aside all limits is something else. That is necessary because he who makes a beginning must be shown that he has not become lord over the life and death of all humanity—but is himself involved in the collapse which he has occasioned.

Nothing finite can cross the frontier from finitude to infinity. But something else is possible: the Eternal can, from its side, cross over the border to the finite. It would not be the Eternal if the finite were its limit. All religions witness to this border crossing, those of which we say that they transmit law and vocation to the peoples. These are the perfecting forces from the Unlimited, the Law-establishing, the founding and leading of all being, which make peace possible. These are they which lead out of the narrows to the crossing of the frontier. These are they which give a consciousness of calling and thereby reveal the essential boundary line amidst the confusion of factual boundary lines. These are they which warn against wishing to storm the last boundary line, the frontier to the Eternal. These perfecting forces are ever there. But they can only become effective if one opens himself to them.

27
What Am I?

AN AUTOBIOGRAPHICAL ESSAY: EARLY YEARS

The fact that I was born on August 20, 1886, means that a part of my life belongs to the nineteenth century, especially if one assumes the nineteenth century to end (as one should) with August 1, 1914, the beginning of the First World War. Belonging to the nineteenth century implies life in relatively peaceful circumstances and recalls the highest flourishing of bourgeois society in its productive grandeur. It also implies aesthetic ugliness and spiritual distintegration. It implies, on the one hand, revolutionary impulses directed against this self-complacent period and, on the other hand, a consciousness of the Christian humanist values which underlie even the antireligious forms of this society and which made and make it possible to resist the inhuman systems of the twentieth century. I am one of those in my generation who, in spite of the radicalism with which they have criticized the nineteenth century, often feel a longing for its stability, its liberalism, its unbroken cultural traditions.

My birthplace was a village with the Slavic name Starzeddel, near Guben, a small industrial town in the province of Brandenburg, at the Silesian border. After four years my father, a minister of the Prussian Territorial Church, was called to the position of superintendent of the diocese of Schönfliess-Neumark. Superintendent was the title of the directing minister in a group of parishes, with functions similar to those of a bishop but on a smaller

From Paul Tillich, *My Search for Absolutes*, (New York: Simon and Schuster, Touchstone), 23–54. Reprinted by permission of Simon and Schuster, Inc. Copyright © 1967 by Simon and Schuster, Inc.

scale. Schönfliess was a place of three thousand inhabitants, in eastern Brandenburg. The town was medieval in character. Surrounded by a wall, built around an old Gothic church, entered through gates with towers over them, administered from a medieval town hall, it gave the impression of a small, protected, and self-contained world. The environment was not much different when, from my twelfth to fourteenth year, I stayed as a pupil of the humanistic Gymnasium, and as a boarder of two elderly ladies, in Königsberg-Neumark, a town of seven thousand people with the same kind of medieval remains but bigger and more famous for their Gothic perfection.

These early impressions may partly account for what has been challenged as the romantic trend in my feeling and thinking. One side of this so-called romanticism is my relationship to nature. It is expressed in a predominantly aesthetic-meditative attitude toward nature as distinguished from a scientific-analytical or technical-controlling relation. It is the reason for the tremendous emotional impact that Schelling's philosophy of nature made upon me—although I was well aware that this philosophy was scientifically impossible. It is theologically formulated in my doctrine of the participation of nature in the process of fall and salvation. It was one of the reasons why I was always at odds with the Ritschlian theology which establishes an infinite gap between nature and personality and gives Jesus the function of liberating man's personal life from bondage to the nature within us and beside us. When I came to America I found that Calvinism and Puritanism were natural allies of Ritschlianism in this respect. Nature is something to be controlled morally and technically, and only subjective feelings of a more or less sentimental character toward nature are admitted. There is no mystical participation in nature, no understanding that nature is the finite expression of the infinite ground of all things, no vision of the divine-demonic conflict in nature.

When I ask myself about the biographical background of this so-called romantic relation to nature, I find three causes which probably worked together in the same direction. First, I find the actual communication with nature, daily in my early years, in my later years for several months of every year. Many memorable instances of "mystical participation" in nature recur in similar situations. A second cause of the romantic relation to nature is the impact of poetry. German poetic literature, even aside from the romantic school, is full of expressions of nature mysticism. There are verses of Goethe, Hölderlin, Novalis, Eichendorff, Nietzsche, George, and Rilke which never have ceased to move me as deeply as they did when I first heard them. A third cause of this attitude toward nature came out of my Lutheran background. Theologians know that one of the points of disagreement between the two wings of the Continental Reformation, the Lutheran and the Reformed, was the so-called "Extra Calvinisticum," the doctrine that the finite is not capable of the infinite (*non capax infiniti*) and that consequently in Christ the two natures, the divine and the human, remained outside each other. Against this doctrine the Lutherans asserted the "Infra Lutheranum"—namely, the view that the finite is capable of the infinite and consequently that in Christ there is a mutual in-dwelling of the two natures. This difference means that on Lutheran ground the vision of the presence of the infinite in everything finite is theologically affirmed, that nature mysticism is possible and real, whereas on Calvinistic ground such an attitude is suspect of pantheism and the divine transcendence is understood in a way which for a Lutheran is suspect of deism.

Romanticism means not only a special relation to nature; it means also a special relation to history. To grow up in towns in which every stone is witness of a period many centuries past produces a feeling for history, not as a matter of knowledge but as a living reality in which the past participates in the present. I appreciated that distinction more fully when I came to America. In lectures, seminars, homes I visited, and personal conversation with American students I found that an immediate emotional identification with the reality of the past was lacking. Many of the students here had an excellent knowledge of historical facts, but these facts did not seem to concern them profoundly. They remained objects of their intellect and almost never became elements of their existence. It is the European destiny to experience in every generation the wealth and the tragedy of historical existence and consequently to think in terms of the past, whereas America's history started with the loss both of the burden and of the richness of the past. She was able to think in terms of the future. It is, however, not only historical consciousness generally which was emphasized by the romantic school; it was the special valuation of the European Middle Ages through which romanticism was deeply influential in the intellectual history of the last one hundred years. Without this influence I certainly would not have conceived of the idea of theonomous periods in the past and of a new theonomy in the future.

Two other points of biographical significance ought to be mentioned in connection with the years in Schönfliess and Königsberg. The first is the effect which my early life in a parish house had upon me, standing as I did with a confessional Lutheran school on the one side and on the other a beautiful Gothic church in which Father was a successful pastor. It is the experience of the "holy" which was given to me at that time as an indestructible good and as the foundation of all my religious and theological work. When I first read Rudolf Otto's *Idea of the Holy* I understood it immediately in the light of these early experiences and took it into my thinking as a constitutive element. It determined my method in the philosophy of religion, wherein I started with the experiences of the holy and advanced to the idea of God and not the reverse way. Equally important existentially as well as theologically were the mystical, sacramental, and aesthetic implications of the idea of the holy, whereby the ethical and logical elements of religion were derived from the experience of the presence of the divine and not conversely. This made Schleiermacher congenial to me, as he was to Otto, and induced both Otto and myself to participate in movements for liturgical renewal and a revaluation of Christian and non-Christian mysticism.

Existence in a small town in eastern Germany before the turn of the century gave to a child with some imaginative power the feeling of narrowness and restrictedness. I have already referred to the surrounding wall as a symbol of this. Movement beyond the given horizon was restricted. Automobiles did not exist, and a secondary railway was built only after several years; a trip of a few miles was an event for man and beast alike. The yearly escape to the Baltic Sea, with its limitless horizon, was the great event, the flight into the open, into unrestricted space. That I had chosen, later, a place at the Atlantic Ocean for the days of my retirement is certainly due to those early experiences. Another form of escape from the narrowness of my early life came in making several trips to Berlin, the city in which my father was born and educated. The impression the big city made on me was somehow similar to that of the sea: infinity, openness, unrestricted space! But beyond this it was the dynamic character of life in Berlin that affected me, the immense amount of traffic, the masses of people, the ever-changing scenes, the inexhaustible possibilities. When, in the year 1900, my father was called to an important position in Berlin, I felt extreme joy. I never lost this feeling; in fact, it was deepened when I really learned of the "mysteries" of a world city and when I became able to participate in them. Therefore I always considered it a good destiny that the emigration of the year 1933 brought me to New York, the largest of all large cities.

Still deeper in their roots and their effects than restrictedness in space and movement were the sociological and psychological restrictions of those years. The structure of Prussian society before the First World War, especially in the eastern part of the kingdom, was authoritarian without being totalitarian. Lutheran paternalism made the father the undisputed head of the family, which included, in a minister's house, not only wife and children but also servants with various functions. The same spirit of discipline and authority dominated the public schools, which stood under the supervision of local and county clergy in their function as inspectors of schools. The administration was strictly bureaucratic, from the policeman in the street and the postal clerk behind the window, up through a hierarchy of officials, to the far-removed central authorities in Berlin—authorities as unapproachable as the "castle" in Kafka's novel. Each of these officials was strictly obedient to his superiors and strictly authoritative toward his subordinates and the public. What was still lacking in discipline was provided by the Army, which trespassed in power and social standing upon the civil world and drew the whole nation from earliest childhood into its ideology. It did this so effectively in my case that my enthusiasm for uniforms, parades, maneuvers, history of battles, and ideas of strategy was not exhausted until my thirtieth year, and then only because of my experiences in the First World War. But above all this, at the top of the hierarchy, stood the King of Prussia, who happened to be also the German Emperor. Patriotism involved, above all, adherence to the King and his house. The existence of a parliament, democratic forces, socialist movements, and of a strong criticism of the Emperor and the Army did not affect the conservative Lutheran groups of the East among whom I lived. All these democratic elements were rejected, distortedly represented, and characterized as revolutionary, which meant criminal. Again it required a world war and a political catastrophe before I was able to break through this system of authorities and to affirm belief in democratic ideals and the social revolution.

Most difficult to overcome was the impact of the authoritarian system on my personal life, especially on its religious and intellectual side. Both my father and mother were strong personalities. My father was a conscientious, very dignified, completely convinced and, in the presence of doubt, angry supporter of the conservative Lutheran point of view. My mother, coming from the more democratic and liberal Rhineland, did not have the authoritarian attitude. She was, however, deeply influenced by the rigid morals of Western Reformed Protestantism. The consequence was a restrictive pressure in thought as well as in action, in spite (and partly because) of a warm atmosphere of loving care. Every attempt to break through was prevented by the unavoidable guilt consciousness produced by identification of the parental with the divine authority. There was only one point at which resistance was possible—namely, by using the very principles established by my father's authoritarian system against this system itself. And this was the way I instinctively chose. In the tradition of classical orthodoxy, my father loved and used philosophy, convinced that there can be no conflict between a true philosophy and revealed truth. The long philosophical discussions which developed belong to the most happy instances of a positive relation to my father. Nevertheless, in these discussions the breakthrough occurred. From an independent philosophical position a state of independence spread out into all directions, theoretically first, practically later. It is this difficult and painful breakthrough to autonomy which has made me immune against any system of thought or life which demands the surrender of autonomy.

In an early polemic between Karl Barth and myself, he accused me of "still fighting against the Grand Inquisitor." He is right in asserting that this is a decisive element of my theological thought. What I have called the "Protestant principle" is, as I believe, the main weapon against every system of heteronomy. But Karl Barth must have realized in the meantime that this fight never will become unnecessary. History has shown that the Grand Inquisitor is always ready to reappear in different disguises, political as well as theological. The fact that I have equally often been accused of neo-orthodoxy and of old liberalism is understandable in view of the two strong motives I received in the years under discussion: the romantic and the revolutionary motives. The balancing of these motives has remained the basic problem of my thought and of my life ever since.

In the year 1900 we moved to Berlin. I became a pupil at a humanistic Gymnasium in Old Berlin, passed my final examinations in 1904, and was matriculated in the theological faculties of Berlin, Tübingen, and Halle. In 1909 I took my first, in 1911 my second theological examination. In 1911 I acquired the degree of Doctor of Philosophy in Breslau and in 1912 the degree of Licentiat of Theology in Halle. In the latter year I received ordination into the Evangelical Lutheran Church of the province of Brandenburg. In 1914 I joined the German Army as a war chaplain. After the end of the war I became a Privatdozent of Theology at the University of Berlin, the beginning of my academic career. Reviewing these fifteen years of preparation, interrupted and at the same time completed by the war, I found abundant material for philosophical reflection. But I must restrict myself to some observations about the impact of these years on my own development.

In Königsberg, as well as in Berlin, I was a pupil in a "humanistic Gymnasium." A Gymnasium, compared with American institutions, consists of high school plus two years of college. The normal age for finishing the Gymnasium is eighteen. A humanist Gymnasium has as its central subjects Greek and Latin. My love of the Greek language was a vehicle for my love of Greek culture and especially the early Greek philosophers. One of my most enthusiastically prepared and best received courses had as its subject matter the pre-Socratic philosophy. The problem of the humanistic education is its relation to the religious tradition which, even without a special religious instruction, is omnipresent in history, art, and literature. Whereas in the United States the basic spiritual conflict is that between religion and scientific naturalism, in Europe the religious and humanistic traditions (of which the scientific world view is only a part) have been, ever since the Renaissance, in continuous tension. The German humanistic Gymnasium was one of the places in which this tension was most manifest. While we were introduced into classical antiquity in formal classes meeting about ten hours a week for about eight years, we encountered the Christian tradition at home, in the church, in directly religious instructions in school and outside the school, and in indirect religious information in history, literature, and philosophy. The result of this tension was either a decision against one side or the other, or a general skepticism or a split consciousness which drove one to attempt to overcome the conflict constructively. The latter way, the way of synthesis, was my own way. It follows the classical German philosophers from Kant to Hegel and has remained a driving force in all my theological work. It has found its final form in my *Systematic Theology*.

Long before my matriculation as a student of theology I studied philosophy privately. When I entered the university I had a good knowledge of the history of philosophy and a basic acquaintance with Kant and Fichte. Schleiermacher, Hegel, and Schelling followed, and Schelling became the special subject of my study. Both my doctoral dissertation and my thesis for the degree of Licentiat of Theology dealt with Schelling's philosophy of religion. These studies seem to foreshadow a philosopher rather than a theologian; and indeed they enabled me to become a professor of philosophy of religion and of social philosophy in the philosophical faculties of Dresden and Leipzig, a professor of pure philosophy in Frankfurt, a lecturer in the philosophical departments at Columbia and Yale, and a philosopher of history in connection with the religious-socialist movement. Nevertheless I was a theologian, because the existential question of our ultimate concern and the existential answer of the Christian message are and always have been predominant in my spiritual life.

The fifteen years from 1904 to 1919 in various ways contributed to this decision. My experiences as a student of theology in Halle from 1905 to 1907 were quite different from those of theological student Leverkuhn in Thomas Mann's *Doctor Faustus* in the same period. There was a group of great theologians to whom we listened and with whom we wrestled intellectually in seminars and personal discussions. One thing we learned above all was that Protestant theology is by no means obsolete but that it can, without losing its Christian foundation, incorporate strictly scientific methods, a critical philosophy, a realistic understanding of men and society, and powerful ethical principles and motives. Certainly we felt that much was left undone by our teachers and had to be done by ourselves. But this feeling of every new generation need not obviate the gratefulness for what it has received from its predecessors.

Important influences on our theological existence came from

other sides. One of them was our discovery of Kierkegaard and the shaking impact of his dialectical psychology. It was a prelude to what happened in the 1920s when Kierkegaard became the saint of the theologians as well as of the philosophers. But it was only a prelude; for the spirit of the nineteenth century still prevailed, and we hoped that the great synthesis between Christianity and humanism could be achieved with the tools of German classical philosophy. Another prelude to the things to come occurred in the period between my student years and the beginning of the First World War. It was the encounter with Schelling's second period, especially with his so-called Positive Philosophy. Here lies the philosophically decisive break with Hegel and the beginning of that movement which today is called Existentialism. I was ready for it when it appeared in full strength after the First World War, and I saw it in the light of that general revolt against Hegel's system of reconciliation which occurred in the decades after Hegel's death and which, through Kierkegaard, Marx, and Nietzsche, has become decisive for the destiny of the twentieth century.

But once more I must return to my student years. The academic life in Germany in these years was extremely individualistic. There were no dormitories for students and few, impersonal activities for the student body as such. The religious life was almost completely separated from the life of the churches; chaplains for the students did not exist and could hardly be imagined. The relation with the professors and their families was sporadic and in many cases completely absent. It is this situation which made the fraternities in Germany much more important than they are in this country. My membership in such a fraternity with Christian principles was not only a most happy but also a most important experience. Only after the First World War, when my eyes became opened to the political and social scene, did I realize the tremendous dangers of our prewar academic privileges. And I looked with great concern at the revival of the fraternities in post-Hitler Germany. But in my student years the fraternity gave me a communion (the first one after the family) in which friendship, spiritual exchange on a very high level, intentional and unintentional education, joy of living, seriousness about the problems of communal life generally, and Christian communal life especially, could daily be experienced. I question whether without this experience I would have understood the meaning of the church existentially and theoretically.

The First World War was the end of my period of preparation. Together with my whole generation I was grasped by the overwhelming experience of a nationwide community—the end of a merely individualistic and predominantly theoretical existence. I volunteered and was asked to serve as a war chaplain, which I did from September 1914 to September 1918. The first weeks had not passed before my original enthusiasm disappeared; after a few months I became convinced that the war would last indefinitely and ruin all Europe. Above all, I saw that the unity of the first weeks was an illusion, that the nation was split into classes, and that the industrial masses considered the Church as an unquestioned ally of the ruling groups. This situation became more and more manifest toward the end of the war. It produced the revolution, in which imperial Germany collapsed. The way in which this situation produced the religious-socialist movement in Germany has often been described. I want, however, to add a few reflections. I was in sympathy with the social side of the revolution even before 1918, that side which soon was killed by the interference of the victors, by the weakness of the socialists and their need to use the Army against the communists; also by inflation and the return of all the reactionary powers in the middle of the twenties. My sympathy for the social problems of the German revolution has roots in my early childhood which are hard to trace. Perhaps it was a drop of the blood which induced my grandmother to build barricades in the revolution of 1848, perhaps it was the deep impression upon me made by the words of the Hebrew prophets against injustice and by the words of Jesus against the rich; all these were words I learned by heart in my very early years. But whatever it was, it broke out ecstatically in those years and remained a continuing reality, although mixed with resignation and some bitterness about the division of the world into two all-powerful groups between which the remnants of a democratic and religious socialism are crushed. . . .

Another remark must be made here regarding my relation to Karl Marx. It has always been dialectical, combining a Yes and a No. The Yes was based on the prophetic, humanistic, and realistic elements in Marx's passionate style and profound thought, the No on the calculating, materialistic, and resentful elements in Marx's analysis, polemics, and propaganda. If one makes Marx responsible for everything done by Stalin and the system for which he stands, an unambiguous No against Marx is the necessary consequence. If one considers the transformation of the social situation in many countries, the growth of a definite self-consciousness in the industrial masses, the awakening of a social conscience in the Christian churches, the universal application of the economic-social method of analysis to the history of thought—all this under the influence of Marx—then the No must be balanced by a Yes. Although today such a statement is unwelcome and even dangerous, I could not suppress it, as I could not suppress my Yes to Nietzsche during the time in which everything which deserves a No in him was used and abused by the Nazis. As long as our thought remains autonomous, our relation to the great historical figures must be a Yes and a No. The undialectical No is as primitive and unproductive as the undialectical Yes.

In the years after the revolution my life became more intensive as well as extensive. As a Privatdozent of Theology at the University of Berlin (from 1919 to 1924), I lectured on subjects which included the relation of religion to politics, art, philosophy, depth psychology, and sociology. It was a "theology of culture" that I presented in my lectures on the philosophy of religion, its history and its structure. The situation during those years in Berlin was very favorable for such an enterprise. Political problems determined our whole existence; even after revolution and inflation they were matters of life and death. The social structure was in a state of dissolution; human relations with respect to authority, education, family, sex, friendship, and pleasure were in a creative chaos. Revolutionary art came into the foreground, supported by the Republic, attacked by the majority of the people. Psychoanalytic ideas spread and produced a consciousness of realities which had been carefully repressed in previous generations. Participation in these movements created manifold problems, conflicts, fears, expectations, ecstasies, and despairs, practically as well as theoretically. All this was at the same time material for an apologetic theology.

It was a benefit to me when, after almost five years in Berlin, my friendly adviser, the minister of education, Karl Becker, forced me against my desire into a theological professorship in Marburg. During the three semesters of my teaching there I encountered the first radical effects of neo-orthodox theology on theological students: Cultural problems were excluded from theological thought; theologians like Schleiermacher, Harnack, Troeltsch, Otto were contemptuously rejected; social and political ideas were banned from theological discussions. The contrast with my experiences in Berlin was overwhelming, at first depressing and then inciting: A new way had to be found. In Marburg, in 1925, I began work on my *Systematic Theology*, the first volume of which appeared in 1951. At the same time that Heidegger was in Marburg as professor of philosophy, influencing some of the best students, Existentialism in its twentieth-century form crossed my path. It took years before I became fully aware of the impact of this encounter on my own thinking. I resisted, I tried to learn, I accepted the new way of thinking more than the answers it gave.

In 1925 I was called to Dresden and shortly afterward to Leipzig also. I went to Dresden, declining a more traditional theological position in Giessen because of the openness of the big city both spatially and culturally. Dresden was a center of visual art, painting, architecture, dance, opera, with all of which I kept in close touch. The cultural situation was not much different when, in 1929, I received and accepted a call as professor of philosophy at the University of Frankfurt. Frankfurt was the most modern and most liberal university in Germany, but it had no theological faculty. So it was quite appropriate that my lectures moved on the boundary line between philosophy and theology and tried to make philosophy existential for the numerous students who were obliged to take philosophical classes. This, together with many public lectures and speeches throughout Germany, produced a conflict with the growing Nazi movement long before 1933. I was immediately dismissed after Hitler had become German Chancellor. At the end of 1933 I left Germany with my family and came to the United States.

In the years from 1919 to 1933 I produced all my German books and articles with the exception of a few early ones. The bulk of my literary work consists of essays, and three of my books—*Religiose Verwirklichung, The Interpretation of History*, and *The Protestant Era*—are collections of articles which themselves are based on addresses or speeches. This is not accidental. I spoke or wrote when I was asked to do so, and one is more often asked to write articles than books. But there was another reason: Speeches and essays can be like screws, drilling into untouched rocks; they try to take a step ahead, perhaps successfully, perhaps in vain. My attempts to relate all cultural realms to the religious center had to use this method. It provided new discoveries—new at least for me—and, as the reaction showed, not completely familiar to others. Essays like those on "The Idea of a Theology of Culture," "The Overcoming of the Concept of Religion in the Philosophy of Religion," "The Demonic," "The Kairos," "Belief-ful Realism," "The Protestant Principle and the Proletarian Situation," "The Formative Power of Protestantism," and, in America, "The End of the Protestant Era," "Existential Philosophy," "Religion and Secular Culture" and my books *Dynamics of Faith* and *Morality and Beyond*—these were decisive steps on my cognitive road. So were the Terry Lectures which I delivered at Yale in October 1950 under the title "The Courage to Be." This method of work has the advantages referred to, but it also has its shortcomings. There is even in a well-organized work such as my *Systematic Theology* a certain inconsistency and indefiniteness of terminology; there is the influence of different, sometimes competitive motives of thought, and there is a taking for granted of concepts and arguments which have been dealt with in other places.

The first volume of *Systematic Theology* is dedicated "to my students here and abroad." *The Protestant Era* could have been dedicated "to my listeners here and abroad"—that is, to the numerous nonstudent audiences to whom I spoke in addresses, speeches, and sermons. Looking back at more than forty years of public speaking, I must confess that from the first to the last address this activity gave me the greatest anxiety and the greatest happiness. I have always walked up to a desk or pulpit with fear and trembling, but the contact with the audience gave me a pervasive sense of joy, the joy of a creative communion, of giving and taking, even if the audience was not vocal. But when it became vocal, in periods of questions or discussions, this exchange was for me the most inspiring part of the occasion. Question and answer, Yes and No in an actual disputation—this original form of all dialectics is the most adequate form of my own thinking. But it has a deeper implication. The spoken word is effective not only through the meaning of the sentences formulated but also through the immediate impact of the personality behind these sentences. This is a temptation because one can use it for methods of mere persuasion. But it is also a benefit, because it agrees with what may be called "existential truth"—namely, a truth which lives in the immediate self-expression of an experience. This is not true of statements which have a merely objective character, which belong to the realm of "controlling knowledge," but it is valid of statements which concern us in our very existence and especially of theological statements which deal with that which concerns us ultimately. To write a system of existential truth, therefore, is the most difficult task confronting a systematic theologian. But it is a task which must be tried again in every generation, in spite of the danger that either the existential element destroys systematic consistency or that the systematic element suffocates the existential life of the system.

To begin life anew in the United States at forty-seven years of age and without even a minimum knowledge of the language was rather difficult. Without the help of colleagues and students at Union Theological Seminary and the assistance of German and American friends it might easily have been disastrous. It was for over eighteen years that I taught at the Seminary, and after my retirement age I continued my bonds of friendship with Union Seminary.

It was first of all a shelter at the moment when my work and my existence in Germany had come to an end. The fact that shortly after my dismissal by Hitler I was asked by Reinhold Niebuhr (who happened to be in Germany that summer) to come to Union Seminary prevented me from becoming a refugee in the technical sense. Our family arrived in New York on November 4, 1933. At the pier we were received by Professor Horace Friess of the philosophy department of Columbia University, who had asked me in Germany to give a lecture in his department. Ever since 1933 I had been in close relation to the Columbia philosophers, and the dialectical conversation across Broadway (the street separating Columbia and Union) never ceased but rather developed into an intensive cooperation. It was Union, however, that took me in as a stranger, then as visiting, associate, and full professor. Union Seminary was not only a shelter in the sense of affording a community of life and work. The Seminary is a closely knit community of professors and their families, of students, often likewise with their families, and of the staff. The members of this fellowship meet one another frequently in elevators and halls, at lectures, in religious services and social gatherings. The problems as well as the blessings of such a community are obvious. For our introduction into American life all this was invaluable, and it was also important for me as a counteraction against the extreme individualism of one's academic existence in Germany.

Union Seminary, moreover, is not an isolated community. If New York is the bridge between the continents, Union Seminary is the lane of that bridge, on which the churches of the world move. A continuous stream of visitors from all countries and all

races passed through our quadrangle. It was almost impossible
to remain provincial in such a setting. Union's world-wide outlook
theologically, culturally, and politically was one of the things for
which I was most grateful. The cooperation of the faculty had
been perfect. During eighteen years at Union Seminary I had
not had a single disagreeable experience with my American colleagues. I regret only that the tremendous burden of work prevented us from enjoying a more regular and more extensive
exchange of theological ideas. The work at the Seminary was
first of all a work with students. They came from all over the
continent, including Canada. They were carefully selected, and
their number was increased by exchange students from all over
the world. I loved them from the first day because of their human
attitude toward everything human (including myself); because
of their openness to ideas, even if strange to them, as my ideas
certainly were; because of their seriousness in study and self-
education in spite of the confusing situation in which they found
themselves in a place like Union Seminary. The lack of linguistic
and historical preparation produced some difficulties, but these
were overbalanced by many positive qualities. Union Seminary
is not only a bridge between the continents but also a center of
American life. Its faculty, therefore, is drawn into innumerable
activities in New York and in the rest of the country, and the
more so the longer one is on the faculty. It is obvious that in spite
of the great benefits one can derive from such contacts with the
life of a whole continent, the scholarly work is reduced in time
and efficiency.

Beyond all this, Union Seminary gives to its members a place
of common worship. This was a new experience for me, and a
very significant one. It provided for the faculty an opportunity to
relate theological thought to their own, and to the general, devotional life of the Church. It created for the students the possibility of experiencing this relation of thought to life and thereby
of judging the one in the light of the other. It placed upon me
the obligation of expressing myself in meditations and in sermons
as well as in the abstract theological concepts of lectures and

essays. This added in a profound way to the thanks I owe to Union Theological Seminary.

For external and practical reasons it became impossible to maintain the relationship to artists, poets, and writers which I enjoyed in postwar Germany. But I have been in permanent contact with the depth-psychology movement and with many of its representatives, especially in the last ten years. The problem of the relation between the theological and the psychotherapeutic understanding of men has come more and more into the foreground of my interest partly through a university seminar on religion and health at Columbia University, partly through the great practical and theoretical interest that depth psychology aroused in Union Seminary, and partly through personal friendship with older and younger analysts and counselors. I do not think that it is possible today to elaborate a Christian doctrine of man, and especially a Christian doctrine of the Christian man, without using the immense material brought forth by depth psychology.

The political interests of my postwar years in Germany remained alive in America. They found expression in my participation in the religious-socialist movement in this country; in the active relationship I maintained for years with the Graduate Faculty of Political Science at the New School for Social Research, New York; in my chairmanship of the Council for a Democratic Germany during the war; and in the many religio-political addresses I gave. In spite of some unavoidable disappointments, especially with the Council, politics remained, and always will remain, an important factor in my theological and philosophical thought. After the Second World War, I felt the tragic more than the activating elements of our historical existences, and I lost the inspiration for, and the contact with, active politics.

Emigration at the age of forty-seven means that one belongs to two worlds: to the Old as well as to the New into which one has been fully received. The connection with the Old World had been maintained in different ways: first of all through a continuous community with the friends who had left Germany as refugees like myself, whose help, criticism, encouragement, and unchanging friendship made everything easier and yet one thing—namely, the adaptation to the New World—more difficult. But it was my conviction, confirmed by many American friends, that a too quick adaptation is not what the New World expects from the immigrant but rather the preservation of the old values and their translation into the terminology of the new culture. Another way of keeping contact with the Old World was the fact that for more than fifteen years I had been the chairman of the Self-help for Emigrés from Central Europe, an organization of refugees for refugees, giving advice and help to thousands of newcomers every year, most of them Jews. This activity brought me into contact with many people from the Old World whom I never would have met otherwise, and it opened to view depths of human anxiety and misery and heights of human courage and devotion which are ordinarily hidden from us. At the same time it revealed to me aspects of the average existence in this country from which I was far removed by my academic existence.

A third contact with the Old World was provided by my political activity in connection with the Council for a Democratic Germany. Long before the East-West split became a world-wide reality, it was visible in the Council and with many tragic consequences. The present political situation in Germany—as distinguished from the spiritual situation—lost nothing of this character. I saw it as thoroughly tragic, a situation in which the element of freedom is as deeply at work as is the element of fate, which is the case in every genuine tragedy. This impression was fully confirmed by my two trips to Germany after the Second World War. I lectured at several German universities, in 1948 mainly at Marburg and Frankfurt, in 1951 mainly at the Free University in Berlin. Of the many impressions these visits gave me, I want to point only to the spiritual situation in Germany, which was open, surprisingly open, for the ideas which are discussed in this volume. An evidence of this was the speed with which my English writings were translated and published in

Germany. This way of returning to Germany is the best I could imagine, and it made me very happy.

But in spite of these permanent contacts with the Old World, the New World grasped me with its irresistible power of assimilation and creative courage. There is no authoritarian system in the family—as my two children taught me, sometimes through tough lessons. There is no authoritarian system in the school—as my students taught me, sometimes through amusing lessons. There is no authoritarian system in the administration—as the policemen taught me, sometimes through benevolent lessons. There is no authoritarian system in politics—as the elections taught me, sometimes through surprise lessons. There is no authoritarian system in religion—as the denominations taught me, sometimes through the presence of a dozen churches in one village. The fight against the Grand Inquisitor could lapse, at least this was so before the beginning of the second half of this century.

But beyond this I saw the American courage to go ahead, to try, to risk failures, to begin again after defeat, to lead an experimental life both in knowledge and in action, to be open toward the future, to participate in the creative process of nature and history. I also saw the dangers of this courage, old and new ones, and I confess that some of the new ones began to give me serious concern. Finally, I saw the point at which elements of anxiety entered this courage and at which the existential problems made an inroad among the younger generation in this country. Although this situation constitutes one of the new dangers, it also means openness for the fundamental question of human existence: "What am I?" the question that theology and philosophy both try to answer.

Looking back at a long life of theological and philosophical thought, I ask myself how it can compare with the world of our predecessors in the last generations. Neither I myself nor anybody else can answer this question today. One thing, however, is evident to most of us in my generation: We are not scholars according to the pattern of our teachers at the end of the nineteenth century. We were forced into history in a way which made the analysis of history and of its contents most difficult. Perhaps we have had the advantage of being closer to reality than they were. Perhaps this is only a rationalization of our shortcomings. However this may be, my work has come to its end.

28
Behold, I Am Doing a New Thing

Thus says the Lord
Who made a way through the sea,
A path through the mighty waters.

Remember not the former things,
Neither consider the things of old.
Behold, I am doing a new thing,
Even now it is springing to light.
Do you not perceive it?
A way will I make in the wilderness
And rivers in the desert!
                    —ISAIAH 43:16, 18–19

L ET US LISTEN to words of the Old and New Testaments which speak of the new that God makes in life and history.

Behold the days come, saith the Lord,
That I will make a new covenant
With the house of Israel
And with the house of Judah.
Not like the covenant which I made with their fathers
On the day that I took them by the hand

From Paul Tillich, *The Shaking of the Foundations* (New York: Charles Scribner's Sons), 176–86. Reprinted by permission of Charles Scribner's Sons. Copyright © 1948 by Paul Tillich.

To bring them out of the land of Egypt;
Which my covenant they brake,
So that I had to reject them.
But this shall be the covenant
That I will make with the house of Israel after those days,
    says the Lord:
I will put my law within them
And write it in their hearts;
And I will be their God
And they shall be my people. . . .
For I will forgive their guilt
And I will remember their sin no more.
                                        —JEREMIAH 31:31–34

(Thus says the Lord God:) . . .
I will give them a new heart,
And I will put a new spirit within them.
I will remove their heart of stone
And will give them a heart of flesh.
                                        —EZEKIEL 11:19

(Thus says the Lord God:) . . .
I ignore the troubles of the past.
I shut mine eyes to them.
For, behold, I create new heavens and a new earth.
The past shall be forgotten
And never come to mind.
Men shall rejoice forever in what I now create.
                                        —ISAIAH 65:16, 17

But let us not omit the tragic words of the Preacher.

Vanity of vanities, says the Preacher,
Vanity of vanities; all is vanity.

What has been is what shall be;
What has gone on is what shall go on;
And there is nothing new under the sun.
Is there a thing of which it is said:
Lo, this is new?

It was already in existence in the ages
Which were before us.
—ECCLESIASTES 1:2, 9–10

And this is the answer the apostle gives:

Therefore if any one is in Christ, he is a new creation. The old has passed away; behold, all things have become new.
—II CORINTHIANS 5:17

(And Jesus said to them:) . . . No one puts a piece of new cloth on an old garment, for the patch tears away from the garment, and a worse tear is made. Neither is new wine put into old wineskins; if it is, the skins burst and the wine is spilled, and the skins are destroyed; but new wine is put into new wineskins, and so both are preserved.
—MATTHEW 9:16–17

And finally, let us listen to the seer of the New Testament:

Then I saw a new heaven and a new earth; for the first heaven and the first earth had passed away. . . . And I saw the holy city, the New Jerusalem, coming down . . . and I heard a great voice from the throne saying: Behold, the dwelling of God is with men . . . he will wipe away every tear from their eyes and death shall be no more, for the former things have passed away. . . . Behold, I make all things new.
—REVELATION 21:1–5

Let us meditate on the old and the new, in ourselves and in our world. In these Biblical texts the new is contrasted with the old: the old is rejected, and there is stated, in passionate words, expectation of the new. Even the Preacher, who denies the possibility of anything really new on earth, does not hide his longing for the new, and his disappointment in not being able to find it. Why do these writers feel and speak in this way? Why do they prefer the new to the old, and why do they believe that God is the God of the new? Why do they demand and expect the new birth, the new heart, the new man, the new covenant, the New Jerusalem, the new heaven and the new earth?

They do not announce the new because they believe what

many people of the last decades have believed: that the later things are better than the former things simply *because* they are later; that new developments are more divine than old ones, because they are nearer to a final perfection; that God guarantees a perpetual progress, and that for this reason He is the God of the new. Against such illusions the disappointed words of the Preacher are true for all history. And certainly such illusions are not the content of the prophetic and apostolic preaching concerning the new. What is the content of their expectation? What do they mean when they warn us not to consider the things of old? What are those old things, and what are the new things which they ask us to see and to accept?

"Old" sometimes means that which lasts through all times, that which is today as it was in the past and as it shall be in all the future. There is something that does not age, something that is always old and always new at the same time, because it is eternal. God is sometimes called the "ancient of days" or the "Redeemer of old." The wisdom of old and the law of God, which are as old as the foundations of the earth, are praised just because they are old; nothing new is set against them as no new God is set against the God of old. "Old" as it is used here means "everlasting," pointing to that which is not subject to the change of time.

But in the texts we have read from the words of the unknown prophet of the exile, in the forty-third chapter of Isaiah, "old" means just the opposite. It means that which passes away and shall not be remembered any more—the destiny of everything created, of the stars as well as of the grass in the field, of men as well as of animals, of nations as well as of individuals, of the heavens as well as of the earth. They all become old and pass away. What does it mean to say that somebody or something becomes old? All life grows; it desires and strives to grow, and it lives as long as it grows. Men always have been fascinated by the law of growth. They have called that which helps growth good, and they have called that which hinders it evil. But let us look more deeply into the law of growth and into its tragic nature.

Whether we observe the growth of a living cell or of a human soul or of a historical period, we see that growth is gain and loss at the same time; it is both fulfillment and sacrifice. Whatever grows must sacrifice many possible developments for the one through which it chooses to grow. He who wants to grow as a scientist may have to sacrifice poetic or political possibilities which he would like to develop. He has to pay a price. He cannot grow equally in all directions. The cells which adapt themselves to one function of the body lose the power to adapt themselves to other functions. Periods of history which are determined by one idea suppress the truth of other possible ideas. Every decision excludes possibilities and makes our life narrower. Every decision makes us older and more mature. Youth is openness. But every decision closes doors. And that cannot be avoided; it is an inescapable destiny. Life makes decisions in every moment; life closes doors in every moment. We proceed from the first minute of our lives to the last minute, *because* we are growing. The law of growth lends us greatness, and therefore tragedy. For the excluded possibilities belong to us; they have a right of their own. Therefore, they take their vengeance upon our lives which have excluded them. They may die; and with them, great powers of life and large resources of creativity. For life, as it grows, becomes a restricted power, more rigid and inflexible, less able to adapt itself to new situations and new demands. Or, on the other hand, the excluded possibilities may *not* die. They may remain within us, repressed, hidden, and dangerous, prepared to break into the life process, not as a creative resource, but as a destructive disease. Those are the two ways in which the aging life drives toward its own end: the way of self-limitation, and the way of self-destruction. Often the two ways merge, carrying death into all realms of life.

Let us consider one of these realms—our historical situation, the life of our period. Our period has become what it is through innumerable decisions and, therefore, innumerable exclusions. Some of the excluded possibilities have died away, depriving us of their creative power. Many of them have not died, and after having disappeared for a time, are now returning destructively. The former greatness of our period has produced its present tragedy and that of all who live within it. Even those who are young amongst us are old, in so far as they belong to an aged period. They are young in their personal vitality; they are old because of their participation in the tragedy of our time. It is an illusion to believe that youth *as youth* has saving power. When the ancient empires aged and died, their youth did not save them. And our younger generation will not save us, simply by virtue of the fact that it is young.

We have made many decisions in order to become what we are. But every decision is tragic, because it is the decision against something which cannot be suppressed with impunity.

At the beginning of our period we decided for *freedom*. It was a right decision; it created something new and great in history. But in that decision we excluded the security, social and spiritual, without which man cannot live and grow. And now, in the old age of our period, the quest to sacrifice freedom for security splits every nation and the whole world with really daemonic power. We have decided for *means* to control nature and society. We have created them, and we have brought about something new and great in the history of all mankind. But we have excluded ends. We have never been ready to answer the question, "For what?" And now, when we approach old age, the means claim to be the ends; our tools have become our masters, and the most powerful of them have become a threat to our very existence. We have decided for *reason* against outgrown traditions and honored superstitions. That was a great and courageous decision, and it gave a new dignity to man. But we have, in that decision, excluded the soul, the ground and power of life. We have cut off our mind from our soul; we have suppressed and mistreated the soul within us, in other men, and in nature. And now, when we are old, the forces of the soul break destructively into our minds, driving us to mental disease and insanity, and effecting the disintegration of the souls of uncounted millions, especially in this country, but also all over the world.

From the very beginning of our period we have decided for the *nation*, as the expression of our special way of life and of our unique contribution to history. The decision was great and creative, and for centuries it was effective. But in that decision we excluded mankind and all symbols expressing the unity of all men. The former unity was broken, and no international group has been able to reestablish it. Now, in the old age of our period, the most powerful nations themselves claim to represent mankind, and try to impose their ways of life upon all men, producing, therefore, wars of destruction, which will perhaps unite all mankind in the peace of the grave.

Our period has decided for a *secular* world. That was a great and much-needed decision. It threw a church from her throne, a church which had become a power of suppression and superstition. It gave consecration and holiness to our daily life and work. Yet it excluded those deep things for which religion stands: the feeling for the inexhaustible mystery of life, the grip of an ultimate meaning of existence, and the invincible power of an unconditional devotion. These things *cannot* be excluded. If we try to expel them in their divine images, they reemerge in daemonic images. Now, in the old age of our secular world, we have seen the most horrible manifestation of these daemonic images; we have looked more deeply into the mystery of evil than most generations before us; we have seen the unconditional devotion of millions to a satanic image; we feel our period's sickness unto death.

This is the situation of our world. Each of us should realize that he participates in it, and that the forces in his own soul which make him old, often in early years, are part of the forces which make our period old. Each of us strengthens these forces, and each of us is a victim of them at the same time. We are in the desert of which the prophet speaks, and none among us knows the way out. Certainly there is no way out in what some idealists tell us: "Make decisions, but don't exclude anything! Take the best in *all* possibilities. Combine them. Then will our period become young again!" No man and no nation will become young again in that way. The new does not appear from a collection of the elements of the old which are still alive. When the new comes the old must disappear. "Remember not the former things, neither consider the things of old," says the prophet. "Behold, all things are become new," says the apostle. Out of the death of the old the new arises. The new is created not out of the old, not out of the best of the old, but out of the *death* of the old. It is not the old which creates the new. That which creates the new is that which is beyond old and beyond new, the Eternal.

"Behold, *I* am doing a new thing, even now it is springing to light. Do you not perceive it?" If the new were a part of the old, the prophet would not ask, "Do you perceive it?" for everybody would see it already. But it is hard to perceive. It is hidden in the profound mystery which veils every creation, birth as well as rebirth. It springs to light—which is to say that it comes out of the darkness of that mystery.

Nothing is more surprising than the rise of the new within ourselves. We do not foresee or observe its growth. We do not try to produce it by the strength of our will, by the power of our emotion, or by the clarity of our intellect. On the contrary, we feel that by trying to produce it we prevent its coming. By trying, we would produce the old in the power of the old, but not the new in the power of the new. The new being is born in us, just when we least believe in it. It appears in remote corners of our souls which we have neglected for a long time. It opens up deep levels of our personality which had been shut out by old decisions and old exclusions. It shows a way where there was no way before. It liberates us from the tragedy of having to decide and having to exclude, because it is given before any decision. Suddenly we notice it within us! The new which we sought and longed for comes to us in the moment in which we lose hope of ever finding it. That is the first thing we must say about the new: it appears when and where it chooses. We cannot force it, and we cannot calculate it. Readiness is the only condition for it; and readiness means that the former things have become old and that they are driving us into the destruction of our souls just when we are trying most to save what we think can be saved of the old.

It is the same in our historical situation. The birth of the new is just as surprising in history. It may appear in some dark corner of our world. It may appear in a social group where it was least expected. It may appear in the pursuit of activities which seem utterly insignificant. It may appear in the depth of a national catastrophe, if there be in such a situation people who are able to perceive the new of which the prophet speaks. It may appear at the height of a national triumph, if there be a few people who perceive the vanity of which the Preacher speaks. The new in history always comes when people least believe in it. But, certainly, it comes only in the moment when the old becomes visible *as* old and tragic and dying, and when no way out is seen. We live in such a moment; such a moment is *our* situation. We realize this situation in its depth only if we do not continue to say, "We know where the new will come from. It will come from *this* institution, or *this* movement, or *this* special class, or *this* nation, or *this* philosophy, or *this* church." None of these, of course, is excluded from being the place where the new will appear. But none of these can guarantee its appearance. All of us who have looked at one of these things as the chosen place of the new have been disappointed. The supposedly new always proves to be the continuation of the old, deepening its destructive conflicts. And so I repeat: the first thing about the new is that we cannot force it and cannot calculate it. All we can do is to be ready for it. We must realize as profoundly as possible that the former things have become old, that they destroy our period just when we try most courageously to preserve the best of it. And we must attempt this realization in our social as well as in our personal life. In no way but the most passionate striving for the new shall we become aware that the old is old and dying. The prophets who looked for the new thing. He is doing were most passionately and most actively involved in the historical situation of their nation. But they knew that neither they themselves nor any of the old things would bring the new.

"Remember not the former things, neither consider the things of old," says the prophet. That is the second thing we must say about the new: it must break the power of the old, not only in reality, but also in our memory; and one is not possible without the other. Let me say a few words about this most sublime point in the prophetic text and in the experience of every religion. We cannot be born anew if the power of the old is not broken within us; and it is not broken so long as it puts the burden of guilt upon us. Therefore religion, prophetic as well as apostolic, pronounces, above all, forgiveness. Forgiveness means that the old is thrown into the past because the new has come. "Remember not" in the prophetic words does not mean to forget easily. If it meant that, forgiveness would not be necessary. Forgiveness means a throwing out of the old, as remembered *and* real at the same time, by the strength of the new which could never be the saving new if it did not carry with it the authority of forgiveness.

I believe that the situation is the same in our social and historical existence. A new which is not able to throw the old into the past, in remembrance as well as in reality, is not the really new. The really new is able to break the power of old conflicts between man and man, between group and group, in memory and reality. It is able to break the old curses, the results of former guilt, inherited by one generation from another, the guilt between nations, between races, between classes, on old and new continents, these curses by which the guilt of one group, in reality and memory, permanently produces guilt in another group. What power of the new will be great and saving enough to break the curses which have laid waste half of our world? What new thing will have the saving power to break the curse brought by the German nation upon herself before our eyes? "Remember not the former things," says the prophet. That is the second thing which must be said about the new.

"Behold, *I* am doing a new thing." "*I*" points to the source of the really new, to that which is always old and always new, the Eternal. That is the third thing which must be said about the new: it bears the mark of its eternal origin in its face, as it did when Moses came from the mountain with the tablets of the law, opening a new period of history. The really new is that which has in itself eternal power and eternal light. New things arise in every moment, at every place. Nothing is today as it was yesterday. But *this* kind of new is old almost as soon as it appears. It falls under the judgment of the Preacher: "There is no new thing under the sun." Yet sometimes a new thing appears which does not age so easily, which makes life possible again, in both our personal and our historical existence, a saving new, which has the power to appear when we least expect it, and which has the power to throw into the past what is old and burdened with guilt and curse. Its saving power is the power of the Eternal within it. It is new, really new, in the degree to which it is beyond old and new, in the degree to which it is eternal. And it remains new so long as the eternal power of the Eternal is manifest within it, so long as the light of the Eternal shines through it. For that power may become weaker; that light may become darker; and that which was truly a new thing may become old itself. That is the tragedy of human greatness in which something eternal appears.

When the apostles say that Jesus is the Christ, they mean that in Him the new eon which cannot become old is present. Christianity lives through the faith that within it there is the new which is not just another new thing but rather the principle and representation of all the really new in man and history. But it can affirm this only because the Christ deprived Himself of everything which can become old, of all individual and social standing and greatness, experience and power. He surrendered all these in His death and showed in His self-surrender the only new thing which is eternally new: love. "Love never ends," says His greatest apostle. Love is the power of the new in every man and in all history. It cannot age; it removes guilt and curse. It is working even today toward new creation. It is hidden in the darkness of our souls and of our history. But it is not completely hidden to those who are grasped by its reality. "Do you not *perceive* it?" asks the prophet. Do *we* not perceive it?

Paul Tillich was born in Prussia in 1886. He taught philosophy and theology at the universities of Marburg, Dresden, Leipzig, and Frankfurt. A leader of the Religious Socialist movement, his activities brought him into conflict with Nazism and he was requested to leave Germany in 1933, shortly after Hitler assumed power. From 1933 to 1955 Dr. Tillich taught at Union Theological Seminary in New York. Between 1955 and 1962 he was University Professor at Harvard, and in the latter year he became the John Nuveen Professor of Theology at the Divinity School of the University of Chicago. Dr. Tillich's works include *The Shaking of the Foundations, The New Being,* and *The Eternal Now,* all available from the Scribner Library. He died in 1965.

F. Forrester Church is the senior minister of the Unitarian Church of All Souls in New York City. A graduate of Stanford University, Harvard Divinity School, and Harvard University, where he received his Ph.D. in 1978, Dr. Church is the editor or author of fifteen books, including *Father and Son: A Personal Biography of Senator Frank Church of Idaho.* He lives in Manhattan with his wife and four children.